Rings of desire

to Amy

hoping your Circus adventures
Continue to grow.

lots of love,

Stewart & Mary
x x x

MANCHESTER
UNIVERSITY PRESS

Rings of desire

Circus history and representation

Helen Stoddart

MANCHESTER UNIVERSITY PRESS

Manchester and New York

distributed exclusively in the USA by St. Martin's Press

Published by Manchester University Press
Oxford Road, Manchester M13 9NR, UK
and Room 400, 175 Fifth Avenue, New York, NY 10010, USA
http://www. manchesteruniversitypress.co.uk

Distributed exclusively in the USA by
St. Martin's Press, Inc., 175 Fifth Avenue, New York,
NY 10010, USA

Distributed exclusively in Canada by
UBC Press, University of British Columbia, 2029 West Mall,
Vancouver, BC, Canada V6T 1Z2

British Library Cataloguing-in-Publication Data
A catalogue record for this book is available from the British Library

Library of Congress Cataloging-in-Publication Data applied for

ISBN   0 7190 5233 5   *hardback*
          0 7190 5234 3   *paperback*

First published 2000

07 06 05 04 03 02 01 00   10 9 8 7 6~5 4 3 2 1

Typeset in Photina by Carnegie Publishing, Lancaster
Printed in Great Britain
by Bell & Bain Ltd, Glasgow

For Robert and Gloria Stoddart

Contents

List of Illustrations

Acknowledgements

I would like to thank Keele University whose staff research award granted me leave for 1998/9 as well as funding for my research trip to various circus collections in the United States. My chapter on Fellini ('Subtle, wasted, traces ...') also appears in Frank Burke's *Fellini: A Critical Introduction* (forthcoming from Toronto University Press) and I am indebted to him for his editorial work and various constructive suggestions on this piece. Copyright for this piece is held by the University of Toronto and it is reprinted here with their permission. My colleagues in the English Department have been liberal with their support and encouragement; John Bowen and Anthea Trodd in particular made extremely valuable suggestions on Charles Dickens and the circus and Richard Kirkland supplied crucial Macintosh advice, information and support when I found myself in technical straits. Discussions with students at Keele on various texts have also been very productive for this project and I would especially like to acknowledge Tamarin Penford's perceptive comments which sparked off a train of thought on *Hard Times*. Marius Kwint has generously allowed me to quote from his excellent D. Phil thesis, 'Astley's amphitheatre and the early circus in England, 1768–1830', which itself is forthcoming as an Oxford University Press monograph, and very helpfully alerted me to the Astley's and general circus scrapbooks held in the British Library which became an important source for this book. I would like to make it clear, therefore, that in any instances where we both draw quotations from these primary sources, I owe my tracing of this source to Marius. He has also been a meticulous and thoughtful reader of this manuscript, making many helpful suggestions and saving me from embarrassing errors. Needless to say, if errors remain, they are due to my own oversights and not his. Erin Foley at the World Circus Museum in Baraboo, Wisconsin, Joan Barborak and Robert O'Connor at the

Acknowledgements

Hertzberg Museum in San Antonio and Steve Gossard, the curator of the circus special collection at the State University of Illinois's Milner Library all went to great lengths to locate useful materials for me during my research in the United States and to supply me with illustrations. Steve Gossard has been particularly supportive of the project and has generously donated permission to use the Adah Isaac Menken picture which belongs to his private circus poster collection. The recent International Circus Conference (Refract '99) in London offered very useful insights into the range and variety of contemporary circus and I would like to express my gratitude to the numerous contributors to the conference as well as to Di Robson, its organisor. Finally, thanks are due to ever-patient editors at Manchester University Press, Matthew Frost and Lauren McAllister.

Introduction

The circus is mendacious, eternally opportunistic, at turns demotic and status-seeking, absurd and charming, breathtaking and predictable; prone to material catastrophe and yet driven by unparalleled physical skills and spectacular showmanship. Culturally and geographically it is eclectic, yet also type-ridden. Alternately, sometimes simultaneously, it is conservative, outlawed, conformist and transgressive. Always undeniably a live and fully visible spectacle in which no back- or side-stage tricks are possible, it has also operated some of the most famous of deceits. Deceit may take place not only within some of the acts but, as Marcello Truzzi has acknowledged, for the most part the 'true nature of this organisational structure has been heavily obscured by hosts of romanticised fictions and histories, especially by those circus fans who have sought to perpetuate knowledge of it'.[1] This seems to be almost endemic in the circus, a fact illustrated by one of the earliest stories about the foundation of the circus. Maurice Willson Disher is one of several historians of the circus who report Astley's claim that he was able to acquire his first permanent site on Westminster Bridge because he combined his profits from the Halfpenny Hatch riding school with the money from a diamond ring, worth £60, which, apparently, he chanced to discover whilst one day strolling across Westminster Bridge.[2]

All of this makes the circus at once one of the most entertaining and the most frustrating of arts upon which to attempt research, since the memoirs, testimonies and handbills which constitute the clues to its history and development frequently demonstrate enough cavalier indulgence of fancy over fact to make an occasional Gradgrind out of the investigator. The story of Astley's good fortune on Westminster Bridge, like many others, has been passed on by precisely those fans of the circus to whom Truzzi refers who, with very few exceptions to date,

1

have constituted its principal historians so that circus history and circus mythology have become very much entwined. Perhaps the willingness to pass on such narratives is derived from a desire for the circus itself; a recognition that the charm of such tales lies in their capturing of something essential about the circus which is that an audience may always prefer either an enchanting or an alarming fiction (well presented) over a bare-faced fact. This study, however, has not been conceived as an entertainment but as an academic study, and though it certainly does not aim to produce any kind of complete history of the circus (there already exist many volumes which are more extensive scope and more historically detailed than this) the facts and figures which I do include are, I hope, if not indisputable, then have at least been verified by a number of other sources.

Since the scope of this study, as I suggest above, is clearly defined by certain limitations, it seems important to lay these out and to argue their rationale. The history offered is weighted towards the developing years of the circus and the 'Golden Ages' it enjoyed, at different points, in Europe and, later, in North America. A little less attention, therefore, has been given to later (post-1945) twentieth-century issues and developments as well as to the development of circus traditions in, for example, South America, India, North Africa, China and Russia. This is mainly because my concern in the book has been to trace the formative structures, contexts and performances which gradually, if perhaps rather messily and unevenly, shaped the constitution of the genre of popular art which, by the early nineteenth century could be recognised as circus. Plenty of adaptations and innovations to this model are charted in the book and I hope to be able to engage in further research which is able to do full justice to the exciting diversifications and reorientations within circus practices that have taken place, particularly in the twentieth century. However, in directing my focus towards the establishment of the genre and its major adaptations, I have aimed both at demonstrating that the defining structures of circus (its architecture, its key constituent performances and its economic arrangements), most or many of which have survived in some form to the present day, need to be seen in the context of the eighteenth- and early nineteenth-century theatrical legislation, changing attitudes towards the role of popular entertainment, questions about the human body's relationship to nature provoked by increasing industrialisation and increasing curiosity about and awareness of racial, cultural and zoological diversity which paralleled imperial expansion. All of these have been shaping and indeed defining influences on the circus and ones which help us understand the origins of some of its key energies (its opportunism, populism, thirst for danger and physical discipline, defiance of natural laws and fascination with every form and shape of the human body) as well as the ways in which, in turn, these energies mediate to its audiences, in spectacular and dramatic forms, the triumphs and disorientations through which they understand their place and potential as members of a dynamic world which is recognisably modern. The various innovations which have taken place, both in terms of the international diversification and historical adaptations of the circus have functioned to extend, modify or renovate these early energies but not to rewrite them.

Of course my argument here about what the circus does – its characteristic ambitions, machinery and scope – is already beginning to make assumptions about its identity as a coherent and continuous generic form. As Part I of the book demonstrates, however, early manifestations of circus were not anything so organised as this might suggest and it is important to remember that, not only was the early circus (1768–1800) a messy affair, but the term 'circus' has always been used to label an extremely diverse and often jumbled network of performing practices and organisations which incorporated entertainments taken from fairground and theatre. Connections between players did not, therefore, take place on the basis of aesthetic affiliations but rather out of their need to meet the opposition levelled by the patent theatres, anxious about the potential competition. At the same time we must have some idea of what the circus is if we are to identify its practices and contemplate the meaning of significant variations or innovations within them. Marcello Truzzi offers us what seems like a fairly wide-ranging definition when he suggests that according to 'historians, as well as the folk classifications used by the members of the circuses themselves, *a circus is a travelling and organised display of animals and skilled performances within one or more circular stages known as "rings" before an audience encircling these activities.'* [3] Many circus historians would agree that the ring and the performing horse are the very foundations of the circus, but even this relatively flexible definition would exclude many individual and collective modern performances which take place in other kinds of venues or which exclude animals which we have learnt to call circus. At the same time, the glorious and diverse array of acts (clowns, trapeze and high-wire artists, jugglers and so on), though we may find them on vaudeville stages, street corners or country fairs, can be argued to belong to the circus because their performance in some way embodies a characteristic circus energy or aesthetic. In chapter 5, therefore, I try to outline what these aesthetic characteristics are and to suggest the ways in which, for example, absurdity, sensation or danger, take on very particular resonance and meaning within circus shows. Thus, though the circus, in terms of its institutional structures, has ranged from small and precarious family business to multinational company, in the acts which identify them- selves as circus it must always be possible to identify a characteristic circus aesthetic. Though I am acknowledging the difficulty of providing an all-encompassing definition of what does and does not constitute circus, I hope this will not be read as an attempt to duck the question of generic definition and the questions of authenticity and generic faithfulness which accompany such investigation. Rather, this move is more an indication that this study will be more occupied with describing the cultural and representational issues raised both by indi- vidual circus figures and by collective performances which are identified with the circus either by themselves, their contexts or those who view or represent them.

Circus is, above all, a vehicle for the demonstration and taunting of danger and this remains its most telling and defining feature. Physical risk-taking has always been at its heart; the recognition that to explore the limitations of the human body is to walk a line between triumphant exhilaration and, on the other side of this limit, pain, injury or death. The body in the circus is utterly self-reliant; it is preserved by skill and strength only, never by faith, fate or magic. It is no coincidence then that, in *Thus Spoke Zarathustra* (appropriately the work which is most famous for its declamatory and excessive style), Friedrich Nietzsche turns to the circus to find a figure – the tight-rope walker – to allegorise man's precarious journey of development as a crossing over an 'abyss' during which he must face down limitations and exceed his potential.[4] Zarathustra preaches to an expectant crowd gathered in the market square that 'Man is a rope' extended between the two points on either side of the abyss, 'animal and Superman', and the journey between the two is a 'dangerous going across, a dangerous wayfaring, a danger- ous looking back, a dangerous shuddering and staying still'.[5] Nietzsche's interest in this circus figure is an important indicator of the fundamental secularity of the circus for here is an arena in which wonder, awe and faith are all fostered and exercised, yet their focus is invariably exceptional human physical achievement, skill and bravery. There is no place in the circus for any other more powerful agency or any spiritual or mystical belief, indeed the human body in the circus is admired precisely for its independence, resourcefulness and self-reliance: its ability to survive and to reach new heights of ascendancy over nature. At the opposite end of Nietzsche's rope from 'Superman' (the ideal who 'overcomes' restrictions and creates 'something beyond themselves') is the possibility of descending back down the Darwinian ladder to the ape and, thereby, returning 'to the animal'. Just as, for Nietzsche, the apes are 'a painful laughing-stock and an embarrassment' to men and men likewise to 'supermen', the circus too plays out these dynamics of human exceptionalism and descent within the range of standard acts which include at one end the gravity-defying grace and strength of the aerialists and high-wire acts and, at the other, the clumsy, pie-flinging, barbarous clowns. Thus, when the tight-rope walker steps out on his journey across the rope he is quickly interrupted by a clown, 'a brightly-dressed fellow like a buffoon sprang out', who soon precipitates the tight-rope walker's fatal fall into the crowded square, 'like a vortex of arms and legs'.[6] Read in this light, then, the circus is, as I will argue later, far from being a carnivalesque space in which disorder, illegitimacy and inversion reign, but rather one in which there is an incorporation but also a hierarchical ordering of both the forces of chaos and inversion and those of order, ascendancy and power in which the latter invariably maintain the upper hand.

These features of the circus which make it so characteristically modern are also those which suggest its fascinating challenge to representation and thus it is this issue with which Part II of the book is concerned. Circus goes further than other forms of live art (drama, dance or opera, for example) to mobilise physical energies and sensations which fundamentally resist inscription within film and literary language. Not only has it predominantly side-stepped (if only opportunistically) linguistic language for mime, music and physical stunts, it has also traditionally avoided arranging its acts in any kind of narrative form and has favoured, restless, itinerant and temporary structures. It is, therefore, both the most dangerously immediate and physically sensational of forms and, rejecting forms of memorialisation, it is the most ghostly and insubstantial – an object of nostalgia, mourning and projection. The final three chapters of the book focus on the presence of circus metaphors and representations in the work of Dickens, Fellini and in the at once peculiar and familiar twists which Wim Wenders's film *Wings of Desire* lends to the figure of the female aerialist. Still, circus figures run through much important twentieth-century literature and film (in the writings of John Banville, Angela Carter, Thomas Mann, Harry Crews, John Irving, Franz Kafka, Djuna Barnes and the films of Ingmar Bergman) and I hope in future work to pursue both the particular significance of these figures within individual bodies of work as well as what may be their general character.

At first glance these three chapters may appear to bring together a rather odd and eclectic collection of texts and artists. I have not attempted to provide any overview of literary and film portrayals of the circus but rather have opted for a more selective and detailed interrogation of texts which are interesting not only for either their perpetuation or challenging of common circus images or myths, but because they also reveal other problems in or anxieties about the possibilities and limitations of recording ideas, history, events and people through writing and film-making.

Dickens is well known for his enthusiasm for popular entertainments generally and his particular zest for the circus is evidenced in the appearance of numerous players here and there in his fiction and non-fiction writings. *Hard Times* is the work in which Dickens offers us his most sustained portrayal of a small, hand-to-mouth circus with its line-up of absurd and comic characters. The circus itself is absent from much of the central part of the novel but it re-enters the novel through the metaphorical language which is used to describe both the industrial landscape and the characters who inhabit it and who struggle to invent identities within it. During a period characterised by the expansion of both urban habitation and industrial labour, the novel mobilises the specific example of the circus to replay the shifting and highly contended terms of contemporary debates and discourses surrounding the role of popular entertainments in general. Most interestingly, however, the novel recognises the fundamental resistance of circus (as live, mostly non-verbal entertainment) to literary embodiment: it does not record circus performances. Instead, throughout the text, the circus ring becomes a highly resonant and disruptive figure which foregrounds the instabilities and emptiness which haunt literary embodiment, In this respect Dickens gives us one of the most perceptive and radical literary mobilisations of circus.

No film director has been more closely associated with and pre-occupied by the circus than Federico Fellini. Much like Dickens, even when Fellini's films contain no representations of circuses, their extravagant range of grotesque and exquisite characters, together with their penchant for chaotic narratives and spectacular sets, is evocative of the circus. Fellini, however, saves his keenest interest for the clowns whose allegorical potential he explicitly investigates both on paper and on film. Although the film *The Clowns* is ostensibly an act of mourning and preservation of the clowning tradition which Fellini fears may have disappeared, the film's failed attempts to recover, rejuvenate and memo-rialise their performance again only points to the irreconcilable gap between the clowns' frenetic energy and the film's empty reification of it. Again, as with Dickens, the circus works in this film to describe a problem of embodiment, but in doing so it also articulates the peculiar and ambivalent economy of the photographic image; the image through which a person is 'captured' also becomes their effigy.

The final chapter returns initially and briefly to the cultural history of the circus to pull out from it one of its most highly charged and enigmatic of figures: the female aerialist. As I suggest above, of all circus figures aerialists (of all sorts) have been charged with inspiring the noblest and even transcendent of human achievement; indeed, as I will show, the body of the aerialist frequently operates as a sign for the circus as a whole. Just as the circus promotes a public fantasy of itself as a space of exceptionalism, escape and danger in which the rules which seem to govern the world outside have no currency, the body of the aerialist is weighed down by no regulation and is governed only by its singular self-discipline and strength. The fantasies of liberation immanent in these performances are overset with further significance when they are gendered female since the acts clearly involve both a display of the female form and a spectacular announcement of physical power and self-reliance which has, literally and metaphorically, flown in the face of social convention. Finally, these figures (both male and female) at times also offer an intriguing confusion of gender attributes as they perform, a confusion which is evidenced in the rhetoric sur-rounding the promotion and critical appreciation of their acts. This blurring of gender distinction has worked to promote a further level of inquisitiveness about the 'natural' limits and potential of the human body amongst spectators and artists who seek to represent these performers.

I have focused in such detail on Wim Wenders's film *Wings of Desire* in my final chapter because it seems at first to offer a radical revision of precisely such idealistic fantasies of the transcendent body which have so frequently been generated by aerialists. At the start of the film the female aerialist at the centre of its narrative is very obviously seen to be subject both to the economic pressures and restrictions which circumscribe the circus in which she performs and to the tyrannical ringmaster who directs and controls the terms of her performance. As the film progresses, however, Wenders's aerialist becomes increasingly abstract as he shapes her (with reference to Walter Benjamin's 'Angel of History') into an allegorical figure within his broader artistic conceptualisation of the the nature of progress and its relationship to memory, narrative and the historical moment or crisis in German history. Thus Wenders's aerialist embodies an idea *about* history – the promise of future potential which is harboured by present danger – but she cannot enact or imagine what the fruit of this promise might be. Whereas in Dickens and Fellini we will see how circus figures operate as registers for the failures of embodiment immanent within their respective modes of inscription, in Wenders's film the aerialist's increasingly abstract and undecipherable form becomes a symbol of the resistance of the present moment and of our failure to read in it the future which it will yield: a future which is both incrypted and, as yet, unyielding to the process of narration. Throughout Part II, therefore, I am exploring some of the reasons why the circus has been so attractive to artists who are drawn to, or even nostalgic about, unabashed celebration of human physical presence and potential and yet whose operation within particular forms of narrative inscription has precisely resulted in the erosion or incryption of 'presence'. Thus, this book demonstrates how the circus is definitively modern: modern in its organisational structures and performative energies, but modern also for the way that these performances have furnished us with figures which draw attention to the limitations of the very forms of inscription and narration through which we continually attempt to describe ourselves as such.

Introduction

Notes

1 Marcello Truzzi, 'The decline of the American circus: the shrinkage of an institution', in M. Truzzi (ed.), *Sociology in Everyday Life* (Englewood Cliffs, Prentice-Hall, 1968), p. 315.
2 Maurice Willson Disher, *Greatest Show on Earth* (London, G. Bell and Sons, 1937), p.25. The story has its origin in a puff of 1769, BL *Astley's Cuttings from Newspapers*, vol. 1, item 1169.
3 Truzzi, 'Decline of the American circus', p. 315.
4 Friedrich Nietzsche, *Thus Spoke Zarathustra: a Book for Everyone and No One*, trans. R. J. Hollingdale (Harmondsworth, Penguin Books [1885], 1969), pp. 41–9.
5 Nietzsche, *Thus Spoke Zarathustra*, p. 43.
6 Nietzsche, *Thus Spoke Zarathustra*, pp. 47–8.

I

Cultural history and aesthetics

1

Origins

During April of 1768 a newspaper advertisement urged its readers to make their way to Philip Astley's 'riding school' in Lambeth Marsh at the Halfpenny Hatch (and, it cautioned, 'not the DOG and DUCK' in St George's Fields, Southwark where Mr and Mrs Wolton's trick riding took place) to see the 'activity on horseback' performed by the former 'Serjean[t] Major in his Majesty's Royal Regiment of Light Dragoons'.[1] With its oddly circumspect tone this bill now seems a rather modest and perhaps even inauspicious opening for what would become one of the most brazen of entertainment forms. None the less, the modern circus, as opposed to the Roman one, is generally acknowledged to have its origin in these experiments with trick horse-riding on the Surrey side of the Thames.[2] In some ways it is unrepresentative that Astley is so frequently singled out from his contemporaries as both the first star and point of origin of the circus. Not only had acts of the kind Astley was to bring together under the eventual appellation 'circus' been familiar sport in the now declining traditional British fairs since at least the beginning of the seventeenth century (tumbling, rope-dancing, juggling, animal tricks and so on), but even within Astley's own specialism was he preceded by other exhibitors of trick riding such as Thomas Johnston (from 1758), Mr Sampson (1767) and Thomas Price (1767).[3] Nevertheless, as Marius Kwint points out, Astley's significance lies not so much in any aesthetic or artistic innovation, but rather in his origination of an institutional form for the organisation and display of acts which had previously been characterised by their dispersed, itinerant and singular nature. It was his method of marshalling the convergence of audience and performers within a distinctive performance space which, having proved financially rewarding, marked out the following constituent features of what is recognised today as the 'circus'.[4] Firstly, the situating of the entertainment inside a circular arena had the dual function of both creating a centrifugal force through the galloping horse which bolstered the balance of its rider and, perhaps more crucially, transformed the equestrian performances from a public spectacle from which people wandered towards and away (dropping payment if they so wished into circulating hats), to a pay-on-entry arena which was physically fenced off in order 'to exclude the gaze of non-payers'.[5] Secondly, Astley threw himself enthusiastically into publicising his enterprise through the press, by handing out advertising bills and by traipsing through London with his wife, shouting his attractions in order to pull in crowds. So, whilst Astley, as the first real circus impresario, would go on to contribute much to the development of what made the circus distinctive aesthetically and generically, he also established it as an art form which, as Kwint has argued, was 'comparatively highly commercialised from the start'.[6]

A number of crucial developments in the formation of the circus took place during the lifetime of Astley. The first of these was the rapid growth of the circus as an institution for entertainment beyond Astley's itself. Clearly Astley regarded the circus as his own invention and indeed, as Jacob Decastro tells in his memoirs, throughout his career was extremely 'jealous' of what he came to regard as his 'birth-right'.[7] He did not take kindly therefore to the setting up of rival establishments, of which there were quickly quite a few.[8] At the same time, although Astley's name may have dominated this first epoch of the circus, it is also important to acknowledge that these competitors were greatly significant since, in competition, Astley reacted to and imitated them as much, if not more, than he innovated and invented himself. Acts were improved and multiplied in the various competitors' attempts to outdo each other and draw in greater crowds.

The most important of these figures was Charles Hughes, a former employee of Astley's, who set up a rival equestrian establishment in 1772 – the British Horse Academy – at Blackfriars' Bridge, just up the road from Astley's.[9] It was from Hughes's relocated enterprise, The Royal Circus by the Obelisk in St George's Circus, Lambeth, that, by 4 November 1782, the circus would receive its name: 'The Royal Circus and Equestrian Philharmonic Academy' – Astley's was still an 'amphi-theatre'. It was in this building that the standard ring size of 13 metres (or 42 feet) was established. Hughes together with Charles Dibdin, an actor and dramatist, would prove to be a heavily influential figure in the next phase of the circus (post-1782) when it acquired a specific generic identity and thereby expanded and outgrew its initial association solely with Astley's to become an entertainment form in its own right. [10]

Even in his first year of shows, and before the competition from Hughes and Dibdin, Astley himself had not only filled out his programme to two hours in length by introducing non-equestrian acts, but had also brought 'a representational note into what had been a mere exhibition of skill' with a drama depicting Elliot's charging of the French troops in Germany in 1761 and with 'A Prologue on the Death of a Horse' (a horse appears to be dead but is summoned up again to serve its country). This provided a 'clear, albeit sentimental, demonstration of control over other creatures that took its place in the circus alongside human bodily skill at an early stage'.[11] However, Hughes and Dibdin contributed much to elaborating the theatrical, musical and representational dimensions of circus and some would say those associated with the Royal Circus excelled in relation to Astley in terms of their artistry and performance skills whilst Astley in the end was left with the more successful circus only because his skills as an impresario were unsurpassed during his lifetime.[12]

The circus flourished during this period and this was partly as a result of its acquiring an international dimension. Astley had performed in Paris on a seasonal basis between 1772 and 1778, but the circus proper began in Europe when, at the close of the war in 1783, Astley added a French branch (Amphithéâtre Astley) to his enterprises and was shortly granted, on 8 December 1786, a temporary arena at Versailles by the royal family.[13] He also built the Cirque du Palais Royale (1787), although this was commandeered between 1791 and 1802 (during the years of Revolution) by Antonio Franconi, an Italian bird trainer, and his two sons, Laurent and Henri. They went on to lead the development of the circus across Europe and built many more permanent circus buildings themselves, mostly in Paris. By the time Astley came back in 1802 after the Peace of Amiens to reclaim his grounds, Franconi had established his own permanent circus, and his family, together with Louis Dejean, would eventually take over Astley's and build many more circus-based amphitheatres (Cirque d'Hiver, Cirque d'Eté, Cirque Medrano). Meanwhile Charles Hughes was to be an important mainspring in the establishment of a Russian circus tradition since he performed and taught there after being commissioned in 1793 to buy bloodstock for the imperial stables. Amphitheatres were specially commissioned by Empress Catherine to be built in St Petersburg and Moscow for Hughes. Around the same time (1792) the beginnings of an American circus were being forged by John Bill Ricketts, who had been an apprentice to Hughes when he worked in Philadelphia. By the 1800s, nine British cities possessed permanent circus buildings and, by the time of the Regency, there were as many as that in London alone.

Though the circus rapidly propagated itself on a national and international scale during this period, it was persistently impeded by its physical and legal precariousness. Whilst a standard for the dimensions and layout of the circus and its architecture was eventually set, its material infrastructure quickly acquired associations of impermanence. Astley's alone suffered four catastrophic fires (three in Astley's lifetime) each of which, since he was always vastly underinsured, brought the proprietor to the brink of ruin.[14] Franconi's Cirque Olympique in Paris, over which he had taken charge again after the French Revolution, burnt down in 1826 during Andrew Ducrow's period of management, whilst the fourth fire at Astley's (1841) would be the end of him. By this stage, however, Astley's had become one of the best-equipped stages in the country and the fourth and last Astley's which opened in 1843 lasted right through to the time of 'Lord' George Sanger at the end of the century when it closed as a circus in 1893.

Throughout this period, and up until 1843, all non-patented, that is minor theatres, were prevented under the law from presenting straight prose drama which meant that circuses continually found themselves in difficult but mostly evasive relations with the law (see chapter 4, 'Legitimacy', below). Circuses (like many other forms of popular entertainment) got around the law (by virtue of its vagueness) rather than fell in with it or fell foul of it. They did this partly through careful selection of geographical spaces (for example south of the Thames in London) which were not so rigorously policed and by selecting acts without spoken prose dialogue which were not explicitly covered by existing theatrical legislation. All this was helped along by the fact that, as Kwint points out, the law was 'haphazardly and incompetently enforced'.[15]

Finally, it is important to note the extent to which the early circus was dominated, not only by the presence of the horse, but by equestrian drama. Initially equestrian acts had been privileged within the programmes of entertainment offered by the circus, though in number these were gradually reduced towards the end of the century, eventually making a come-back in 1807 before reaching their peak in the 1830 and 40s with the great military spectacles and equestrian dramas or hippodramas (the most popular of which were 'Timour the Tartar', 'The Battle of Waterloo' and 'Mazeppa') which dominated that period. Indeed the third Astley's which opened in 1804 (and underwent a major refit of the stage between 1817 and 1818) already allowed for horses to take a greater role in productions since it had a reinforced stage, stage elevations, platforms and bridges to accommodate the weight of the animals (see figure 1). This combination was quickly popularised and performed at the Holborn Amphitheatre and the Hippodrome. Though initially in the circus a separation was maintained between stage and ring acts, when the distinction melted away the action began to move freely between the two, and, with the involvement of horses in this movement, 'hippodrama' was born, though it was also a form which existed independently of the ring. Antony Hippisley Coxe, has described this as a 'bastard entertainment' born of a 'misalliance between the theatre and the circus' which, he believes, 'actually inhibited the development of the circus' because the principles which govern each are so fundamentally different.[16] None the less, although horses held a key position in the circus until the 1860s when other, more 'exotic' kinds of animals were introduced, it is also true that, by the turn of the eighteenth century, the circus had acquired a generic identity. The mix of acts which would go on for a century and a half to make up the entertainment form recognised as circus had been fused together, though of course like all generic entertainments the nature of this fusion would evolve and adapt through historical change and cultural adaptation.

In a slightly uncanny turn of events both Astleys, father and son, died in the same bed in Paris; Astley senior died on 20 October 1814 aged seventy-two and, almost seven years to the day later, John died on 19 October 1821. W. Davis took over the running of the amphitheatre for a short while but was quickly succeeded by Andrew Ducrow (1798–1842) in 1825 who was to oversee Astley's running until 1841 in what came to be known as the 'Golden Era' of the British circus.[17] In the period of the Astleys, as I have outlined above, the circus was consolidated into a distinct and relatively coherent form which, after 1820, became, some have claimed, the pre-eminent Victorian entertainment with artistic and physical expertise, audiences, venues

Figure 1
*Astley's
Amphitheatre,*
Pugin and
Rowlandson
1808

(nationally and internationally), cultural references and status multiplying considerably.

Andrew Ducrow, the son of circus strong man, Peter Ducrow (the 'Flemish Hercules'), had been a child prodigy of the circus ('The Infant Wonder' or the 'Little Devil') and had completed most of his training as an equestrian performer abroad, mainly in France. Unlike Philip Astley, Ducrow was always a performer and an innovator, as was his second wife, Louisa Woolford. One nineteenth-century commentator remarked that at Astley's from '1823 to 1843 there was little occurred at this theatre requiring especial mention' but the truth is that, although Ducrow's directorship may have, until its final hours, been absent of great upheaval or revision, his management brought not only physical/institutional but also an artistic and cultural readjustment for circus as a whole.[18] He launched an extensive building programme to erect permanent circuses in the provinces while the circus basked in a level of financial success, respectability, stability and royal patronage (the Royal Family attended in 1828) it had not previously known.[19] As Dickens put it, Ducrow arose 'to shed the light of classic taste and portable gas over the sawdust of the circus', though Maurice Willson Disher suggests that his style, at times both grandiose and bluff, made him a 'character more improbable than any of those Dickens was inventing'.[20]

Artistically he was most famous for his 'poses plastiques', a kind of dramatic equestrianism in which he mimed popular versions of famous characters from myth, history and literature on horseback. His equestrian version of Byron's *Mazeppa, and the Wild Horse; or The Child of the Desert*, first performed on 4 April 1831, was very much in this vein.[21] Willson Disher claims that 'No other spectacle mounted at Astley's, no other play staged in any theatre of the world, was acted so far and wide and so persistently' as this one and indeed, by 1875, it was being performed 'everywhere on earth where the sawdust and ring could lay its fence'.[22] Both this and his other famous adaptation of *The Courier of St Petersburg* (1827), which involved a messenger straddling two horses riding round the ring accumulating ever more (usually up to nine) horses, each of which bears the national flag of a different country. This continued to be performed internationally until late into the 1890s.[23] Ducrow then, can be seen as consolidating the (connected) pantomimic, equestrian and internationalist dimensions of circus spectacle whilst at the same time lending it a certain cultural respectability, through his demotic dramatisations of myth, opera, history and literature which, though they may not have constituted the majority in the audience, proved an irresitable combination for the Victorian middle classes. As Cunningham puts it, 'without Ducrow it would hardly have been possible for Dickens to celebrate Astley's.'[24]

A disastrous fire at Astley's in August 1841 precipitated Ducrow's mental breakdown and his untimely death some months later on 27 January 1842. By this stage however, Ducrow and other proprietors had established a number of both temporary and permanent circus buildings in provincial towns and cities up and down the country. The most widely known of these were Cooke's (which was to take over the lease of Astley's in 1853 for several years, after William Batty, Ducrow's successor), Sanders, Samwell's, Holloway's, Wild's and Hengler's, which, in 1871, set up shop in London.[25] Circus programmes of the period suggest that the content of these various companies' shows was fairly similar, though with their main emphasis being on equestrian drama and pantomime, each working and reworking a now established repertoire of generic acts and set-pieces performed by players who would move between various troops in the course of their careers.[26] Most followed the pattern of wintering in a permanent or temporary wooden theatre in the city before embarking on a summer of touring and tenting (often coinciding with local fairs); both types of venue could house around 1,500 people per performance. Frequently they were accompanied by travelling menageries such as Wombwell's and Atkin's who would set up their booths filled with animals and human oddities around the main circus tents.

The 1850s and 60s then, were decades of great and nation-wide expansion for the British circus, but this was greatly spurred on by the arrival of hot competition from both France and North America. The Franconi family, who had succeeded Astley at the Cirque Olympique in Paris following the Revolution, brought their 'Cirque Nationale de France', but it was the enormous 3,000–5,000 seater North American touring circuses such as Hernandez and Stone (who arrived in 1853) and Howes and Cushing (1857), which perhaps had the greatest impact. Americans had been performing on British circus stages for some time, indeed it was Ducrow who was responsible for making Isaac Van Amburgh the first real star in Britain of wild-animal taming acts, but now in American circus companies they were to have an impact on the scale and scope of both circus acts and institution.[27]

Experiments in equestrian display would appear to have been taking place in the United States by about 1771, with records giving details of performances by a Mr John Sharp in Salem, Boston and New York in November 1771 and Mr Faulks and Jacob Bates, in 1771 and 1772 respectively, in Philadelphia.[28] However the main reason given for the later development of what could be called an American circus is the interruption caused by the years of Revolution during which an Act of Congress (1774) had prohibited public exhibitions and entertainments. Subsequently there were equestrian performances in a small purpose-built construction in Philadelphia by Thomas Pool in August of 1785, but it would not be until the arrival of Charles Hughes's protégé, John Bill Ricketts, in late 1792 that, what had previously been simply equestrian and human/animal tricks, would become interspersed with clowning in a manner which qualified as circus. Almost immediately (22 April 1793) Ricketts' circus received the sanction of the first President, himself an expert horseman, who proved to be a long-standing and loyal patron of Ricketts and of the circus in general. The need of this unofficial entertainment to acquire the official sanction of the head of state was not the only thing which the early American circus had in common with the British one. It too was initially a city-based (Philadelphia and New York) entertainment which took place in speedily constructed, semi-permanent buildings and consisted of equestrian acts interspersed with other human and animal entertainments including American adaptations of 'The Taylor Riding to Brentford' and 'The Metamorphosis of a Sack' and various pantomimes, dances and burlettas, though the latter were quite rapidly abandoned and a pared-down, more economic and less stage-bound version of the circus emerged more quickly than it had done in Europe.

Though Ricketts and his brother Francis performed with very little serious competition, the acquisition of great prosperity was hampered by the same kinds of problems which had faced Hughes and Astley. His eventual departure from Philadelphia in 1801 was precipitated by a fire which completely destroyed his amphitheatre there. After a short but eventful stay in Guadeloupe he attempted to sail back to England but was lost at sea when his ship went down. A taste for circus entertainment, however, had been whetted and considerable numbers of European performers, mainly French and English, made their way to the States to continue where Ricketts had left off, bringing with them all the elements (acrobatic, equestrian, clowning and so on) of a generic form which had, as we have seen above, by this stage been fully shaped and established in Europe. By the late 1820s, however, Americans themselves began to operate their own circuses and from this period on there emerged several significant developments and adaptations which would prove to distinguish the American circus from its counterparts in other continents: the use of tents rather than permanent or semi-permanent buildings, the construction of highly ornate circus wagons during street parades, the transportation by rail and the multiplication of circus rings from one to three.

In 1825 J. Purdy Brown of Delaware was the first American circus proprietor to take his circus on the road with a tent, thereby paving the way for a fully peripatetic circus which was free to leave the expensive city amphitheatres, where they may have been committed to sometimes unprofitably lengthy runs, and travel into often entertainment-starved rural areas, moving on to a new town every few days, depending on when the audience of a particular town was exhausted. As the population and the North American roads system expanded, so did the number of circuses which were able to move themselves about using horses and wagons increase in number. Since many of these troupes were rather small, this rapid movement from place to place reduced the pressure on them to produce constant innovation in the nature and variety of the entertainments presented. The bigger circuses demarcated separate activities into separate but adjoining tents with the 'big top' being used for the main show, an adjacent smaller menagerie tent (for the exotic animals and 'freak show') and side show tents containing carnival shows such as sword swallowers, snake charmers, fat ladies and so on. Additional tents functioned as canteens and horse stables.

By the 1830s the American circus had also adopted and transformed the tradition of a street parade of circus bands and wagons on arrival in each town. These were no ordinary wagons. Speaight suggests that the inspiration for their highly opulent and elaborate design came from the coaches used to mobilise the European royalty from the Renaissance period onwards. It is difficult to deny the evidence of the regal and imperial aspirations in these richly coloured wagons which were frequently decorated with carved dragons, eagles and the symbols of various continents and which were often drawn by camels or elephants as well as horses. The spectacular force of the wagons rapidly increased so that by the 1870s the wagons, some of which now included figures which telescoped mechanically in and out of the top of them, had become so elaborate that they began to constitute an entertainment and an art form in themselves.[29] At their peak the parades for the big circuses such as Ringling Brothers Barnum and Bailey could be up to three miles long and might take several hours to pass.

The vast geographical spaces to be covered by the American circus and the move mentioned above towards more economic tours consisting of shorter stops in larger towns and cities meant that, for the bigger circuses, transport by rail soon emerged as a more attractive and faster option than pulling multiple wagons over often half-formed or weather-damaged tracks and roads. A Dr Gilbert A. Spaulding of the Spaulding and Rogers show made a tentative beginning in 1856, but the tracks and carriages of the period were primitive and his tour was more hindered than helped by the experiment.[30] It would not be until the late 1860s that others followed Spaulding's initiative with the real breakthrough taking place in 1871 with P. T. Barnum's then partners, Dan Castello and William Coup, persuading him that a larger than normal circus in possession of its own uniquely fashioned rail cars would be worthy of (indeed might bolster) his name; the Ringling Brothers eventually moved completely to rail transport in 1890. Thus the railway trains came to consolidate some of the defining features of the North American circus during the period which would constitute its Golden Age (1871–1915): panoramic spectacle, self-containment and organisational efficiency on an enormous scale. The trains, carrying between 2 to 109 cars per circus (20–25 wagons per engine), embodied the most spectacular (and self-publicising) form of modern mechanised speed produced by the industrial era. They increased the size of audiences by cutting out stops at small towns but ferrying in small-town audiences with special 'day tripping' trains. Time efficiencies were achieved as the circuses travelled by night allowing performers to sleep on the trains' passenger cars (previously performers had also slept in their horse-drawn wagons) rather than in hotels, so that they could perform the next day. The speed at which the trains travelled, however, meant that the new form of transport carried attendant dangers and the famous train crashes of 1882 (Sells Brothers), 1885 (Adam Forepaugh), 1892 (Ringling) and the worst in 1918 (Hagenbeck-Wallace) ensured that the image of the train crash accompanied that of the fire, the collapsing stand or tent and the furious, escaping wild animal into the visual mythology of the dangers of the circus both in and outside the ring.

Only the biggest circuses (Ringling Brothers Barnum and Bailey, Cole Brothers, Dailey Brothers and finally Clyde Beatty) owned their own freight, whilst the others had to hire theirs from railway companies. Few of the latter survived the Depression, after which rail transport was reduced and smaller circuses turned to trucks and lorries, the preferred form from then until the present day. Experiments with motorised transport began in 1918 and had begun to prove successful by 1926 when the Downie Brothers circus went on the road with thirty-eight trucks and accompanying vehicles and by the 1930s all but the biggest moved this way with other forms of mechanised vehicles such as the famous Bulldog Macks doing the work formerly performed by work-horses.[31] In Europe, however, where the spaces to be covered between shows have not been quite so vast, Bertram Mills was one of very few circuses to move by rail (between 1933 and 1955).[32] Mills had been inspired by the impressively efficient loading and unloading systems he had witnessed on a visit to John Ringling in the United States and a memory of Barnum and Bailey's famous continental tour of 1898 for which four trains and sixty-one special circus cars had been commissioned and built in England.[33] The North American railroad circus, then, consolidated an image of American wealth, ambition and systematic organisation on a grand scale which, whilst it clearly impressed practitioners and general public, was generally rejected, along with the three ring circus, itself to be seen partly as an offshoot of the railroad circus in that the new means of transport had a greatly increased capacity for carrying equipment of all sorts.

Finally, between 1871 and 1881, the American circus introduced both the three-ring circus (see chapter 2, 'Structures') and, with it, an extra entertainment in the form of the 'midway': a tunnel of carnival exhibition stalls which lined a pathway of about 300 feet towards the front entrance of the big top, for which it also functioned to drum up business. These were made up of a combination of acts which, as we have seen, in early circus would have been part of the main show (human oddities, exotic animals, marionette shows, sword swallowers, tattooed women and men), as well as dioramas, wax figures, mechanical wonders and rare objects, though interest in these museum-style exhibits had somewhat subsided by the early 1880s. Yet the live side-shows, since they clearly involved a different form of audience attention and had become increasingly unacceptable to middle-class sensibilities, were gradually edged out of the central show to become optional, pay-as-you-go extras on the midway. The emphasis on large-scale spectacle in the three-ring circuses meant that acts which involved speed, danger and multiple performers were moved to the top of the bill ahead of traditional clown and novelty acts such as the learned pig, the contortionists and so on. In the dubious educational spirit of Barnum's American Museum of which they were an offshoot, midway side-shows were frequently accompanied by a 'lecturer' who acted as a guide to the exhibits, talking them up whilst peddling suspect life histories and bogus science.[34] Not only did the impact of these performers depend precisely on their individuality, which became spectacular when marketed as uniqueness or oddness, but, since their attraction was augmented by a verbal explanation (of origins, technique or of a propitious accident), this kind of more intimate audience/spectacle engagement became difficult to accommodate within an entertainment in which narration played an increasingly diminishing part. Equally, there is importance in this separating off of major and minor circus acts into central and marginal spaces in the second half of the nine-teenth century because it suggests an implicit privileging of acts in which individual bodies which are exceptional for certain kinds of achievement (grace, beauty, strength, skill) over others where excep-tionalness is marked by abnormality (smallness, tallness, fatness, gender anomalies, birth defects) or self-mutilation (tattoos, sword-swallowing). Whereas curiosity for such exhibitions seems to have waned in Europe by the end of the nineteenth century, they continued to be popular in the United States as 'ten-in-one' shows within touring carnivals and fairs, with the last remaining 'freak show' disbanding only in 1995.[35]

It was on the circus midway, however, that the grifters operated: gamesters, pickpockets, card sharks and con men of all sorts who duped a gullible general public ('towners') out of their dollars, nearly always with the knowledge and sanction of the circus proprietors and local authorities who would receive a cut of the takings. These fraudsters were at first seen as part and parcel of the circus's renegade appeal, and indeed were, in a way, close cousins of Barnum who believed that the public voluntarily and knowingly participated in his scams or 'humbugs' precisely because they were entertaining and relatively harmless. By the turn of the century many communities began to feel that the balance had shifted too far towards the con men and even big circuses such as Hagenbeck-Wallace and Howes Great

London were regarded with suspicion, as places of swindling, immorality and danger.

The turning point, in terms of the moral disapproval with which the circus was surrounded by the 1890s, came with the growing pre-eminence of the Ringling Brothers who, from setting off on their first road show in 1882 and their first circus in May 1884, became the successors to Barnum (who died in 1891) as the dominant names in the railroad era of the American circus. By the time James Bailey had returned from his 1898 five-year European tour of 'The Greatest Show on Earth', he discovered that his absence had worked to strengthen the arm of the Ringlings, who had always been his main and fiercest competitors. John Ringling, who by 1905 had already negotiated a half share of Bailey's Forepaugh-Sells Circus, made a good deal on the purchase of 'The Greatest Show on Earth' (as well as the rest of the Forepaugh-Sells show) in October, 1907, following Bailey's death in April 1906. Eventually, in 1929, on the eve of the Great Depression, John Ringling would also take over the grouping of all the other big railroad shows (Hagenbeck-Wallace, Sells-Floto, John Robinson, Sparks and Al G. Barnes) which had been joined together in the 1920s by Jerry Mugivan, Bert Bowers and Ed Ballard under the heading the American Circus Corporation and was based in Peru, Indiana. The family business which had been most successful in building a circus empire also presided over the decline of the railroad shows during the Depression, and the subsequent receding from the Golden Age, as each of the five big circuses withdrew from the railways in the course of the 1930s. Finding himself unable to make the repayments of the money he had borrowed to take over the syndicate, John Ringling was forced to relinquish control over it in 1932, though in 1938 his nephew John Ringling North regained the dominant position again for the Ringling family. However, the subsequent years, until the abandonment of touring shows in 1956, proved to be very tough ones, marked as they were by the labour disputes of 1938, followed by the war years and, within this, the infamous Hartford fire of 1944 in which 168 people were killed.

The early popularity and success of the Ringlings was in large part due to the sweeping changes they made to the regulation of dubious practices and business associations which had become synonymous with circus shows. They banned all forms of grifting from their lots and made public their insistence on value for money. Circus employees were issued with a printed list of strict regulations stipulating proper behaviour (with reference to drinking, smoking, dress and associations with the opposite sex) at all times, and for this they, and other shows which followed their example, earned the title 'Sunday School Shows'. But the clean-out proved highly profitable since it allowed the Ringlings to set about selling the circus as morally wholesome, family entertainment and marketing the respectability of their shows in comparison with their shady competitors, to whom they showed no mercy; it became a way both of rebranding the circus in the popular imagination and of extending Ringling domination of the marketplace.[36]

As you would expect of an art form which had so far invested so heavily in the promotion and development of modern technology, the circus and, most notably the Ringlings, were involved in early cinema screenings; the technology which, many have suggested, succeeded and usurped the circus as the pre-eminent form of popular Western entertainment. In 1897, using a machine bought from Edison, the Ringling Brothers set up an extra tent on their lot which would, ominously perhaps, be called the 'Black Top' (due to the necessity of conducting the screenings in darkness). The tent contained a cinematograph, an early film projector which showed a boxing match, Corbett-Fitzsimmons, which had taken place in March of 1897.[37] Still, at this stage these early films with their poorly composed, flat, black and white images suggested no serious competition for the circus, but must rather have been valued for their novelty and for the extra cachet which the display of pioneering technology of vision must have brought to the circus.[38] Nevertheless, in the late nineteenth century, most big American towns and cities had built opera houses for the purposes of housing travelling theatrical companies and by the turn of the century the Vaudeville stage and large-scale amusement parks became serious rivals to the circus, even before the advent of sound in the cinema in 1927. The physical incompatibility of the two forms also quickly became apparent since overheated projectors which blew up constituted a further serious incendiary threat to the circus; this, together with increasing levels of demand and new health and safety legislation drove cinema exhibition towards its own auditoriums.[39]

Meanwhile in the United Kingdom, though circuses and circus acts continued to tour widely, many of what had been permanent circus buildings became less distinguishable from other forms of popular theatre. Many of the star aerial acts (discussed in my final chapter), for example, took place in London theatres such as the Royal Alhambra and Holborn or Crystal Palace, above the audience's heads, rather than in a ring, and this was also the case in the United States and the rest of Europe.[40] The top-billing acts of the second half of the nineteenth century were not the extensive equestrian dramas and pantomimes of Ducrow's era; circus, as I have already suggested, had by this stage established its various recognisable generic component parts (clowns, acrobats, aerialists) who, as named stars in their own right, were not necessarily confined to performing either in the ring or committed to any ring in particular. In this respect Astley's lasted longer than most since, although Cooke had given it up in 1860 and for a decade it returned to being a conventional theatre, in 1871 it fell under the management of colourful figure of 'Lord' George Sanger who had the interior rebuilt in order to accommodate seating for 4,000 and who presided over its running until it was converted into a music hall in 1893. Sanger's programme was dominated by opulently staged pantomime (with only occasional hippodramas) and as such it became an important feature of the Victorian Christmas calendar. What is important in these various changes to the ways people experienced the circus is that a discernible separation clearly took place between the institution of circus as it emerged in the late eighteenth century (as entertainments on horseback, taking place in a ring, mixed with clowning, acrobatics and animal tricks) and the idea of circus as a set of characteristic performances. In other words, a gap emerges between *the* circus and circus, a gap which would widen and complicate in the twentieth century as the infrastructures and audiences which had so enthusiastically supported the classical circus in the West throughout the nineteenth century began to weaken. Circus has not only begun to adapt and mutate, again, into different forms, but has also impacted on other forms of art and entertainment (cinema, ballet, opera, contemporary dance) into which it has, at times, been incorporated. However, it would be a mistake to read this change as any kind of return to pre-Astleian days before these disparate acts were collected under one roof since the status and associations of these acts were entirely transformed by the establishment of circus as a distinct generic form of entertainment.

In the post-war period there have been two major and connected developments within the reshaping of the circus in both Europe and the United States. Firstly, a combination of bad publicity and high-profile animal-rights campaigning around the issue of circus animals has resulted in intense media and, in the United Kingdom, RSPCA scrutiny of circus animal-keeping practices as well as the outright banning by many local authorities of circuses with animal acts. Traditional British circuses such as Cottle's, Chipperfield's, Roberts's and Miller's, which have tended to operate on quite a small scale, have been forced either to adapt or to supplement their tours with shows abroad. A major boon to these companies in the last decade has, however, been the exodus of highly skilled and state-trained performers from the former Soviet Union and Eastern Bloc countries who have been widely promoted by British circuses such as Jay Miller's and Bobby Roberts's.

Secondly, there has been a growing excitement of interest in what has popularly been dubbed the 'new circus'. Though there exist huge variations in both scale and style within the 'new circus'; what unites them all is their rejection of animal performances as well as a common genesis in the alternative arts of the 1970s, particularly street theatre, mime and dance – all of which of course are, at the same time, deeply traditional in their origins. Some of the performers, such as Pierrot Pillot-Bidon, founder of the French company Archaos and Katja Schumann of the highly successful Big Apple Circus in the United States, were the renegade children of the traditional circus, but others have learnt their skills outside the established circus families in circus schools such as (in London) Circus Space or have simply moved into circus after training in dance or theatre. Two off-shoots of this broadening of the availability of skills have been, firstly, that there is now more artistic interchange between circus and other performance-based arts so that circus skills are more in evidence within contemporary dance, opera and theatre. Secondly, the 'new circus' is frequently more theatrical and narrative or theme-based than circuses have been since the nineteenth century.

Notes

1 4 April, BL *Astley's Cuttings From Newspapers*, vol. 1, item 4. Although the Halfpenny Hatch no longer exists, historians have demonstrated, with reference to Horwoods 1799 map of London, that it partly corresponds to what is now the Cornwall Road in Lambeth with the White Hart public house now occupying the space that was once Astley's. For a reproduction of this map see Paul Bemrose, *Circus Genius: A Tribute to Philip Astley*,

1742–1814 (Newcastle-Under-Lyme, Priory Publications, 1992), pp. 16–19.

2 The most detailed account of these is contained in the first chapter of Rupert Croft-Cooke and Peter Cotes, *Circus: A World History* (London, Macmillan, 1976), pp. 7–38. George Speaight also stresses that these were by no means the origin of the modern circus since they differed in both scale of performance and in content, offering as they did mainly chariot racing and games. See Speaight's *The History of the Circus* (London, Tantivy Press, 1980), p. 11.

3 For further details about these acts see George Speaight *History of the Circus*, pp. 21–3, Paul Bemrose, *Circus Genius* pp. 15–17 and Howard Loxton, *The Golden Age of the Circus* (London, Grange Books, 1997), pp. 10–11. Amongst some of the most notorious venues for such itinerant fair performers were Southwark Fair, St Bartholomew's Fair, the Frost Fair, the May Fair, Vauxhall Gardens, and Sadler's Wells Theatre (in Paris the fairs were at St Laurent, St Ovide and St Germain) and of course public houses such as the Three Hats in Islington. Theatre spaces had been scarce since the Civil War in 1642.

4 'it must be recognised that he actually originated very little himself ... But Astley's reputation rests not so much on what he originated as on how he developed the elements of entertainment that he had inherited' George Speaight, *History of the Circus*, p. 31. Other historians of Astley reinforce this point. See, for example, Marius Kwint, 'Astley's amphitheatre and the early circus in England, 1768–1830', D. Phil thesis, Oxford University, 1994, pp. 17–20.

5 Kwint, 'Astley's amphitheatre', p. 17. Speaight suggests that Dobney's Bowling Green in Islington, where Thomas Price had his riding school in 1767, had a 'proper ring surrounded by seated spectators' *A History of the Circus*, p. 31.

6 Kwint, 'Astley's amphitheatre', p. 17.

7 Jacob Decastro, *The Memoirs of J. Decastro, Comedian* (London, Sherwood Jones & Co., 1824), p. 25.

8 Mr and Mrs Wolton, for example, whom Kwint credits with bringing in the 'circus' characteristic variety of entertainments into the ring' for the first time by interspersing his horse-riding with rope-dancing, tumbling and pistol-shooting. Kwint, 'Astley's amphitheatre', p. 21.

9 Maurice Willson Disher describes Hughes indeed as 'Astley's best horse-man' but adds that he was 'a dark, envious man'. Many other sources indicate that he was possessed of, at best, a determined and stormy personality. M. Willson Disher, *Greatest Show on Earth* (London, G. Bell and Sons, 1937), p. 30.

10 Hughes was disadvantaged in relation to Astley in that, because he didn't own his own site, he constantly had to negotiate with Landlords which, as Decastro notes, produced constant tension and ill-feeling: 'every day

produced soemthing disagreeable, and the social compact of union which had existed was entirely broken through; hence the misfortunes of that concern arose, as each party acted in direct opposition to the general welfare of one another, and consequently of the general concern.' This was exacerbated by the fact that Hughes was reported to be 'a man of irritable temper', 'possessing a spirit of opposition'. He constantly worked against Dibdin until 'negligence and confusion prevailed'. Finally, during the early 1790s 'the popularity of the place diminished every day', 'the treasury failed' and a 'general desertion took place.' See Decastro, *Memoirs*, pp. 119–20. When Hughes took off to work for Empress Catherine in Russia in 1793 no rent was paid on the circus and it was returned to the owner, Colonel West's widow, who leased it to George and James Jones in 1794. It burned down in 1805 only to reopen the following year. It was then leased to Robert Elliston who changed its name to the Surrey Theatre and the ring was removed in 1810. It became a circus again in 1814 when Dibdin temporarily took over the lease, then in 1816 the ring was removed for ever.

11 Kwint, 'Astley's amphitheatre', p. 19.
12 See Speaight, *A History of the Circus*, p. 35–7.
13 See BL *Astley's Cuttings*, vol. 1, item 525.
14 After the Riding School, south of Westminster Bridge, which he began in May 1769, he moved to his first covered amphitheatre (Astley's Amphitheatre Riding House – renamed the Royal Grove in April 1786) in 1779. This burnt down on 16 August, 1794 and a second amphitheatre was opened as 'The Amphitheatre of Arts' on Easter Monday 1795. Speaight confirms that 'Pony Races in Astley's' (Guildhall Library, *c.* 1795) is perhaps the only remaining print of the second Astley's amphitheatre, though see Kwint pp. 207–8 for a likely watercolour print of this building. see George Speaight, 'Astley's amphitheatre', *Theatre Notebook*, 42 (1988), p. 76. Another fire on 2 September 1803 destroyed the building. BL *Astley's Cuttings*, vol. 2, item 254a reports insurance was worth £1,700 which meant a loss of £28,000. Astley was back in business by 2 April (Easter Monday) 1804.
15 Kwint, 'Astley's amphitheatre', p. 141.
16 Antony Hippisley Coxe, 'Equestrian drama and the circus', in David Bradby *et al.* (eds), *Performance and Politics in Popular Drama* (Cambridge, Cambridge University Press, 1980), p. 109.
17 See Willson Disher, *Greatest Show on Earth*, p. 157.
18 A series of articles printed under the pseudonym 'W' in *The Theatrical Journal* of 1849 are reproduced in Ray Toole Stott, *Circus and Allied Arts: a World Bibliography* (Derby, Harpur and Sons, 1971), vol. 4, appendices A–D (pp. 291–303), p. 295.
19 For details of these see Hugh Cunningham, *Leisure in the Industrial Revolution c. 1780–1880* (London, Croom Helm, 1980), p. 34. One of several

frequently recounted anecdotes about Ducrow involves his dismissal, whilst on a regional tour, of Sheffield's Master Cutler and his Town Council as a 'set of dirty knife-grinders' insisting that he 'only waited upon crowned heads'. Apparently this misjudgement of the class status of his circus cost him his season in Sheffield. Thomas Frost, *Circus Life and Circus Celebrities* (London, Chatto & Windus, 1881), pp. 63–4.

20 Charles Dickens, 'Astley's' (1835), *Dickens' Journalism: Sketches by Boz and Other Early Papers, 1833–39*, ed. Michael Slater (London, Phoenix, 1996), p. 106. Disher, *Greatest Show on Earth*, p. 103.

21 Disher gives a full account of the main features of this drama (comic characters, mounted sword-fighting, costumes, moving panoramas and so on), *Greatest Show on Earth*, pp. 117–25.

22 Disher, *Greatest Show on Earth*, pp. 122–3.

23 Coxe reports the continued existence of the 'courier act' in more recent times at the Swiss circus, Knie's. see *A Seat at the Circus* (London, Macmillan, 1980), p. 59.

24 Cunningham, *Leisure in the Industrial Revolution*, p. 34.

25 Hengler's, which performed under many variations of the title 'Hengler's Colossal Hippodrama and Grand Cirque Variety', eventually and successfully converted the Palais Royal, London (now 'The London Palladium') into a circus. see John Turner's exhaustive history of this circus, *Historical Hengler's Circus*, 4 vols (Formby, Lingdales Press, 1989–90).

26 See BL *A Collection of Programmes, Cuttings From Newspapers Relating to Performances in Various Circuses From 1772–1858*. Scrapbook, 2 vols.

27 Van Amburgh's status and fame were confirmed by Queen Victoria's apparent obsession with him. Disher reports that in 1839 she went to see him at Astley's seven times in two months and was moved to have Sir David Wilkie paint his portrait in 1844 when he visited Windsor, *Greatest Show on Earth*, p. 144.

28 For more details of these performers see Isaac Greenwood, *The Circus, its Origins and Growth* (New York, Dunlop Society, 1898), Stuart Thayer, *Annals of the American Circus* (Manchester, Michigan, Rymack Print Co., 1976), R. W. G. Vail, *Random Notes on the History of the Early American Circus* (Worcester, Massachussetts, American Antiquarian Society, 1934), pp. 60–2, Leonidas Westervelt, *The Circus in Literature* (New York, the Author, 1931), pp. 14–20.

29 Robert Withington, however, cautions against labelling circus parades as 'pageants' since they seek 'only to entertain' and therefore lack 'even a semblance of allegory or symbolism' as well as a either a 'civic occasion' to mark and a 'unifying spirit' which could be derived from this. This is only partially true since many circus wagons were highly biblical and allegorical in their depictions of bible illustrations, historical and mythological figures and, although the parades themselves may have been somewhat disparate in their use of themes, the circus 'spectaculars' or

Origins

'specs' in the United States have frequently been thematically focused around incidents of historical moment or spurious ethnographic conceptions. See Robert Withington's chapter 'Pageantry in the United States' in *English Pageantry*, vol. II (Cambridge, MA, Harvard University Press [1926], 1963). see also David M. Bergeron, *English Civic Pageantries* (London, Edward Arnold, 1971), pp. 9–122.

30 See 'Freeman H. Hubbard, '100 Years of Circus Trains', *Railroad*, April 1956, pp. 12–27.

31 See Bob Parkinson, 'Concerning mechanisation of the circus', *Bandwagon*, June 1967, pp. 30–1 and Fred D. Pfening, Jr, 'Tractors and trucks on circuses', *Bandwagon*, Jan./Feb. 1965, pp. 16–17.

32 See Cyril B. Mills, 'Bertram Mills Circus: rail travel in Great Britain', *Bandwagon*, Nov./Dec. 1983, pp. 36–8, and Cyril Bertram Mills, *Bertram Mills Circus: Its Story* (Bath, Ashgrove Press, 1983), pp. 61–8.

33 Charles Henry Jones, 'Transporting the greatest show on earth: the 1898 tour of England', *The Ludgate*,1898, reprinted in *Bandwagon*, Mar./Apr. 1968, pp. 13–16.

34 For book-length studies of these shows see Ricky Jay, *Learned Pigs and Fireproof Women* (New York, Villard Books, 1986) and Leslie Fiedler, *Freaks: Myths and Images of the Secret Self* (New York, Simon & Schuster, 1978).

35 See Roger Corman, *The Last American Freak Show* (BBC TV, 1995).

36 See David Lewis Hammarstrom, *Big Top Boss: John Ringling North and the Circus* (Urbana and Chicago, Illinois University Press, 1992), pp. 1–21.

37 John Culhane, *The American Circus: An Illustrated History* (New York, Henry Holt & Company, 1990), p. 157.

38 Noël Burch describes the aesthetic poverty of these early films of the 1894–1906 period in *Life to those Shadows* trans. Ben Brewster (London, BFI Publishing, 1990), pp. 113–16.

39 According to Don Stacey, early British circuses, most notably Chipperfields also incorporated film screening at about the same period using bioscope technology. He also cites the 1909 Cinematograph Act which introduced fire regulations to the display of films in the United Kingdom, '100 years of cinema and the circus: part 1', *King Pole*, December 1996, p. 6.

40 For further details of these venues see Steve Gossard, *A Reckless Era of Aerial Performance: The Evolution of the Flying Trapeze* (Normal, Illinois, the Author, 1994).

2

Structures

It has already been established that the shape and dimensions of the circus space confirmed the primacy of equestrianism within circus performance. Whilst to a great extent a circular ring of 42 feet/ 13 metres in diameter has remained a constant to all circuses, it is also true that significant developments and variations have occurred around the relationship of this ring to a stage, the machinery attached to it, its lighting and the organisation of seating circumjacent to it, all of which are registers of changes in the kind of shows performed and the nature and size of the audiences which have attended them.

Initially the circus was an open-air construct (though some seating was covered) which meant that it was limited to daytime performances and summer stints only (usually from Easter Monday until tours abroad from September onwards). The addition of a roof to Astley's riding ring by 1779 from some 'lumber salvaged from an election hustings' brought financial as well as aesthetic benefits.[1] Now, not only were shows protected from inclement weather and could therefore carry on through a winter season and for evening performances, but the opportunities now available for greater varieties of theatrical spectacle which did not simply rely on the agility or skill of the human body considerably expanded with the introduction of artificial lighting which could be manipulated to enhance performances but also to produce specific effects. The circus was quick to exploit this facility and, as Kwint points out, by 1779/80 Ombres Chinoises and shadow plays became part of Astley's programme which, exhibited in a darkened auditorium, produced the circus's 'first cinematic effect'.[2] In the early period of the circus candles and oil lamps were used and etchings of the first Astley's Royal Grove revealing a central circular candelabra which could be hoisted up and down over the ring. The first records of gas lighting are at the New Theatre, Philadelphia in November 1816 and at Astley's and the Covent Garden Theatre in 1817–18 season, although smaller travelling shows on both sides of the Atlantic were reliant on candles and kerosene or paraffin sources until the 1880s due to the costs and logistics of gas installation.[3] Indeed at times gas lighting was so exciting that, rather than simply enhancing the clarity of spectacle, which it did considerably, it also became a source of spectacle in itself when many gas flares were shot up into the circus space simultaneously and colossal candelabras, such as the one in Thomas Cooke's Philadelphia amphitheatre which, in 1837 reportedly held 2,500 gas lights. Astley's Amphitheatre in London was lit by '200,000 jets of gas', adding to the 'glittering effect of the auditorium'.[4] Coxe reports that the American clown Dan Rice ran some experiments with dynamo-driven electricity as early as 1852, however electricity was not systematically mobilised until the 1880s following Charles F. Brush and Thomas Edison's development of the carbon arc electric lamp and incandescent electric light, respectively, in 1879.[5] Indeed it appears that Howe's London Circus, Sanger's Royal Menagerie and Cooper, Bailey and Company's International Allied Shows was chosen by Brush as the forum for the first public display of lighting in the United States when on 15 April 1879 the circus was not only electrically lit, but also contained a light parade.[6]

The fact that the circus was the first American show to be electrically illuminated is testimony not only to its popularity and cultural significance at the time, but is also of wider significance in a number of ways. Firstly, its association with electric lighting underlines its connection to the emerging technologies of vision and spectacle which would, in a little over a decade, produce the cinema. Visibility of the spectacular has always been the substance and the means of verification ('seeing is believing') of the circus, and electrical lighting simply allowed the audience to appreciate more intensely all the aspects of spectacle which defined its glory – the size and colour of its spectacles, the skill and beauty of its performers and the diversity of its participants (human and animal). Secondly, through its electrical experiments, the circus became historically aligned with modernity and the processes of technological innovation which helped to define it. Loeffler uncovers a newspaper advertisement of 1879 for a subsequent performance of the Great London Circus which proclaims its use of the 'Immortal ELECTRIC LIGHT!' which is the 'invention that set the whole world ablaze with excitement' and is therefore 'Worth Travelling 1,000 Miles to Look

At!'.[7] Not only does the circus attempt to make itself synonymous with a technology which, like circus itself, would shortly be taken up around the 'whole world', but as a mechanism that produces 'Night Made Bright as Day' and which puts the 'Sun Itself into the Blush', this association consolidates the circus's drive to demonstrate visually the human capacity to dominate the natural world and to challenge the dual oppressions of mortality and darkness. Of all arts and entertainments during this pre-cinema period, the circus was the one most wholeheartedly wedded to what would emerge as the spirit of modernity, even whilst the contents of its shows offered broadly familiar, even ritualistic entertainments.

In the United States pride in American innovations in electric lighting was articulated through a belief in the superiority of American circus over its European counterparts. For example Loeffler quotes a claim in the Philadelphia *Record* of 18 April 1879 that the generating engine developed by Brush to power Cooper and Bailey's circus was 'by far ahead of anything that now exists in Europe. For the want of this secret the people of France and England have been forced to use a machine for each separate light required.'[8] In fact, it would be some time before electricity fully replaced gasoline lighting, with even the largest American circuses such as Barnum and Bailey and Ringling Brothers leaving off the considerable financial commitment involved until the years between 1907 and 1909. Gradually improvements were made in technology so that by the 1970s a huge array of theatrical effects would be available to lighting designers lending circus directors greater subtlety and scope for expression in the presentation of acts and spectacles. Lighting, therefore, allows for a kind of editing so that linkages between disparate acts are now smoother as the focus, for example, may fall on an individual performer who holds the attention of the audience and leads them into the next scene which has been prepared in the darkness, a technique used particularly in three-ring circuses in which one or two of the rings may be thrown into darkness at any given time. The option of invisibility and of tight focusing is also particularly important in the staging of aerial acts when performers take their place in the dark and are thus revealed to the audience already suspended in the air, as if by magic.[9]

Perhaps one of the most interesting aspects of the circus's architectural development is the role of a stage as a supplementary performance space alongside the ring. Astley's first amphitheatre established the archetypal arrangement of a combination of ring and small proscenium stage, surrounded by two levels of seating. Far from dying on the vine immediately, however, the stage, for a while, increased in size and importance. In fact, as Speaight points out, the stage in Astley's third amphitheatre was bigger than any other in the English theatre of the period.[10] Not only did many of the most influential early artistic directors have their roots in the minor theatres of the day (for example Charles Dibdin and Grimaldi Snr), but the pantomimes and melodramas produced were of a similar nature. What was unique to this circus combination of stage and ring, however, was the hippodrama, one of the first examples of which, *The Brave Cossack*, is mentioned above.[11] Since the horses moved between the two on specially built ramps, the stages had to be specially reinforced in order to bear the considerable weight involved, but also often included several levels as did Astley's 1818 stage when Grieve added an adjustable stage. Franconi's new post-1826 circus included a stage with mechanically moveable floors and ramps to facilitate the post-Napoleonic military spectacles, then the standard fayre of such places. It seems that even when George Sanger tried out the conjoining of three rings in 1860 (some twenty years before Barnum's), he still held on to the stage, two of which were placed on either side of the central ring.[12] Until the emergence of the hippodrama action had either taken place on the stage or in the ring but now, with the introduction of ramps, action flowed from one to the other so that, as Martin Meisel observes, 'the battle did not need to appear between the horses legs'. Interestingly Meisel argues that, since one of the key features of these dramas was that they involved mixing 'domestic drama and individual vignettes with explosions and climactic battles' in the ring which often ended with a 'triumphant tableau' on stage, this effect could be compared with the kinds of cinematic techniques mobilised in epic cinema such as *Birth of a Nation* (D. W. Griffith, 1915, US) which move an audience's attention rapidly between wide panoramic shots and close shots of individuals as well as between frozen and frenetic action.[13]

So for most of the nineteenth century the stage remained as a kind of unbroken umbilical cord connecting the circus with the theatrical roots of some of its performers and facilitating the spectacular enactment of the military backgrounds of others. An examination of physical theatrical structures is important not only for an understanding of the aesthetic parameters of the dramas which took place in these arenas, but also for thinking about how audiences approached these perform-ances. Marcello Truzzi has suggested that 'whereas the carnival is an extension of the medieval fair', the circus is 'essentially an extension of the theatre', and in this sense it was Astley and Hughes who were formative in constructing the circus as a theatrical, private space, albeit a peculiarly shaped one.[14] This is an all-important distinction to bear in mind when considering the relevance of Mikhail Bakhtin's ideas on the carnivalesque to the analysis of both the circus and its repre-sentations since Bakhtin makes it clear that carnival is by definition a form of social ritual or 'pageantry' and as such it 'knows no footlights'.[15] Thus circus and circus texts may *perform* or represent some of the inversions and *mésalliances* which Bakhtin identifies as features of car-nival processions, but they do so as carnivalesque art rather than as (temporarily) socially subversive carnival. Commentators such as Hippesley Coxe have argued that because there is no backstage or proscenium arch in what we now define as the circus, the performance can be seen, 'from all sides' so that 'the audience holds the spectacle in its midst' and yet at the same time is very much separated from it.[16] However, it is also important to remember that historically this has not always been the case and that considerations of nineteenth-century examples of encounters with the circus such as those of Dickens and Wilkie Collins should be placed in the context of amphi-theatres (or hippodramas) where elements of the entertainment were sectioned off as proscenium stage performances.

Even though the hippodrama as such faded out in Great Britain at the end of the nineteenth century, its main principles, formal and thematic, had already been absorbed into the North American circus in the form of the circus spectacle, or 'spec' as it would come to be known. Ricketts and subsequent small travelling circuses had used pantomime performances as finales for their shows up until the Civil War but the connection to the European hippodrama was made in 1853 when Seth B. Howes booked members of the Franconi troupe to put on 'Franconi's Hippodrome'. This involved the reinstatement of the hippodrome track around the perimeter of the performance circle and of course the arrangement of rings which best served the shape of the hippodrome processional was the three-ring circus, offering as it did a Roman-style tournament track with stages in the centre in which to perform dramatic scenes. Conventionally these spectacles have been and, in some cases still are, used to open the shows and constitute yet another variation on the pageantry of the pre-circus street parade, and large financial investments are made in the purchasing of props, costumes and, later, special effects to maximise the visual impact of the show.

From the outset circus seating arrangements have always catered for class distinction with differential ticket pricing functioning to separate out spaces for different social classes in very conventional theatrical fashion with stalls (or pit), gallery (usually two-tiered) and private boxes for the wealthy and nobility. By the 1780s the prices of these closely corresponded to the cost of comparable four-level theatre seating in Drury Lane but, at the bottom end, still a little more than fairground show entrances which were threepence to sixpence, as opposed to the circus which started at sixpence for standing room and moved up to three shillings for boxes.[17] Audiences numbers varied. When Astley first started shows at the riding school he was playing to a small crowd of perhaps a couple of hundred who were fitted on to three rows of wooden seats around a sixty-foot ring. Travelling family-based circuses such as Samwell's, Cooke's, Sanders's and Wild's always tended to be a little smaller than the amphitheatres holding up to 1,000–1,500 people in their temporary buildings. However, as the circus increased in popularity towards the end of the century, so too did its crowd capacity grow so that by the time Ducrow took over the third Astley's his theatre could hold 2,500 per sitting. By the end of the nineteenth century even tenting shows such as Powell and Clarke's, which travelled around the country fairs, were reaching a capacity audience of 7,000. The biggest influence on the burgeoning dimensions of the circus audience, and on the spectacular capacity of the ring to embody a notion of sheer size, came with the arrival of the tenting American circuses in the 1850s.

Whilst the European circuses of the eighteenth and early nineteenth century sought, in their choice of names for themselves, to impress their importance on prospective audiences by emphasising their royal and noble aspirations ('The Royal Grove', 'The Royal Circus', 'William Cooke's Circus Royal', 'Cirque du Palais Royale', 'The Royal Amphitheatre'), by the 1850s this naming process began to reflect a growing investment in the commercial value of audience capacity and grandness of scale. For example Hengler's Circus which prospered during the 1850s travelled under a series of different headings such as 'Hengler's Colossal Hippodrama and Grand Cirque Variety', 'Hengler's Colossal

Moving Hippodrama and National Circus' and 'Hengler's Mammoth Circus and Great Equestrian Exhibition'.[18] Even its catchphrase 'Amusement for the Million and Rational Recreation' reflects a switch to more demotic and pragmatic ambitions as an impression of royal appointment is traded in for a democratically minded image of a judiciously balanced, mass entertainment.

The Americans seem partly to have been responsible for this equation of size with democracy and with this an emphasis also on the modern and internationalist nature of their tenting circuses, witnessed in the following verse composed for a Howes and Cushing United States Circus advertising bill of 1857:

> Here are strange wonders! Olympia to Columbia yields,
> Exchanged, are modern acres for Elysian fields;
> Tents now take precedent of ponderous Marble Halls,
> Thousands are encircled within its woven walls;
> The flags of every nation flutter in the breeze,
> A universal Brotherhood it thus at once decrees;
> By Brother Jonathan the Gothic times are sent
> To black oblivion and to their Mighty Tent;
> They all the world invite to witness acts of daring,
> And boldly now assert their cirque beyond comparing.[19]

The sweeping replacement of Olympia, the valley of the ancient European games, by a made-up American equivalent is dramatised here in terms of an architectural revolution which frees up circus performance from an attachment to a stifling theatrical past exemplified by cold, immobile, and deathly marble and dark, 'Gothic times'. It is placed instead within the more harmonious space of the 'woven' tent which 'encircles' rather than orders its occupants and which accommodates an internationalism and fraternity which is figured as natural to it in the form of the enlivening 'breeze' which animates the national flags arranged throughout. Paradoxically, that which made the circus distinctly American (the 'United States Circus') was also that which marked it as internationalist. It should also be added, however, that the verse is a little disingenuous since when in London the circus played at the Alhambra Palace as part of its national tour.[20]

So the 1850s saw a period of expansion in the audience capacity of the larger tenting circuses moving from, for example, the 'portable equestrian Palace' toured by Hernandez and Stone in 1853 which held approximately 3,000 people, to Howes and Cushing's 1857 circus which held around 5,000.[21] It was not simply the case that the capacity of the American circus was only driven by a greater appetite for profits but, as we shall see later, it was also the case that their new style of circus – the nature and contents of the acts performed – worked best in the more spacious, airy tent than in the enclosed auditoriums pioneered by Hughes and Astley, though these two had certainly attempted to maximise audience numbers within these more intimate structures. Sanger's experiments with two and three adjacent rings have already been mentioned, but the greatest revolution in the physical scale of the circus's performance space, as opposed to merely what happened inside it, came with Barnum's pioneering three-ring circus of 1881. This introduced what would become an American standard within the entertainment, and the circus achieved a size never to be equalled: James Bailey's European tour of the Greatest Show on Earth had a capacity of 15,000.[22] Once the 42-foot ring had become established as the unalterable foundation of the circus, for practical reasons previously mentioned, simply expanding the ring to accommodate bigger shows was not an alternative so the three- or sometimes four-ring set-up seemed the only solution. Often a track ran round the outside of the ring on which parades would take place and stages were often also present for acrobatic performances. Of course the existence of three rings with simultaneous entertainment in each also transformed the nature of spectatorship since it now became impossible to take in the whole performance at once and an appreciation of individual acts was replaced by impression of the show as a whole. As Truzzi puts it, the spectator was soon 'compelled to receive more than his money's worth'.[23] Perhaps Barnum also calculated that the spectator who had been impressed with the generosity of a show which gave him more than he had paid for would pay again to catch what had eluded his attention the first time. With Barnum we see the introduction of an economy of excessive consumption combined with gratuitous waste as well as a temporary consolidation of panoramic spectacle (mirrored in the now all-important circus parades which preceded the shows on the streets of the town/city visited) over more theatrical, character-based drama.

At the same time it is worth suggesting that, since it provided no unity of vision, the organisation of the rings in this fashion may have been panoramic in shape but was really closer to an animated triptych which perhaps has its closest parallel in Abel Gance's epic cinematic experiment in simultaneous projection, *Napoléon* (1927, Fr.). Since the two stages which provided the link between the three rings were also performance spaces, however, the audience was frequently being challenged by five simultaneous acts (figure 2), although, as we can see from the circus programmes of the day, occasionally a star performer, such as Berta Beeson and her high-wire act in the Sells-Floto Circus (figure 3) would be privileged over the others by being granted the centre ring while the others were shut down.

These programmes offer fascinating insights into the structures according to which circus acts were organised as different performers can be seen to have been combined, offset and privileged in relation to each other, depending on whether they occupied (in order of importance) their own ring, the central or outer ring or an adjoining stage. As the illustration demonstrates, the full panoramic view of the five simultaneous acts was the preserve of the top-price ticket customers in the Grand Stand and 'Reserved' stands (kept for local businessmen, officials and their families) whilst those in the 'general admission' stands got the best view only of the act nearest to them and a blocked view of the centre, most important, ring. Far from a fully democratised spectacle being on offer, therefore, the three-ring circus, as Susan Stewart has observed, reinstates a hierarchy of viewing according to ticket pricing and social status.[24] Thus a peculiar economy of vision and blockage emerges wherein no one in the audience is able to absorb the excess of simultaneous visual spectacles before them. Whereas the grand stand audience select the acts to which they will or will not devote their attention, the general audience is given a proper view only of the act immediately before them, though it glimpses the others in a diminishing perspective beyond them. Thus the three-ring circus structurally limits general choice and scope of vision whilst at the same time it fetishises the distant or inaccessible view which is available only in partial or diminished form. The first audience has the luxurious impression of more being made available than they could possibly take in, the second of being offered less than is available.

The programmes themselves constituted a guide, a complement and a distraction to the barrage of sights, sounds and information contained in the rings. Not only must the audience inevitably have struggled to keep up with the acts paraded before them, but the programmes, whilst on a certain level were informative (detailing the name and a description of the act as well as supplying a full narrative account of the opening spectacle – see figure 3), also offered an excess of information which, as the illustrations demonstrate, often paralleled the three-ring performance itself. The central picture gave a key to the acts on each stage in each display whilst on either side of this would be, on top, a piece of circus wisdom (figure 2) or an advert (figure 3) and, underneath, more elaborate details on each act. In this way the increasingly mute North American circus with its big-scale, physical acts was supported by a written text which doubly addressed the spectator as both a consumer of the circus (and, through self-promoting headlines, of one circus in particular) and as a commercial consumer within the wider marketplace.

As is obvious even from these rough plans from Sells-Floto, the size of both tents and audiences rocketed. Speaight reports that an 1840s circus tent would have been around 85 feet in diameter, moving to 150 feet in the 1870s and by the 1890s circuses such as Adam Forepaugh's and Barnum and Bailey were between 360 and 460 feet long (including 6-by-60 foot middle pieces) and roughly 180 feet wide. Whereas Barnum's single-ring show of 1872 held an audience of approximately 5,000, by the 1890s they could squeeze in over 14,000.[25] The growing size of the tents also had a knock-on effect on travel schedules and personnel since not only did moves between towns necessarily become more rapid because potential audiences, especially in smaller towns and cities, were more quickly exhausted, but also larger, more highly organised and efficient crews were needed to erect and dismantle the tents. Increasingly it became the case that almost as much, if not more, time and energy was spent on these processes of physically moving and reconstructing the space of performance than was expended on the shows themselves. Although European tours were also embarked upon occasionally, the three-ring formation was never as popular here as it was in the United States so the practice, with the exception of a few experiments, did not catch on elsewhere.

In the twentieth century, as I outline in chapter 1, 'Origins', urban planning and transport development in the West have made it difficult for the big travelling shows (with seating for 2,000 or more) to survive, though in Europe the Swiss-based Circus Knie remains one of very few large-scale tenting shows to survive and prosper. Indeed, worldwide, India stands out as an exceptional environment for the touring/tenting shows in that, nation-wide there are still around seventeen companies

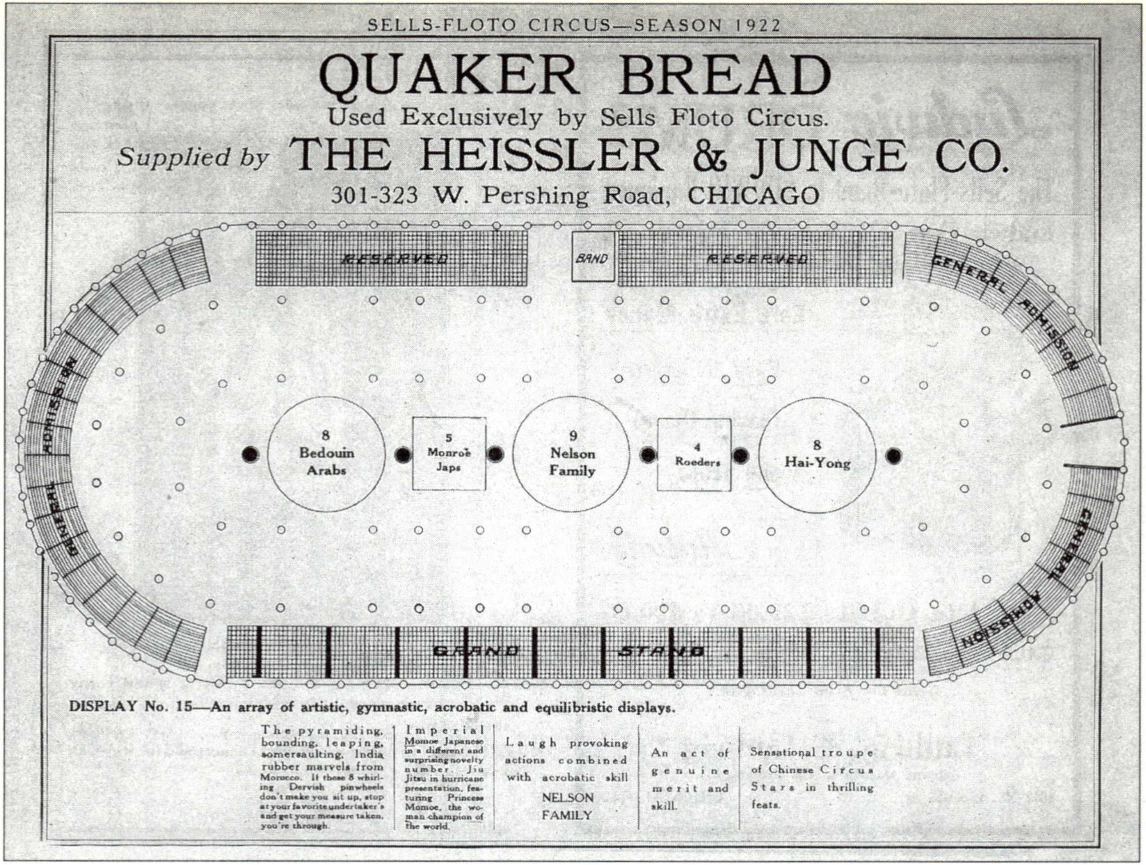

Figure 2 Three-ring circus plan including Quaker Bread advertisement printed in the Sells-Floto Circus program of 1922

DANGER IN EVERY STEP

During the running of the Sells-Floto hippodrome races which close the performance, there is probably not two persons sitting in the grand stand who could decide which is the most dangerous of the many different races. Many people think the Roman chariot race is the one, others, owing to the sharp turns, the jockey race. But the real race, with danger every moment to the man or woman, is the thrilling Roman standing race. Let it be understood that the rider has but two legs, with eight legs moving under him. It is not only horsemanship that is needed, but exceptional balancing power is required as well. Everything is moving at a high speed and the slightest stumble means injury, if not death to the rider.

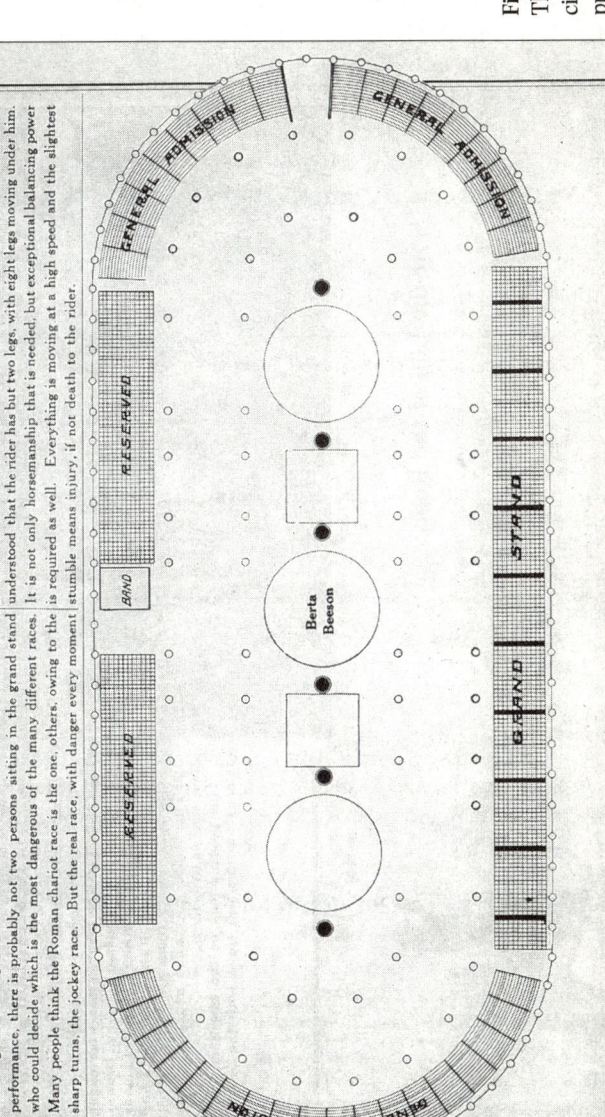

Berta
Beeson

DISPLAY No. 16—High over head Berta Beeson, "The Girl Who Keeps You Guessing," dances alone upon a slender thread of silver. The whole show stops and gasps and holds its breath while MLLE. BEESON gives a superb and dainty exhibition on the tight wire the equal of which the world has never seen.

Figure 3
Three-ring
circus plan
printed in
the
Sells-Floto
Circus
program of
1922

with personnel upwards of 200 people (Gemini, Jumbo's, Empire, Great Royal) travelling around at any given time.[26] For the substantial populations of India's cities in which illiteracy levels (especially in the north) are high, the spectacular, colourful, musically noisy, physically dynamic and very lengthy circus shows constitute a comparable mode of address to Indian cinema, though the latter now exceeds the circus in terms of popularity. Until the recent break-up of the Soviet Union, tenting circuses there numbered fourteen; again within a nation in which many languages are spoken, through state investment from the Ministry of Culture, the circus thrived alongside ballet as a national entertainment.[27] In the rest of Europe and the United States, however, touring circuses have been pared down, though some circuses continue to play to mass audiences in alternative, permanent venues such as theatres and warehouses since most of the long-standing purpose-built circus buildings have now been pulled down.[28]

Notes

1 A. H. Saxon, *Enter Foot and Horse: A History of the Hippodrama in England an France* (New Haven and London, Yale University Press, 1968) p. 10.
2 Kwint, 'Astley's amphitheatre', p. 37.
3 Robert Loeffler, 'Candles, flares, gas, electric all used to light the circus', *White Tops*, May/June 1984, 27–38, p. 28.
4 Loeffler, 'Candles, flares ...', pp. 28–9 and *London Illustrated News*, 28 October 1871.
5 Hippesley Coxe, *A Seat at the Circus*, p. 37. Speaight claims the first use for Manders's Menagerie in 1867, *A History of the Circus*, p. 46.
6 Loeffler, 'Candles, flares ...', p. 29. During the period 1901–11 J. J. Meyer is credited with revolutionising circus lighting through his innovation of a gas generator which was used at a number of shows including Barnum and Bailey, Ringling Brothers and Forepaugh-Sells. He sold out in 1911 to Bolte (to form Bolte and Meyer Co. of Chicago) which would go on to light most of the early circuses electrically. Bill Metzger, 'Early circus lighting', verticle file, Circus World Museum.
7 Loeffler, 'Candles, flares ...', p. 30.
8 Loeffler, 'Candles, flares ...', p. 30.
9 See Karl G. Ruling, 'Three ring lighting', *Lighting Dimensions*, Nov. 1995, pp. 95–7.
10 Speaight, *A History of the Circus*, p. 38.
11 Probably first performed at Astley's in 1807. see BL *Astley's Cuttings*, vol. 3, item 86, 8 May 1807.
12 Speaight, *A History of the Circus*, p. 44.

13 Martin Meisel, *Realisations: Narrative, Pictorial and Theatrical Arts in Nineteenth-Century England* (Princeton, Princeton University Press, 1983), pp. 214–5.

14 Truzzi, 'The decline of the American circus', p. 315.

15 Mikhail Bakhtin, *Problems in Dostoevsky's Poetics*, trans. and ed. Caryl Emerson (Manchester, Manchester University Press, 1984), p. 122.

16 Hippesley-Coxe, 'Equestrian drama and the circus', p. 109.

17 Speaight, *The History of the Circus*, p. 44. Kwint also points out that many unskilled workers wouldn't have been able to afford even the sixpence admission charge so a special unadvertised price of threepence was maintained for servants and children, 'Astley's amphitheatre', p. 73.

18 Turner, *Historical Hengler's Circus*, vol. 2, p. 64, p. 73, p. 108.

19 August 1857, BL *A Collection of Programmes*, vol. 2, item 153.

20 See 12 April 1856, BL *A Collection of Programmes*, vol. 2. item 155 and 8 November 1858, item 235.

21 See 1853, BL *A Collection of Programmes*, vol. 2, item 129.

22 Stephen Sharpe, '100 years ago: Barnum & Bailey on tour', *King Pole*, 121, December 1998, p. 18.

23 Truzzi, 'The decline of the American circus', p. 318.

24 Susan Stewart, *On Longing: Narratives of the Miniature, the Gigantic, the Souvenir, the Collection* (Durham, NC, and London, Duke University Press, 1993), p. 12.

25 Speaight, *The History of the Circus*, p. 137.

26 See Sreedharan Champad, 'The circus in India', *King Pole*, 104 (1994), pp. 35–6. See also John Irving's novel *A Son of the Circus* (London, Bloomsbury, 1994) which involves a comic fictional account of several circus performers, including a dwarf family, based on his own research in Gujurat.

27 For more information on the organisation of the Soviet Circus see David Davies, 'Circus in the USSR', *King Pole*, 79, 1988, pp. 12–14.

28 *King Pole* gives details of the British touring circuses in any given year and published a full list of all British tenting shows between 1940 and 1980 in *King Pole*, 54, 55, and 56, 1982.

3

Economics

The economic history of circus is one dominated by entrepreneurship and advertising. Clearly methods or organisation have altered enormously since the days of Astley and at the same time it is impossible to generalise when scale and ambitions have varied so greatly. Despite the existence of so many myths surrounding circuses which foreground the congenial family-style camaraderie of its workers (for whom their work is a way of life rather than a job, at the expense of their labour) the circus has never been an entertainment borne out of luxury but rather one driven by a need to expand and survive. Probably the concept of the family-style organisation of the circus has its origins in Astley's establishment of what had become known as the 'benefits system' and had been adopted generally by theatrical touring company as Dickens demonstrates frequently in his portrayal of the Crummles in *Nicholas Nickleby*.[1] Rather than pay his employees in fixed weekly salaries they were granted instead the full use of the company and auditorium on a particular evening designated as being 'For the Benefit of Mr. Mulligan', as a result of which they would be given the chance to shine especially well by being given a particular prominence in the performance and would then receive the profits from that show.[2] This generosity was also extended to local charities, even when travelling, and had the clear advantage of minimising the wages bill and local expenses. Shows were held to support specific causes but also money regularly went into local community projects such as house-building. Kwint points out that the 'obligations of the benefit, from which the principal performers stood to gain the most, tended to tie them to the community'.[3] The performers' star status and the financial remuneration which resulted, depended on a regular and loyal audience cultivated over a season, but the bonds of mutual support formed by the fixed amphitheatres also functioned to bolster the reputation and respectability of the circus. At the same time the benefits system provided circus performers with a kind of mutual insurance which allowed them to transcend particular conflicts and rivalries between companies in times of disaster. For example, when the Royal Circus burnt down in August 1805, John Astley allowed its performers to hold their benefits at Astley's in acknowledgement of the fact that his performers had been granted the same favour by the Royal Circus following Astley's fire of September 1803.[4]

As the circus grew rapidly in size and attracted ever larger audiences its presence in a community had knock-on effects on local businesses such as farriers and saddlers, though typically, that these were not all circus-related business was desirable since pleasure seekers heading south of the river for their entertainment also boosted rates of drinking and prostitution at the same time as they proved easy victims for thieves who targeted the area. As Kwint suggests, despite attempts to cultivate an image of respectability and positive investment, 'in all its public postures the circus was continually aware that people might perceive it to have a darker side'.[5] The suggestion here is that these gestures were made less in the name of earnest philanthropy than good business sense. Charity events brought in high-profile members of the local community whose attendance could be drawn attention to and translated as approbation for both the patron and the entertainment on offer. Financially, then, in order to maximise its profits the circus was caught in a double-bind which produced a tension between simultaneous reliance on both high-minded charitable promotion and almost unavoidably illicit activity because a portion of the audience would be reassured by the former whilst some would always be excited by the latter.

The high physical risks associated with circus performance inside the tent have always been mirrored in the dangers of financial investments in the running of the circuses which may just as well flip between glories and mighty falls. For this reason circuses have never been run by people who already have money and respectability, but rather by opportunists who have neither and therefore have nothing to lose. The race between Hughes and Astley in the 1780s to outdo each other in terms of the splendour of their permanent auditoriums helped establish the respectability of the circus as such, but these costs were covered by the continuous reinvestment of most of the profits back into these ever-elaborate and, especially in Astley's case, multiplying buildings.

Whilst Kwint's argument may be generally true that early circuses were 'headed by patriarchs' and that it was the name and force of personality of these figures which were their driving force (as opposed to the theatre which he describes as 'a more civic space, inhabited by a variety of actorly identities') this does not seem to have been consistently the case.[6] When Hughes left London for Russia the Royal Circus was taken over by managers and Astley's itself may have held on to the name of its charismatic founder after his and his son's death, perhaps in recognition of the powerful and lasting pull of the cult associated with his name, but at times, in practice, it was more anonymously managed. It does appear that a large amount of old-fashioned paternalism and its associated values of family loyalty and hierarchy have predominated in the circus and yet at the same time this almost militaristic organisation has also proved to be the perhaps unlikely site for the defiance of restrictive social conventions, or indeed prejudice, in the areas of class, race and gender. The circus has given opportunities for wealth and fame to performers who, almost without exception, came from poor or unprivileged backgrounds, giving many a leg-up also to successful theatrical careers in which wages and status were higher. As Kwint points out, in the circus 'stars rose substantially on their individual merits, [and] performers under the emerging star system could break through the normal obstacles of gender, race or age'.[7] In contrast to the late eighteenth- and early nineteenth-century theatre where women's wages were two-thirds of men's, in the circus they had parity and, although crude racial stereotyping existed in many of the acts, there appear to have been few practical bars to black performers' careers.[8] So the circus may have worked its own strict and sometimes restrictive codes of operations, and in this sense was by no means a 'class-free utopia', yet at the same time these were not necessarily the same codes and conventions which held sway in society at large.[9]

Advertising, and most especially print-based advertising of various kinds, has not only constituted the fuel which has powered and perpetuated the circus from the outset, but has also become recognised in itself, like the circus wagons, as a part of its art as well as its machinery. At the same time it is fair to say that, although circuses mobilised many existing forms of advertising they also made transformations and innovations in the technologies and scope of nineteenth- and twentieth-century advertising as a whole. The forms which circus advertising have taken have mirrored its own values and aesthetics;

that is, great emphasis has been placed on the use of colour, stunts, sensation, large-scale and spectacular pictorialisation. Astley, for example relied greatly on handing out bills and on newspaper puffs as we have seen, but he also established an annual rowing boat race (or "Prize Wherry") on the Thames between Westminster Bridge and Vauxhall as well as generating much publicity, beginning in 1784, by launching a number of unmanned hot-air balloons ('New Curious Aerostatic Experiments') into the sky, one of which was around 25 feet in circumference.[10] He was canny too in his targeting of particular kinds of audiences. As Kwint points out, Astley, conscious of his need to attract precisely the 'nobility, gentry and others' addressed in his bills in order to secure a level of respectability for his circus in its early and barely legitimate days, chose to use the higher quality of print offered by the *Public Advertiser* and the *Morning Post* rather than simple handbills and he specifically emphasised the circus's promotion of military skills and all-round physical fitness, whilst at the same time suggesting their accessibility beyond the upper and upper-middle class.[11] Even the early circus quickly realised that because of the circus's dubious moral and artistic reputations it was particularly important to plan not simply visually striking advertising and stunts, but ones which could also reach enough of the desired kinds of people and send them the most persuasive of messages about the circus's attractions.

The three most important methods of advertising for the circus then are print-based (posters, bills, newspaper puffs, cards), public-relations exercises (local benefit performances, local sponsorships in exchange for free tickets) and stunts. Initially newspapers were the most important and effective way of achieving maximum circulation since, as Bob Parkinson suggests, 'it was the only media of advertising that was regularly delivered into the hands of the largest number of potential customers'.[12] Naturally the greatest drawback in using early newspapers was the poverty of colour and pictorial possibility available; however, Parkinson outlines the way in which the circus fashioned an art all its own out of initially crude black and white illustrative cuts. Out of this, in around 1815, was born what has been labelled 'display advertising', a term which presupposes the consumer's lack of familiarity with the item being introduced to them visually through the advertising image and, in most cases therefore, the consumers must be persuaded that what they have managed very well without so far must be, if not a necessity, at least desirable. Thus, with the circus and its methods of selling itself, come the technologies of persuasion, selling and stimulation of artificial consumer desires. For obvious reasons these techniques were particularly important for the travelling menageries which toured widely from the beginning of the nineteenth century onwards since their *raison d'être* was the display of exotic and unfamiliar animals. The citizens of a given town who had never seen an elephant, and who had so far survived without seeing one, would have to be sufficiently convinced and intrigued by an advert's representation of one to bring themselves to make a visit. Combining an enticing verbal account of an elephant or a giraffe with an image of it went some way further in making these seemingly improbable creatures concrete in the imagination of the public.

Gradually print advertising became more detailed, more pictorial, occupied more space and was generally superior in all these aspects to other types of advertising and by the 1870s large and varied print styles, multiple columns and elaborate illustrations were commonplace. By the late 1880s in the United States, however, levels of circus advertising declined as rival advertisers from outside the circus, recognising the success of the eye-catching newspaper spreads, all clambered for the same spaces thereby forcing up the cost of column inches. The Ringling Brothers/Bailey competition of the end of the century caused a revival and elaboration of newspaper advertising potential using every inch of space in what were often full-page adverts. The circus too pioneered the use of press agents; Dan Rice hiring the first, David S. Thomas, in 1871.[13] This was followed by the concept of an advertising agency, which secured lower advertising rates and free publicity, as Parkinson observes, with plenty of 'fast talk and complimentary passes'.[14] So the circus, on both sides of the Atlantic, not only advanced the physical materials of print-based advertising (including outdoors bill posters and lithographs) but also worked out the principal relationships of selling which would go on to form the infrastructures of modern western advertising; the first press agents, advertising agencies issuing press releases, publicity information on acts and stars and the careful development of marketing strategy. The circus also followed and exploited wider commercial and media developments in society including radio and television advertising for which special advance agents were assigned.[15] Also, in the 1960s, Ringling Brothers Barnum and Bailey were able to do deals which involved inserting circus flyers into monthly statements for the big mail order companies such as Sears and

Montgomery Ward whilst others arranged for supermarkets to insert them into their shopping bags.[16]

The 1870s in the United States was a hot house for the development of advertising practice; the two key factors in this were, firstly, the entrance of P. T. Barnum in 1870 and, secondly, the transportation of circuses by rail from 1872 onwards. Only the larger circuses could afford to travel by rail, but this new and enormously faster method of transportation meant that those that did travel by rail were more ruthless in their targeting of the larger towns and cities where they would often only perform for one or two large audiences before moving on to the next city. This meant that advertising had to be right and had to be done in advance since there wasn't time for word of mouth publicity to get around. The so-called 'advance men' (general, contracting and press agents) travelling ahead of the show in 'advance cars', up to five in number and with a crew of perhaps sixty men, therefore became indispensable as they set up free publicity, handed out free passes to local business men, gave out story outlines or 'press books' containing ready-prepared stories and photographs to newspaper editors, sent out men to paste up lithograph posters, hang banners, and hand out programmes and bills detailing what the show had to offer. When a circus was to arrive in a city all the free spaces on walls and windows were commandeered by the advance crews who would transform the landscape of the town with between six and eight thousand bills and posters, some of which were composed of between three and one hundred connecting sheets, though at times two companies might converge at which point the walls would become thick with posters as one crew busily plastered over the other's work. During the fierce competition of the 'billing wars' of the 1890s, a car designated as the 'Opposition Car' had the task of tracking the path of a main competitor, anticipating their route and covering over as much of their wall pasting as possible. It was quickly recognised not only that the coloured lithographs were the most effective way of grabbing the public's attention, but also that, as Braathen and Braathen observe, 'the volume of business done was in direct proportion to the amount of advertising done'.[17] In the field of advertising then, the circus in this so-called Golden Era, as in other areas of its development, made pioneering use of the new technologies of image-making and spectacle in constructing colossal, coloured and panoramic advertising images (effectively, therefore, inventing the billboard) which exploited the new techniques of lithography in colour which had been developed by 1840 in London.[18] The posters, the making and distribution of which swallowed up considerable amounts of money, also furnished the public imagination with a series of recurrent and resonant images which became not only forms of early trademarks (such as the Ringlings' famous leaping tiger), but came to characterise public expectations about the circus as an entertainment form, dominated as they were by three kinds of images: dangerous or exotic animals, athletic and scantily clad bodies in motion and laughing clowns.

In P. T. Barnum, however, the circus found a figure who, as we see from the account of Astley and his contemporaries above, did not so much invent modern methods of advertising, but rather adapted and built upon practices of exaggeration, imposture, 'puffing' and the well-publicised stunt on a bigger and more international scale. When Barnum claimed that he 'thoroughly understood the art of advertising' he describes his mastery not so much of the technologies and infrastructures of advertising described above, but of the aesthetics and psychological dynamics between consumers and salesmen which made these technologies successful in the generation of the desire to purchase what was neither necessary nor even what it was advertised to be.[19] This is what Neil Harris has described as Barnum's 'operational aesthetic' which combines the delivery of information with the generation of curiosity, beauty and excitement; in other words, advertising which went beyond the simple display of goods.[20]

Harris points for an example to an early stunt dreamt up to entice people into Barnum's American Museum in New York. Barnum had responded to a beggar by suggesting that, instead of receiving charity, he should earn his money and put him to work with five bricks:

> 'Now,' said I, 'go and lay a brick on the sidewalk at the corner of Broadway and Ann Street; another close by the Museum; a third diagonally across the way at the corner of Broadway and Vesey Street, by the Astor House; put down the fourth on the sidewalk in front of St. Paul's Church, opposite; then, with the fifth brick in hand, take up a rapid march from one point to the other, making the circuit, exchanging your brick at every point, and say nothing to any one.'[21]

Within half an hour of the man commencing his task 'with a military step and bearing' and answering none of the questions asked of him,

Barnum claims he had generated a crowd of around five hundred people 'anxious to solve the mystery'. After an hour or so the crowd had multiplied to fill the nearby pavements also. The 'brick man' then made his way into the museum 'devoting fifteen minutes to a solemn survey of the walls' on his way around and was generally followed in by 'a dozen or more persons' who would buy tickets at the entrance 'hoping to gratify their curiosity in regard to the purpose of his movements'. Repeated on an hourly basis the stunt not only brought new paying customers into the museum but also 'excited considerable talk and amusement' for Barnum on the back of a minimal financial output. At the same time it represents the meeting of advertising and conceptual art wherein the campaign to sell more tickets to the museum has an non-mimetic, indeed almost arbitrary, relationship to the thing advertised and has, as the focus of its energy, not the object for sale but rather the process of selling itself. Within this the generation of 'curiosity' becomes part of a form of dramatic seduction in which, in future such stunts, consumers would increasingly recognise their part as willing dupes. Thus, with Barnum, as it had with Astley before him, advertising had itself become a form of entertainment in which the 'humbug' reflected values which operate more generally in the circus; namely, the persuasion of an audience into a willing suspension of suspicion, allowing for the disguise of the ordinary or banal as the unique, extraordinary or exotic, throughout which 'truth' and mimesis become irrelevancies.

Naturally part of the selling of the circus as an entertainment has always involved the selling of the people who are its performers; in other words, the creation of stars. As we have already seen, star names in the eighteenth- and nineteenth-century circus were consolidated in very much the same fashion as theatrical ones; through privileged advertising, billing, and benefits-taking. Again, however, this period of the American circus established both an institutional infrastructure and a public appetite for stars from which Hollywood would later take its cue. In his promotions of people like Charles Stratton ('General Tom Thumb') and Jenny Lind ('The Swedish Nightingale') Barnum had realised that the moment of actual public performance was just one small element in the making and selling of a star; far more important in some ways was the process of giving the public the impression that they had knowledge of and access to the lives of the performers. In addition to General Tom Thumb's public appearances, for example,

Barnum circulated pictures, cheaply printed biographies (penned by Barnum) and, perhaps most famously, turned his wedding of 1863 into a media event which included a highly publicised celebrity guest list. On trips to Great Britain his celebrity status was established through, again highly publicised, aristocratic and royal introductions through which Stratton was at once elevated and in relation to which he cultivated a cheeky and parodic wit which lent him a demotic appeal. This is perhaps best exemplified by Barnum's account of the first of the Duke of Wellington's apparently frequent spontaneous visits when he happened to find Stratton 'personating Napoleon Bonaparte, marching up and down the platform, and apparently taking snuff in deep meditation' and claiming to be 'thinking of the loss of the battle of Waterloo'.[22] Stratton's stature both leant him licence to impersonate and, by implication, lampoon political leaders, yet it also pre-emptively weakened the impact of this satire since Stratton's hauteur in elevating himself to such lordly positions simultaneously made him the object of laughter.

In the economy of stardom, then, the performer must tread a difficult line between the extraordinary and the banal; they must both be exceptional in some highly visible way, and yet at the same time be seen to possess enough of the attributes of ordinariness to facilitate identification and empathy on the part of the consumer. In large American circuses, the press agents not only carried on in Barnum's footsteps in this way, but at the same time set precedents for the creation of stars which would be taken up and developed by the film industry. For example, many film historians cite Carl Laemmle's planting of a false story about the death of a 'Biograph Girl' (Florence Lawrence), followed by an outraged denial of the event by him, as the first example of media manipulation to generate interest in a named performer.[23] Of course, as we have seen, Barnum had been involved in this sort of press manipulation decades before this incident in 1910. So the circus industry had the infrastructure (press agents and agencies to feed stories, reviews and pictures to the press) which was creating stars some time before the consolidation of a cinema industry in Hollywood, though the development of the star system in Hollywood, like the industry as a whole, had significant knock-on effects on the big circuses of the day and, therefore, by implication, on the way they marketed their stars. From the 1910s through to the mid 1950s, circus stars in the United States acquired unprecedented levels of status and household familiarity, particularly during the 1920s when stars such as May Wirth, Bird Millman, Con Colleano, Alfredo Codona and Lillian Leitzel were seen to possess all the desired charms of the so-called 'jazz age': good looks, romance, highly publicised private lives and a blatant disregard for the threat of death. They were the subjects of glamour photography, advertising campaigns (figure 4), gossip columns and celebrity magazine interviews in the *Saturday Evening Post, Collier's, Time* and *Life Magazine*; speciality circus publications such as *Billboard* have tended to be more trade and less fanzine in style and appeal. In 1918 Bird Millman even became involved in selling war savings stamps. Her wire was fixed between the J. P. Morgan building and the Sub Treasury Building in New York and she danced on the wire to the Navy Yard Band whilst bidding her spectators to exchange their quarters for stamps.[24] Thus circus star images were marketed and manipulated as commodities within the broader economy in the same way as film stars, selling goods and publications at the same time as they gained free publicity for the circuses in which they performed. The function of the star performer, even in the theatre, has always been to stand as a banker of good audiences, and, as circuses grew rapidly in personnel and production values at the turn of the century, it became increasingly important to draw in consistently large audiences of, as we have seen, up to 15,000. As in the film industry after the 1940s, stars 'were a guarantee, or a promise, against loss on investment and even profit on it.'[25] In return for this the big names of the American circus mentioned above received film-star privileges which were unprecedented in the industry. The benefits scheme was of course no longer in operation and stars in the big circuses could negotiate individual salaries and were given individual travelling cars, top billing and so on.

In fact, the circus of the 1920s and 1930s had a great deal in common with the cinema of the 1940s and 1950s; the transcendence of the musical, the celebration of human and mechanical speed and invention, the invention of colour spectacle, the star vehicle and the emergence of a generic form which presents variations on a similar show to a mass national and international audience and which sells both cultural and material commodities. Almost to confirm this, therefore, in the mid 1950s to the mid 1960s the American cinema begins to make films (*The Greatest Show on Earth*, Cecil B. DeMille, 1952, *3 Ring Circus*, Joseph Pevney, 1953, *Billy Rose's Jumbo*, Charles Walters

Figure 4 Advertisement for Grandma Brown's Ginger Tea Tablets featuring Lillian Leitzel printed in the Ringling Brothers Barnum and Bailey Program of 1922

1962), about the circus which display all of the above features and one of which, *Trapeze* (Carol Reed, 1956), was heavily marketed on the basis of its featuring and being produced by a film star, Burt Lancaster, who had a brief early career in the circus and which made much of the fact that Lancaster performed his own trapeze work (as a catcher) in the film.[26] Lancaster is also one of the many celebrities, most of whom had more negligible connections with the circus than he, who were mobilised by Ringling Brothers Barnum and Bailey (Jimmy Durante [1947], Van Johnson [1947], Spencer Tracy [1949], Bing Crosby [1949], John Steinbeck [1954], Ernest Hemingway [1953], Clark Gable [1950]) in their programmes to give eulogies on the glories of circus as an American institution. Lancaster's contribution to the 1951 programme, 'A "First of May Guy"', accompanied as it is by an advert for 'Pabst Blue Ribbon Beer', showing a domestically located Burt serving up barbeque in an apron, is a complex combination of star image establishment, circus endorsement (Lancaster only mentions Ringling Brothers Barnum and Bailey in his article) and product selling.

Yet although the circus was pioneering in its construction of economic infrastructures which were reproduced and adapted by the film industry, it is easy to see why the defining structures and aesthetics of circus performances worked to hamstring its star-making potential in comparison to cinema and television. Firstly, as Richard Dyer points out, theatre and circus may have made the best of innovations in lighting in order to privilege certain staged figures over others through spotlighting, but this proved no match for the film close-up in terms of establishing a sense of intimacy, close proximity and familiarity with the object of the gaze whose eyes and facial expression in general offer signs of interiority – of emotion and personality.[27] Indeed, as the vast multiple-ring circuses of the American Golden Age further stretched the distances between audience and performer, circus stars of the 1920s and 30s produced an inverse relationship between their public popularity and the close visibility of their acts since the more popular and economically remunerative they were, the bigger their audiences were and the further they therefore were from that audience. What has been absent from the circus then, since the passing of figures such as Andrew Ducrow and the losing touch – from the late nineteenth century onwards – with its theatrical roots, has been a capacity for circus stars to generate a sense of both individual personality and charisma within their performances. Circus performers tend, perhaps with the exception of clowns, to present acts and physical stunts through which they are defined (the lion tamer, the magician, the acrobat and so on) rather than perform dramatic roles. This means also that their star profiles have not been informed and, crucially, developed by their association with identifiable character patterns in their casting. Equally, since the most celebrated star acts in the circus have tended to be those associated with physical dangers and therefore are ones in which the necessity of physical strength, stamina, and dare-devilry is obvious (and much vaunted in general publicity for acts), as we will see in the final chapter, these same attributes represented a particular barrier for the marketing of female circus stars. These powers, which made figures like Bird Millman, Lillian Leitzel and Antoinette Concello exceptional, were the same ones which threatened to place them precisely as eccentric or irregular in relation to contemporary codes of approved femininity, so that publicity around individual stars worked very hard to stress their delicacy and lightness.[28]

The days of circus stars achieving celebrity status are long gone in the West and indeed the background of the personnel in circuses may now be quite different in that the relatively recent development of (often state-sponsored) circus training schools and the incorporation of circus skills (such as mime, acrobatics and clowning) into the curricula of dance and drama schools has meant that many circus performers are the product of these rather than established circus dynasties. State sponsorship has been more consistent and long-standing in Eastern Europe; the Russian State Circus School was the first to be established in Moscow in 1927, though others followed in Leningrad, Minsk, Kiev and the Hungarian school in Budapest, though since the collapse of the communism much of their finance has been withdrawn over the last ten years. From the 1980s onwards Le Centre National des Arts du Cirque has been established in France as a state school, so too is L'Ecole Nationale de Cirque in Montreal, though L'Ecole Nationale des Arts du Cirque is financed by a mixture of state and private sponsorship whilst the Circus Space in London is private. In the United States many performers have learnt their skills in community arts education programmes such as those which have sponsored MAKE*A*CIRCUS in San Francisco, The Big Apple Circus in Harlem, Circus Kirk and Circus Kingdom (Lutheran and Methodist Church-sponsored respectively) or at YMCAs such as the ones in Bloomington, Illinois or Wenatchee, Washington.

Not only have these developments in new learning centres for the circus fostered the so-called 'new circus', as well as the dissemination of circus skills and performance styles into other art forms, but in some cases they have also been responsible for the growth in using circus as a tool within community welfare and rehabilitation projects.[29] In many countries around the world, government, local authority and arts council grants have been issued to allow circus workers to teach skills to adults and children in poor or conflicted areas. In 1985 a community circus was set up in Belfast, for example, with part of its remit being specifically to bring together young people from both Protestant and Catholic communities. 'No Fit State Circus', set up in 1995 and based in Cardiff, travels to different communities in Wales, coordinating a fresh story-based production in each space driven by the ideas and talents of 250 or so members of the community who become involved in the show. In 1992 Oxfam and the Red Cross sponsored six circus projects in Ethiopia, led by Marc La Chance of L'Ecole Nationale de Cirque, to teach circus skills to street children whilst at the same time passing on information about hygiene and the dangers of landmines. Interestingly many commercial circuses are also now involved in community projects: Cirque du Soleil runs programmes for children in nineteen inner-city areas around the world and, in the United Kingdom, Zippo's has specifically sought to recruit young homeless people into its Academy of Circus Arts.[30]

In some ways these developments can be compared to those efforts of the eighteenth-centuy circus, described above, to improve its social standing and respectability with local communities by fostering trade agreements and offering charity donations to the needy. At a time when so much recent media publicity has highlighted circus cruelty and outdatedness, such projects bring opportunities not only to nurture new talents and showcase the various fusions which define and distinguish 'new circus', but any reparation of image which results is also good for business generally in that it raises the profile of circus as a whole.[31] Yet public suspicions of vagabondism and outlawry which tainted the circus's early reputation have never entirely been shaken off and these projects in which circus workers promote good citizenship, social and personal responsibility and intra/cross-community bridge-building confirm an ideal rather than a demonising image of the circus, without either being the whole picture. Thus the rise of the 'new circus' and its accompanying institutions, sources of financing, practioners and cross-generic forms, has functioned to open up the possibilities around the future role and shape of circus. On one level it is a multi-million pound business again (Cirque du Soleil) but in other contexts it ranges from being a state-subsidised community art, a traditional, generically defined family entertainment, an avant-garde theatrical practice or a method of engendering civic responsibility and protecting the vulnerable. Circus can at once be experienced as a vehicle for extravagantly expensive spectacle, a small tented show in a derelict urban space or a two-week run in Madison Square Garden.

Notes

1 I rely here on Kwint's extensive account of the benefits system in 'Astley's amphitheatre', pp. 90–101. see Charles Dickens, *Nicholas Nickleby*, ed. Paul Schlicke (Oxford, Oxford University Press [1938–39], 1990) pp. 270–330.

2 20 August 1836, BL *A Collection of Programmes*, vol. 1, item 34.

3 Kwint, 'Astley's amphitheatre', p. 119.

4 13 August 1805, BL *Astley's Cuttings*, vol. 2, item 273D. Decastro discusses his application to Jones, Cross and Hodson at the Royal Circus to perform his benefit there following the 1803 fire in *Memoirs*, p. 88.

5 Kwint, 'Astley's amphitheatre', p. 90.

6 Kwint, 'Astley's amphitheatre', p. 105.

7 Kwint, 'Astley's amphitheatre', p. 113.

8 The most famous of these in the early circus, Pablo Fanque, whose real name was William Darby, is mentioned in many circus histories. He began as an acrobat but was running his own circus by 1853. see advertisement for Pablo Fanque's Amphitheatre, Edinburgh, 23 June 1853, BL *Circus Programmes* vol. 1, item 103, and John Turner, 'Pablo Fanque: "An Artiste of Colour"', *King Pole*, 89, December 1990, 5–9 and 90, January 1991, 3–5.

9 See Kwint, 'Astley's amphitheatre', p. 115.

10 11 March 1784, BL *Astley's Cuttings*, vol. 1, item 527.

11 Kwint, 'Astley's amphitheatre', p. 153.

12 Bob Parkinson, 'The circus and the press', *Bandwagon*, March/April 1963, p. 3.

13 See Rodman Gilder, 'Dan Rice, American clown and humorist', *Theatre Arts*, May 1941, pp. 361–8.

14 Parkinson, 'The circus and the press', p. 8. Also see Ed Zotti, 'Circus advertising: the greatest hype on earth', *Advertising Age*, 12 December 1983, p. 11.

15 See Parkinson, 'The circus and the press', *Bandwagon*, March/April 1963, pp. 3–9.

16 Bill Ballantine 'Spring's Shameless Ballyhoo', *True; The Man's Magazine*, March 1967, pp. 41–3.

17 Sverre O. Braathen and Faye O. Braathen, 'The advance could make or break a circus', *Bandwagon*, January/February 1971, 11–25, p. 13.

18 The first full-colour circus bill is thought to have been used by Raymond and Waring's in 1847. see Fred D. Pfening, Jr, 'Circus bill posting and advance advertising cars', parts 1 and 2, *Bandwagon*, November/December 1973, 4–16 and November/December 1974, 4–14.

19 P. T. Barnum, *Struggles and Triumphs; or, Forty Years' Recollections* (New York, Warren, Johnson & Co., 1973), p. 121.

20 Neil Harris, *Humbug: The Art of P. T. Barnum* (London and Chicago, Chicago University Press, 1973), p. 57.

21 Barnum, *Struggles and Triumphs*, pp. 121–2.

22 Barnum, *Struggles and Triumphs*, pp. 183–4.

23 See, for example, David A. Cook, *A History of Narrative Film* (New York, W. W. Norton, 1981), p. 40, Gorham Kindem, 'Hollywood's movie star system: a historical overview', in Gorham Kindem (ed.) *The American Movie Industry: The Business of Motion Pictures* (Carbondale, Southern Illnois University Press, 1982), pp. 80–2, and Janet Staiger's slightly different reading of the Laemmle incident in 'Seeing stars', in Christine Gledhill (ed.), *Stardom: Industry of Desire* (London, Routledge, 1991), pp. 3–8.

24 Saturday, 6 April 1918, *New York Tribune*. The article also draws attention to the fact that this was the first time a Ringling Brothers Barnum and Bailey act was allowed to be filmed, thus confirming the patriotism and commitment of this circus in making exceptions for the war effort.

25 Richard Dyer, *Stars* (London, BFI Publishing, 1979) p. 11.

26 See, for example, 'Burt is back in the big top', *Friends*, March 1956, pp. 26–7 which describes a photograph of 'Burt' as he 'calls on his fund of circus knowledge to explain intricacies of tricks performed by flying team', p. 26. Interestingly, another publicity article written by Lancaster himself begins with the lines 'My first job was as a circus acrobat. The second was as a salesman', 'Selling the greatest show on earth', *Salesman's Opportunity*, February 1957, pp. 31, 78, 80.

27 Dyer, *Stars*, pp. 16–17.

28 For example, Lillian Leitzel is still rarely mentioned without some additional reference being made to her 'petite' size in which her height and weight (4 feet 9 inches, 95 lbs) and the physical 'grace' acquired from early ballet training are cited. see Marian Murray, *From Rome to Ringling* (Westport, CT, Greenwood Press, 1956) p. 311, 'The fabulous Lilian Leitzel' (sic.), *King Pole*, December 1962, pp. 26–7.

29 Recent examples include Robert LePage's production *The Geometry of Miracles* (1999), which included a webcast, and Opera Factory's production of *The Magic Flute* (1997) in which most of the cast was involved in juggling.

30 Amelia Gentleman, 'Circus lifts girl beggar from low life to high wire', *Guardian*, 30 August 1999, p. 20.
31 The New Millennium Experience Company, for example, commissioned Circus Space in East London to train and accredit the 90 aerialists who have performed in the Millennium Dome's Central Show before a daily audience of up to 12,000 people; almost up to the 15,000 capacity of The Greatest Show on Earth at its peak.

4

Legitimacy and status

It is a relatively common feature of Marxist-influenced criticism of popular culture that it has sought to make an interpretative leap between disrepute and dissent and to assume that the popular may always at some point either voice or at least harbour dangerous politics. So it is easy to see how the circus, so persistently the outlaw in relation to vagrancy and theatrical legislation as well as to middle-class morality, would look to be such a promising object for such analysis. Hugh Cunningham, for example, has argued for a certain interconnectedness between different aspects of essentially pre-industrial popular entertainments (sports, pantomime, circus, menageries) in the first half of the nineteenth century which were all becoming commercial concerns and often shared common personnel as people moved between different activities which were 'further drawn together by the political necessity of defending it' and which also shared 'a consistent radical cutting edge'.[1]

The point about personnel may be true, but there are problems with generalising too far on this basis. Firstly, Cunningham sees it as significant that the Chartist Thomas Frost recalled these entertainments in detail and identified their unity, but in his memoirs 'Lord' George Sanger gives an account under the chapter heading 'The Chartists Spoil Newport Fair' of the Newport uprising of 1839 which makes it very clear that the fair workers were far from sharing the Chartist or the Chartist colliers' radical political agenda.[2] The show people are depicted as respectable citizens driven by the simple but honest desire to 'make a little money' for their families suffering from 'the dread inspired by the miners whose roughness and brutality were at that time proverbial'. The fact that the drama was almost immediately seen as 'an excellent subject for my father's peep show' is absolutely typical of the Sangers' commercial opportunism and Sanger's description of their portrayal of the 'desperate attack on the Westgate Hotel' together with the 'flight of the mob' (the miners) indicates that this peep show portrayal, together with a later one dramatising Thomas Frost's trial for treason and felony, were far from resembling any kind of agitprop theatre for the Chartist cause. Secondly, the necessity for defending the circus from legal restrictions was, for those who worked in them, always a commercial rather than a political one. Not only is there little evidence to suggest that, despite informal connections and camaraderie, those who worked in the circus constituted any kind of united front (either amongst themselves or with other entertainment workers) which might have been labelled political, but, on the contrary as we have seen above, there was much cut-throat competition between circuses as well as a sustained campaign by different circus publicists to distance themselves from the sundry forms of popular entertainment of which in many ways they were a product. Whilst the circus had indeed been an arena for many transgressions, these have rarely been of an overtly political nature, in fact in these terms it has been consistently conservative. Rather it is necessary to adjust the focus somewhat to identify the challenges and perceived social dangers of the circus which have their roots in the risks, juxtapositions and revelations of human and animal bodies which it has consistently offered as entertainment.

Henry Angelo, whose father had been responsible for selecting Astley from a cavalry regiment to perform a display, reports that even in Philip Astley's days of military horsemanship 'the mastery which he obtained over his horse, so astonished the common people in the neighbourhood of Wilton that they thought Corporal Astley was the devil in disguise'.[3] Elsewhere a contemporary commentator exclaims 'What a wicked age this is, and likely to continue so! for no less than two thousand persons nightly walk and ride to the Devil – at Astley's'.[4] Of course the tone of both this and Angelo's reports implies a tongue-in-cheek humour and this is supported by the fact that these diabolical references were made light of through puffs which advertsised particular performers as the 'English Devil' or the 'Scottish Devil'. However, the fact that a demonic association is made suggests that, though there may be no serious moral implication in the reference to the devil, there is something else at stake here besides. The crowd in this case is a 'common' one and its distrust of Astley's performance is perhaps not moral but rather aesthetic in foundation since its basis apears to be a delighted astonishment which is tainted by the suspicion that spectacularly visible accomplishment could readily be associated with devilry in disguise. For the circus, the essential and highly marketed aesthetic categories of the astonishing, the wondrous and the unbelievable would continue for some time to be greeted by a delight tempered by disbelief in what appeared to be near miraculous human achievement; a disbelief which, for want of an alternative aesthetic language, for a time found expresssion in light-hearted references to the biblical terms of dangerous enchantment. The fact that this reference to diabolical influence was a rhetorical fashion rather than a real moral issue is confirmed by the appearance of the following newspaper puff of 1786 from Astley's which suggests that Astley himself was capable of mobilising this rhetoric quite subtely:

> It is remarked by a correspondent, that most places of public amusement are obliged to have several Devils to their aid, while Astley refuses all such diabolical assistance, and is playing the Devil by relying upon Terrestrial Excellence.[5]

In rebuttals to accusations about his reputation, Astley commonly identified with the discourse mobilised by his critics, casting himself playfully in this way as a renegade or subversive precisely for his conformity and respectability within an otherwise roguish industry. What is particularly interesting about this self-promotion is the sly way in which Astley manages both to joke about his innocence from 'diabolical assistance' and, in the same move, to distract his potentially respectable audience from the real dangers and anxieties commonly associated with the circus which focused on their context and environment rather than the contents of particular performances. It is also important to note that in his playful engagement with this rhetorical fashion, Astley emerges as particularly forward-looking since his suggestion that he has eschewed demonic possession for, by implication, 'self possession', anticipates a much more Victorian-sounding equation of moral improvement, physical self control and respectability. It is telling, then, that even very early on in the establishment of this highly secular form of entertainment, religious references operate humourously and rhetorically as a way of both procuring commercial advantage through advertising and, within this, to confirm its excitement over the physical excellence of the purely human body.

Astley's concern for reputation extended only to his own concerns and indeed, contrary to Cunningham's broad claim, he saw an interest in darkening the name of other circus establishments. None the less he also worked to promote the general worthiness and social responsibility of the circus by advertising the vital and edifying skills involved in performance and encouraged the public in regarding circus riding (taught by Astley in his school or through the purchase of his riding manual) as an improving leisure pursuit.[6] The constant emphasis in early advertising bills on the 'manliness' of the equestrian performers, however, is a measure not only of Astley's identification of fashionably martial and marketable skills, but is indicative also perhaps of a slight uneasiness around such spectacular displays of the performing male body which, in consequence, is idealised in very different terms, as I argue in my final chapter, from the female body in similar performances. For example an advertising poster of 1827 marvels that a current production of 'The Courier of St. Petersburg' has 'outstripped and immeasurably surpassed' any previous productions of the drama which had 'hitherto been accounted *Wonderful* in the bold and manly attainment of equitation'. At the same time it warns that the 'unpractised eye' may not appreciate the 'scientific management of the Rein' executed by the rider whose 'light air and agility' of movements, combined with 'firmness' of footing, work to 'banish all fear for his personal safety'.[7] Though it may not be obvious to the lay spectator, it is emphasised, what is truly 'wonderful' about this performer is that he is, paradoxically, not a thing of wonder at all but the result of careful scientific management of balance and gravity. Thus we are not so much invited to admire the beauty of the performance as the technical skill behind it, an admiration which simultaneously flatters its audience by upgrading their reaction from blind wonder to informed 'appreciation' and thereby connoisseurship.

On another level the physical energies involved in these dramas appear to have been importantly symbolic. Kwint and Meisel have both identified familiarly Romantic discourses at work in these shows with Meisel reading dramas such as *Mazeppa* as playing out an ambivalent response to the energies unleashed after the French Revolution with the horse 'ready to shake off or run away with the presumptuous human will', and Kwint suggesting that the equestrian became 'an emblem of conquest but also of civilisation itself' with the horse representing both the wild earth to be conquered and 'the principal muscular force on which commercial and industrial society was built'.[8] The following, as a newspaper account of one of Ducrow's epic equestrian dramas of 1830s, is illustrative of an awareness that some of these broader issues were at stake:

> The performances are of a manly and ennobling character; they breathe throughout a generous spirit. The daring actions of Englishmen are here embodied to the life. We have seen them breathe, and move, and have their being where Englishmen alone would have ventured – where they alone would have struggled – in foreign climes, amidst disaster, and want, and death. We witness lion-hearted deeds – daring feats – generous devoted actions, and we know they are not merely the lying scenes of lying men, but the faithful and just epitome of our nation's history.[9]

Here effeminacy and poor (unfaithful) production values are the connected enemies of a conquering patriotism and expansionism celebrated in the circus. Again this publicity, in conventional theatrical mode, flatters the class of its audience by assuming their appreciation of matters concerning national history. Visible also here are the ways in which the idealisation and aestheticisation of male bodies were given a symbolic, cultural and historic purpose when linked to equitation.

Astley displayed the most overt royalism and worship of the gentry in his desire to confirm the raised status of circus above other popular entertainments and the attendance of any such figures was made much of in publicity materials. His advertising bills conventionally opened with the words 'We are desired to inform the Nobility, Gentry and others, that Mr Astley ...' and went on to mention their patronage in terms which suggested Astley's was their first and favoured choice of entertainment.[10] Astley's Amphitheatre always advertised the patronage of 'her majesty the Queen and Prince Albert' and 'Lord' George Sanger was not the only figure to bestow a knighthood upon himself.[11] This was important for the development of the circus as a whole because, as Kwint points out, it 'set the robustly loyalist tone of the establishment' and thereby distanced it from the 'feared seditiousness of popular London'.[12] This infatuation with occupants of high station not only highlights an important, not necessarily contradictory, thread within the populist fabric of the circus, but also signals a thirst for moral respectability and approval from establishment figures which transferred even into the New World in new, more Republican, forms. John Bill Ricketts, for example, was just as quick to advertise George Washington's attendance at his circus and, as John Culhane suggests,

Washington's famous horse Jack, which he rode during the years of the Revolution, became the 'first sideshow attraction of the circus in America' when Ricketts purchased it for his show in 1797.[13]

The character of the circus, then, needs to be understood in terms of its being a child born and raised in a confinement which proved determining, though not necessarily stifling, since the confinements simultaneously produced intense compensatory energies. Imprisoned by eighteenth-century British theatrical, or rather anti-theatrical legislation, its identity became shaped early on during either habitual outmanoeuvring or compliance with the law, but it rarely resorted to out and out defiance. In 1737 the Theatre Licensing Act had made it illegal for plays to be performed in any but the official patent theatres. The minor London theatres of the period had responded to this by offering productions which were predominantly musical and spectacular and which, since they did not rely on spoken dialogue, could not therefore be classed as drama. Much of what I will be going on to discuss as central to circus aesthetics can be seen to have been moulded during this period of avoidance of theatrical injunctions on speech in performance. A later act of Parliament (the Vagrancy Act, 1744) led to the gaoling of unlicensed performers and on top of this, in 1752 the Disorderly Houses Act forced all local places of public entertainment to acquire a magistrate's permit on an annual basis. Astley fell foul of both these pieces of legislation in 1773 and 1777 respectively. The 1773 prosecution led to the closure of the amphitheatre (he had neither a royal permit to cover stage drama nor a magistrate's permit for dance and music) and this crisis prompted Astley to leave town to tour the provinces.

Though Hughes's entrance, as mentioned above, was in many ways crucial to the formation of the circus as an entertainment form in its own right, his opening of the Royal Circus in December 1782 very nearly precipitated its downfall. His extensive pre-show publicity (and Astley's counter-advertising) made it clear that a stage was to be part of the new circus. Both proprietors were arrested, sent to New Bridewell prison and Astley was subsequently forced to remove his stage.[14] A bitter falling out between the two occurred as Hughes accused Astley of reporting him to the officials.[15] Again this incident had aesthetic consequences with Astley turning instead to alternative forms of spectacle such as fireworks and dancing and left it to his son John to maintain an element of drama in the shows by introducing more narrative into the acts.

There is also evidence, however, of a sort of scramble for legitimacy amongst the minor theatres and circuses. The proprietors of Sadler's Wells, itself a minor theatre, put forward a petition to the House of Lords in 1788 to grant them exclusive rights to summer performances. This followed the prosecution of the Royalty, another minor, which suggested the threat of a less tolerant interpretation of the Disorderly Houses Act than had recently been enjoyed. Astley's and the Royal Circus followed suit, separately, with similar counter-petitions asking that they be named under an amended version of the Disorderly Houses Act as having exclusive rights to stage burlettas. Astley's plea relied less on legal force than on his attempt to establish the respectability and morality of the circus's credentials; finally he mobilised his war veteran's record, backed up by a character reference from the late Colonel Nangle of the 15th Light Dragoons, and enlisted statements from other citizens who pointed out the precarious reputation of Sadler's Wells which stood alone in including a pint of liquor in the price of admittance when no liquor was permitted at either Astley's or the Royal Circus.[16]

At times, during the last two decades of the eighteenth century and the early nineteenth, the circus reached peaks of near hysterical patriotism, in an attempt to marshal their audiences' support in the name of the national interest. For the most part this took the form of staging grand patriotic spectacles or hippodramatic battle re-enactments, particularly in the period immediately following the Napoleonic wars, though at other times national loyalties were reduced to the level of sometimes absurd or casual rhetoric. For example in a letter to the *Morning Herald* in August 1785, Richard Wroughton, then manager of Sadler's Wells, attempts to justify his obviously opportunistic and slightly desperate purchase of a Learned Pig for exhibition there; a pig which Wroughton would later describe as 'an honest Englishman'. Although the signing led to the immediate resignation of five of his star (foreign) performers, who were promptly engaged at Astley's, he argues that "I was obliged either to sacrifice an Englishman to the caprice of these foreigners, or lose their performances for the remainder of the season".'[17] What the incident highlights is the very marked tension between the discourse of patriotism which may have been mobilised opportunistically by circuses with different national bases in response to fashion and political events in order to bolster their status and popular support, and the institutional reality of a popular entertainment which has always been both constitutionally international and, at the same time, strategically xenophobic.

By 1830, the licence which Astley's had acquired to permit it to perform dance and music was extended to include 'other public entertainments of the like kind' and Kwint suggests that the more liberal approach to the licensing of popular entertainments in the subsequent period needs to be understood within the context of its acknowledged commercial success so that 'entertainment was defined less by customary entitlement, and more by what the entrepreneurs could supply'.[18] It wouldn't be until 1843, after the death of both Astleys and Ducrow, that the Theatres Act was passed and with it the patentee's prose drama monopoly finally dismantled. However, by this stage the generic identity of the circus as a mute, musical or pantomimic dramatic form had been established and fully exported around the world and if anything, as we will see, the narrative components of circus shows declined as the century progressed.

C. H. Amidon makes the point that, whereas in Europe theatrical prohibitions which stemmed from royal command functioned to divide legitimate theatre from circus on the basis of the proscription of speech in the latter, in the United States (aside from the specific injunctions during the Revolution mentioned above which were informed more by anticipation of wartime hardship than by morality) objections to the circus were civic, moral and general; that is, since all forms of stage and ring experienced restrictions, it was more common for elements of circus and theatrical performance to be combined.[19] Moral disapproval however was not uniformly exhibited across the States, indeed, as Amidon suggests, although the more Puritan Northeast coast area of New York, Boston and Philadelphia was initially distrustful, Southeastern states were more accommodating, finding the circus's European, vaguely aristocratic and military associations to be dashingly attractive. None the less, although Pennsylvania legislation against theatrical spaces was instigated in 1779, it was lifted again in 1789 following which Washington, himself an aristocratic and horse-loving Southerner, led the way for other prominent public figures to be seen at the circus with his now famous attendances at Ricketts's circus in 1793 and again in 1797.[20] When Lincoln's highly flaunted connection with the clown Dan Rice in the nineteenth century followed Ricketts's association with Washington it became clear that political (especially presidential) patronage of the circus became as significant here for the establishment of the status of the circus as royal and aristocratic attendance had been in England.[21] In the twentieth century, as we saw above, again it was the Ringling Brothers's success in wiping out 'grifting' from their lots and their subsequent marketing of their shows as safe, family entertainment which proved to be one of the key elements in their huge commercial success.

From the 1820s, in the United Kingdom, even before the repeal of the anti-theatrical legislation, the circus generally, but especially the permanent city circuses, was increasingly attended openly by celebrities, people of fashion and royalty. Though not strictly legal it was hardly suspected of inciting dangerous or immoral behaviour. Middle-class patrons may well still have been attracted to the circus because of the frisson of roguishness still attached to it (and which is still attached to it) from its historical reputation whilst, in reality, they were assured of relatively high standards of security and comfort. This is not to say that the idea of danger was not still at the heart of what the circus offered, simply that this was the spectacle of physical danger observed from a distance and a highly qualified eroticism rather than the complicity of participating in illegitimate entertainment.

Though there were similar legal restrictions on circuses in France in that the Comedie Française possessed an effective monopoly over the performance of prose and popular performance genres, from the outset, circuses and circus performers received acquired more kudos there as skilled artists. Many talented British circus figures, most notably Ducrow, spent long periods of their working lives in Europe. In the years immediately preceding the French Revolution Englishness had acquired a certain voguish status amongst polite French society and, since skills in horsemanship were associated particularly with the cult of Englishness, Astley and others were greeted as celebrities by the French Court in Versailles.[22] According to Disher, after the 'politically troubled period from the forties to the eighties, when the excitable public was fed on equestrian dramas' the circus became established as a fashionable entertainment with 'the écuyère of the ring' being 'fêted in the summer as religiously as diva or ballerina in the winter, and the stables of the Cirque D'été in the Champs Elysée, became as fashionable as the coulisses of the opera'.[23]

After the Theatres Act of 1843 circuses (with stages) received legal recognition and thereby, during the years of the great equestrian dramas, enjoyed a brief and relative freedom from legal restraint. Indeed, the legitimacy of the circus per se in the United Kingdom has never since been under threat, and its own defence of its public role and reputation has been correspondingly relaxed. However, certain elements of its theatrical offerings, firstly child performers and aerial acts and, secondly, animal acts have been the object of sustained and, at times, highly emotive public campaigns to ban them. By the 1870s, the combination of the spirit of nineteenth-century reformism coupled with the new enthusiasm in the circus for high-wire performance, aerialism and acrobatics, led to the Dangerous Performances Act of 1879 and a series of further legislation which came in on its coat tail. The bill was then impelled by a series of well-publicised falls on both sides of the Atlantic and provided a list of proscribed acts whilst also making specific gender distinctions. For example, as Steve Gossard points out, Leona Dare's descent in air whilst hanging from a balloon by her teeth had so provoked the British public that, henceforth, men but not women would be allowed to perform this stunt.[24] The Children's Dangerous Performances Bill (1879) also targeted children under fourteen, preventing them from performing potentially life-endangering acts, though, as Carolyn Steedman points out, it did not cover the process of training acrobats.[25] Their apprenticeship into circuses from walking age had been an especial bugbear for campaigners who recognised the excessive manipulation and pain involved in this particular form of child labour. Amye Reade, whose two sensationalist novels of the period, *Ruby; a Novel, Founded on the Life of a Circus Girl* (1889) and *Slaves of the Sawdust* (1892), captures the crusading tone typical of many campaigners, who, like Lord Shaftsbury, had often also been involved in other reformist battles, when she describes her 'mission' to end a 'dark phase of those who are engaged in the circus' by giving these 'white slaves' their 'emancipation'.[26] Their campaigns finally came to fruition with the Prevention of Cruelty Acts of both 1889 and 1894 which focused on the training of acrobats, under the age of sixteen, for the purposes of public performance. This is not to say that child acrobats have not performed in British stage and circus venues since these dates, but it is likely that they will have been trained elsewhere.

Undoubtedly it has been in the area of animal display and performance that the twentieth-century circus has found itself subject to the most rigorous policing, control and inspection and the issue has proved most thorny for the United Kingdom and United States-based circuses, most particularly since the 1970s. This is not the place to debate the case either for or against the inclusion of animals as circus performers, both of which have been extensively and frequently argued elsewhere.[27] However, legislation to control the welfare, husbandry and transportation of animals has not only increased the costs involved in animal-keeping, but has also had the effect of intensifying public scrutiny of circus practices in this area. The recent case in the United Kingdom is of Mary Chipperfield who, together with her elephant trainer, was found guilty in April 1999 of using excessive force in the process of training a chimpanzee and an elephant. Both had been secretly filmed by Animal Defenders who then presented their video evidence to MPs at the Commons in February, coinciding with the period when the Circus Advisory Group to the All Party Animal Welfare Committee were preparing evidence for their report. Channel 4 and BBC 1 both broadcast television documentaries featuring this material.[28] The case provoked a particular crisis of conscience for supporters of animals in the circus since Mary Chipperfield, whose animals are also used in film and television productions, had always been cited in their campaigns as exemplary of good training practice.[29] In 1965, British circuses, under the self-formed organisation of the Association of Circus Proprietors (ACP), attempted to pre-empt and disarm public suspicions about cruelty by declaring themselves open to RSPCA inspection at any time. Since then it has laid down its own code of practice for members and has been able to cite in its defence a recent independent scientific report which supported the case against the outright banning of animals. Even so, the re-establishment of the legitimacy has not been, and therefore seems unlikely to be, achieved.[30] Whilst a few circuses, such as Brighton-based Zippo's, persist with the display of domestic animals such as dogs and horses, the fact that, in 1993, 180 local authorities had banned circuses with animals has led to a widespread conversion to human-only shows.[31] At the same time, at the more radical end of human circus, Archaos were bankrupt between 1991 and 1996 when Bristol City Council cancelled a two-week booking there following tabloid reports about nudity and chainsaw juggling.[32] Over all though, many circuses have considered the financial costs of swimming against the tide of public opinion against animal performing too great, whilst others have taken their shows to other European countries such as France, Denmark, Switzerland and Holland where, though legislation is very similar, public sensibilities are more accommodating of animal displays.

Again then, the circus in both Europe and the United States has been forced to negotiate, even campaign, and to an extent reinvent itself, in order to maintain its commercial survival and legitimacy. The Romantic celebration of man's benevolent mastery over nature symbolised by his ennobling and skilful horsemanship, which, as Kwint has argued, lay at the core of the circus's appeal, no longer has any purchase over contemporary imaginations for whom the dominant public discourses in relation to nature centre on environmental protection (against the force of human exploitation) rather than domination. Ironically this means that the horse, around whose skills and potential the very ring of the circus was measured, and whose employment constituted a way of entertaining the public which precisely allowed for the side-stepping of theatrical legislation, is now being removed in order to regain the legitimacy it once secured.

Notes

1 Cunningham, *Leisure in the Industrial Revolution*, p. 36, p. 37. See also Marius Kwint, 'The legitimization of the circus in late Georgian England', *Past and Present* (forthcoming, 2000).

2 'Lord' George Sanger, *Seventy Years a Showman* (J. M. Dent and Sons, London, 1927), pp. 66–71. Sanger does, however, qualify his portrayal of this drama with a confession that, though he could 'patter volubly enough about the riots and the trial' he really 'knew little about it' and admits that he has 'since lived to see everything granted in the way of liberty that the chartists then asked for, with none of the evil results that people in the old days so freely prophesied would follow', p. 71.

3 Angelo, *Reminiscences*, vol. 1, p. 100.

4 Kwint, 'Astley's amphitheatre', pp. 156–7. August 1785, BL *Astley's Cuttings*, vol. 1, item 688. See also Kwint, p. 248.

5 1786, BL *Astley's Cuttings*, vol. 1, item 918.

6 Philip Astley, *The Modern Riding Master; Or, A Key to the Knowledge of the Horse and Horsemanship, with Several Necessary Rules for Young Horseman* (London, 1775).

7 December 1827, BL *Circus Programmes*, vol. 1, item 74.

8 Meisel, *Realisations*, p. 216, and Kwint, 'Astley's amphitheatre', p. 312.

9 10 May 1834, BL *Astley's Cuttings*, vol. 3, item 1372.

10 See 1772, BL *Astley's Cuttings*, vol. 1, items 52, 53, 61, 62, 81.

11 See 15 May 1840, BL *Circus Programmes*, vol. 1, item 92.

12 Kwint, 'Astley's amphitheatre', p. 20.

13 Culhane, *The American Circus*, pp. 5–6.

14 On 30 December 1782. see BL *Astley's Cuttings*, vol. 1, item 445.

15 Astley publishes a public denial of this. See BL *Astley's Cuttings*, item 435.
16 See 25 June 1788, BL *Astley's Cuttings*, vol. 1, items 1027 and 1029 for Astley's case and his reference respectively. It is also reported by Decastro, *Memoirs*, pp. 39–40, and Thomas Frost reproduces the newspaper letter which argues that the case against the minors 'arises from a principle of morality, which is indeed the only plea of opposition which can be alleged', *Circus Life*, p. 36.
17 1 August 1785, BL *Astley's Cuttings*, vol. 1, item 691.
18 Kwint, 'Astley's amphitheatre', p. 151.
19 C. H. Amidon, 'Behind the scenes with John B. Ricketts', *Bandwagon*, November/December 1874, p. 16.
20 Amidon reads significance into these dates since the first visit (22 April 1793) coincided with Washington's Neutrality Proclamation in the war between France and England and his second during his final period as President when criticism of his presidency was mounting (p. 18). Even for presidents, the circus is seen to work as a safety valve.
21 Dan Rice, born Daniel McClaren (1823–1900), is generally recognised to have been the foremost American clown of the nineteenth century and has often (wrongly) been cited as the source of the figure of 'Uncle Sam', whom he characteristically mimicked. His career spanned the period in which the clown was the pre-eminent performer of the nineteenth century, making him the highest-paid star of the 1850s and 60s, to its decline in the era of the three-ring circus. He is usually cited as the source for Mark Twain's clown depiction in *The Adventures of Huckleberry Finn*, ed. Victor Doyno (London, Bloomsbury [1885], 1996), pp. 197–200. The most reliable source of information on Rice are chapters 33 and 35 of the John Dungeness manuscript, an unpublished manuscript detailing the history of the American circus held in the Hertzberg Collection. see also Culhane, *The American Circus*, pp. 47–62.
22 See 1782, BL *Astley's Cuttings*, vol. 1, item 403. Also Decastro gives an account of John Astley's performance at Versailles for Louis XVI and Marie Antoinette. He records that 'they were so delighted with his manly agility, symmetry of figure, elegance of attitude, and gentlemanly deportment, that they were graciously pleased condescendingly to present him with a gold medal, set with diamonds, . . . and designated him the "English Rose", an allusion to that most accomplished of French dancers, the original "Vestris", who was then styled the "French Rose"', *Memoirs*, p. 45.
23 Disher, *Greatest Show on Earth*, p. 291.
24 Steve Gossard, *A Reckless Era of Aerial Performance: The Evolution of Trapeze* (Normal, Illinois, the author, 1994), p. 19.
25 Carolyn Steedman gives a very full and fascinating account of the discourses surrounding the child acrobat during this period in *Strange Dislocations: Childhood and the Idea of Human Interiority, 1780–1930* (London, Virago, 1995), pp. 96–111.

26 Amye Reade, 'Preface', *Slaves of the Sawdust* (London, F. V. White and Co., 1892).
27 See, for example, Jeanne Rousch, 'Animals under the big top', *The Humane Society News*, spring, 1981, pp. 18–21, David Jamieson and David Davis, 'Animals in the circus', *King Pole*, 120, September 1998, pp. 12–15. The Circus Fans Association of the United States published an official 'Position Statement on Animal Welfare' in *White Tops*, 63:6 (1990), p. 7.
28 *Secrets of the Circus* (Channel 4, 8 April 1999) and *Saving Trudy* (BBC 1, 12 April 1999).
29 See, for example, David Jamieson et. al., 'Animals in the circus: a *King Pole* special', *King Pole*, 67, June 1985, pp. 3–19.
30 The ACP code is reproduced in Jamieson *et al.*, p. 4. see Marthe Kiley-Worthington, *Animals in Circuses and Zoos* (Basildon, Little Eco Farms Publishing, 1990).
31 Vivek Chaudhary, 'Campaign aims to outlaw "world of suffering" for circus animals', *Guardian*, 3 August 1993, p. 5.
32 Nicholas de Jongh, 'French Circus Banned', *Guardian*, 21 July 1990, p. 2.

5

Aesthetics

The process of defining the terms of circus aesthetics is very much like, and is linked to, defining its generic identity. Its aesthetic components and their shifting levels of importance in relation to each other have been subject to much change and adaptation according to institutional transformations and technical innovations over the years. At the same time, however, it should still be possible to give a general account of such features which is flexible enough to accommodate historical and cultural fluctuations.

One of the key distinctions of which to take account in this respect is between representational and non-representational, mimetic and non-mimetic displays, and, as discussed above, these distinctions have a historical context. Whilst the circus before 1782 was an eclectic and opportunistic assemblage of equestrian display, human and animal tricks and burlesque, the importance of the stage after this, during the so-called Romantic era, transformed the nature of the circus spectacle for a considerable period of time until, under the influence of the American circus in the second half of the nineteenth century, it was in some ways returned to its fairground roots where display took precedence over drama. For critics such as Coxe who have attempted to define the circus in terms of its distinction from the theatre, this return to roots represented a vital casting aside of a 'national love of compromise' by the British for an anti-illusionist display of skill:

> Any performance presented on a stage, framed by a proscenium, is a spectacle based on illusion ... Just as the theatre has a parallel in painting, so does the circus have an analogy in sculpture. You can walk round it. It can be seen from all sides. There can be no illusion, for there are eyes all round to prove that there is no deception. The performers actually do exactly what they appear

to do. Their feats of dexterity and balance and strength must never be confused with the make believe world of the actor ... for while an actor says he will 'play his part', the circus artiste tells you he will 'work his act'.[1]

This view of the circus as work and as 'a spectacle of actuality' leads Coxe to a reclassification of the circus as a craft rather than an art because, he believes, it is purely 'demonstrative' and, unlike the theatre, has no 'interpretative' dimension to it.[2]

A number of important and controversial assumptions, however, underpin these claims. Firstly, the inclusion of acts which are also considered to be 'stunts', must lead to a redefinition of the nature of 'performance' within circus shows. To a certain extent the performance theorist Erving Goffman's concept of audience 'framing' is of relevance here.[3] Goffman argues that spectators habitually establish in their own minds separate 'frames' of operation which allow them to distinguish between 'play frames', in which they already recognise what they see as either 'not true' or 'nonexistent' (sic), and those elements of perform-ance which they experience in the social world which have not been transformed into art or fantasy.[4] The performance 'frame' here, then, works to distance the audience from what happens inside its frame and thereby to relieve them of responsibility for what goes on inside it.

Where the circus has been engaged in the presentation of seasonal pantomimic drama, clowning and, to a degree, acrobatics, these frame separations hold. However, we have also seen that one of the defining attractions through which the circus distinguishes itself from other spectacular forms is through both the real presence of its dangers in the form of 'stunt' acts and, until relatively recently, the frisson attached to the human and animal representatives of other cultures whose very existence, despite perhaps fantastic ornamentation, was to be proved rather than disputed by their exhibition in the ring. The circus perform-ance 'frame', therefore, depends on its periodic expansion and contraction in that although the audience are clearly divided physically from the scene of performance, their occasional confrontations with the actual existences of the performers arise out of moments of danger in which the impact of the show depends on the audience's recognition of (and indeed sense of responsibility for) the performer's proximity to human extinction, rather than merely untruth. Goffman's model is useful then partly because it draws attention to the ambiguous relationship circus maintains with the concepts of 'illusion' and 'reality' as it seeks, at different times, to embrace both. Yet Goffman also provides a good example of the way definitions of performance frequently hinge on assessments of an audience's ability to negotiate with and interpret the 'signs' of representation within a performance, rather than focusing on non-representative elements such as physical skill, balance, strength, agility and daring which have tended to be the foundations of the most highly rated circus acts and which have sometimes led to their being grouped as sport rather than craft or art.[5]

This implicit distinction between artistic and physical skill leads us, secondly, to Coxe's reinforcement of what Raymond Williams has demonstrated to be a separation between the terms 'art' and 'work' which has historically specific origins in mid-nineteenth-century shifts in production and exchange values. Art and artists therefore were separated from industry which meant they could be seen as forms of activity 'which were not determined by immediate exchange' and which could be at least conceptually abstracted.[6] Thus, Williams argues, the 'artist' is also to be distinguished from the *'artisan* and *craftsman* and *skilled worker*, who are now operatives in terms of a specific definition and organisation of work'.[7] To classify the circus within these terms as 'work' rather than 'art', is to feed the illusion that 'art' may not be subject to commodification in the same way as it is the circus in which exhibitions of skill are perhaps more obviously driven by a thirst for profit-making. Secondly, Coxe relies on a very selective view of circus history which regards the 'Romantic age' of the circus in which, as discussed above, the stage was as important as the ring and detailed representational dramas predominated, as a temporary if lengthy blip in an entertainment otherwise dedicated to the pure display of effects. The fact that many of the most well known of the so-called 'new' circuses have also returned to forms of narrative story-telling in their shows can either be seen, from this purist view of the circus as a discrete genre, as a further example of cross-generic corruption, or that the 'skills' identified by Coxe as part of the 'craft' of the circus may also, at times be incorporated into a wider agenda of representational drama. Thirdly, the question still remains of whether circus could still be considered art, rather than entertainment, when the acts presented within it are purely demonstrative. It should be pointed out that Coxe is clearly a passionate devotee of the circus and its history; when he describes it as 'simply a craft' next to the 'art' of the theatre he bestows greater value on the 'craft' since for him this term connotes the associated virtues of authenticity, integrity, vitality and honesty as opposed to art's implied artifice and effeteness.

The relative value attached to art and entertainment respectively has been an issue which has dominated debates about the relationship between 'high' and 'low' or popular culture, especially within debates in film and literary studies, since the 1970s and it seems that some of the same issues and assumptions are at stake here.[8] The first assumption is that art must necessarily, by virtue of being representational, offer the spectator a space between something assumed to be 'reality' or 'actuality' on the one hand and the artistic rendering of some aspect of that world within representation. It is this once-removal from the world that facilitates the activity of reflection, interpretation and critique so that art offers us not simply a piece of life but also a way of thinking about it. Forms of avant-garde art such as Brechtian theatre may reject the compulsion to reflect or explain the world as it is, preferring instead to offer a ruptured, fragmented and direct art from which stems a more intellectually active spectator. Nevertheless, a space for cerebral activity is still seen as being an important credential in the establishment of the text's complexity and the centrality of the body (rather than the word) to these forms was regarded as a fresh opportunity for exploring the body's expressive potential.[9]

For Brecht, abstract or non-figurative forms of representation may also be defended in these terms for their capacity to engender in a spectator/viewer a reassessment or readjustment of some aspect of their relationship to the world around them by 'turning the object of which one is to be made aware, to which one's attention is to be drawn, from something ordinary, familiar, immediately accessible, into something peculiar, striking and unexpected'. Thus the object is made momentarily 'incomprehensible' only so that it may be stripped of the assumptions which had previously surrounded it and, thereby, rendered 'the easier to comprehend'.[10] The difference in forms of popular culture is that they are defined by a series of aesthetic qualities which threaten to seduce, overwhelm or anaesthetise its spectators with fear and are therefore without the final goal of fresh comprehension.[11] In the case of the circus it is the first two of these which pertain most strongly since the circus, without exception, engenders a relationship of spectacular immediacy with its audience and, as I will suggest, the adjectives which surround it indicate that its aesthetics prioritise effect over thought. The question remains, however, of whether these aesthetics of pure effect, rather than analysis, mean that circus is necessarily entertainment rather than art and whether the former may not be valued on its own terms in a way which does not necessarily make it the poor relation of the latter.

The surrealist dramatist and theorist of the theatre Antonin Artaud extols the value of 'pure effects' in his championing of Balinese theatre's stress on the primacy of mime and physical gesture in contrast to western theatre's 'subservience ... to the lines'.[12] Artaud is fascinated by the potential of this theatre to offer 'a new bodily language no longer based on words', but rather on 'signs which emerge(s) through the maze of gestures, postures, airborne cries' which, being directly relayed through the body, has 'an exact meaning that only strikes one intuitively, but violently enough to make any kind of translations into logical, discursive language useless'.[13] Still, Artaud's repetition of his notion that the Balinese actors' bodies and their costumes are 'moving hieroglyphs', a figure repeated in 'The Theatre of Cruelty', indicates his desire to identify these bodies as the objects of interpretation, though the meanings they harbour, like the hieroglyph itself, may always contain a certain disclosure since, in 'supply(ing) us with some of the mind's most secret perceptions' they constitute pointers to what, for Artaud, has been long since repressed in 'the West'.[14] Thus, in the 'codes' of Artaud's new language for the theatre, the elements of ritual and gestural, non-textual performance are highly prized and in this sense he draws attention to their affinity with circus performance which, as we have seen, has always worked through each of these. In the notion of the body as hieroglyphic he offers us the suggestion that the performing body, stripped of verbal language, may harbour meanings for an audience and which may indeed exist as an element of their immediate effect rather than despite it. None the less, his high regard for such techniques is founded on an orientalist opposition between East and West which sees eastern performance styles as expressive and with open access to the unconscious in relation to a West which is characterised by logocentrism and its accompanying repressions. This means that the conventional aspect of ritual only appears radical and surprising when it is culturally 'other'; therefore circus, with its familiar character types and strict division between spectator and performer, smothers its dangers in the cotton wool of familiarity and minimises the direct shocks which could be felt by its audiences.[15]

Other dramatists, however, have attempted to extricate circus techniques from the highly commercial and demotic institution to which they have traditionally belonged in order to rearticulate them within other contexts. Thus, in an interestingly Brechtian turn, their function and effect may be reviewed and redefined in ways which have been considered radical in either artistic or political terms. An example of the latter is Vladimir Mayakovsky's play *Moscow Is Burning* which was commissioned in 1930 by the Soviet Central Agency of Circuses to mark the 25th anniversary of the 1905 Revolution.[16] It was performed in the First Moscow State Circus in April of that year (a week after Mayakovsky's suicide), included a number of well-established circus performers in its cast and followed the conventional circus show which had formed the first half of the evening's bill. The play mobilises essentially pantomimic techniques as the vehicles for its satirical portrait of Imperial Russia, working through rallying songs, clowning (for the tsar's officials and policemen), a series of tableaux (a huge pyramid representing pre-Revolutionary society with Tsar Nicholas at the top and 'schackled workers' [p. 82] at the bottom) and spectacular circus stunts ('a worker swings from one trapeze to another, hurling down pamphlets' while the policemen chasing him find their weapons have caused them to become entangled in the rigging). The Tsar himself was played by a 'gaunt circus dwarf' (p. 74). At the same time, the sense of continuity which marks the conventional circus pantomime's narrative structure has been replaced by montage style in which the juxtaposition of spectacular enactments is supported by the use of cinematic projections (sometimes multiple projections) throughout the play. The latter not only reflects the influence of Soviet cinematic practices (most specifically Sergei Eisenstein's 'Montage of Attractions') on the reinvention of circus spectacle as it is presented here but, at one point three simultaneously projected images of, respectively, a 'moving train', a 'horse-drawn tram' and a 'busy factory' captures the conflicting elements of the Soviet economy in which the speed and mechanisation necessary in a modern industrialised society must grapple with and update the parts of the country which were still agrarian.[17] The circus's physical machinery, as well as its dramatic figures and structures, constitute for both Mayakovsky and Eisenstein a radical theatrical *language* within which a critique of capitalism may be articulated and is therefore not merely a set of metaphors put to satirical use. As we have seen, then, in political terms, circus as a dramatic form is neither necessarily radical or reactionary; its language of 'show', having absorbed and adapted numerous cultural and historical traditions has proved open to widely differing ideological inflections.

Naturally this suggests the necessity of outlining what the elements of the circus's language are and what values, if any, may be inherent in its fundamental terms. A trawl through any collection of circus advertising from almost any period will turn up a very similar collection of adjectives being used to depict the delights on offer. These can be divided up into attributes (exoticism, gorgeousness, skill, novelty, magnificence, danger, display, beauty, action, spectacle) and effects (sensation, delight, wonder, humour, suspense, astonishment) and these in turn may be described through a series of related critical characterisations (realism, comedy, absurdity, burlesque, anomaly, orientalism, eclecticism, melodrama). Most of these terms have featured within the previous discussion of the circus's history, and from this it has been clear that not all of these terms have been of equal value or presence at any given time or place. The shifting priority of some over others is of significance here. It will also be important to distinguish between the meaning of these terms as they refer to the circus and their use in relation to other art forms.

Realism may sound to the contemporary circus-goer like an odd and incongruous term for describing any aspect of circus performance, even given the notorious critical flexibility, some might claim vagueness, of its application. It is a term with only temporary relevance to the circus, lasting only as long as the hippodrama had its day, and has most relevance when limited to its pre-Romantic (early eighteenth-century) sense of constructing 'realisations'; that is, giving elaborate form to events, ideas or fictions, without the obligation of offering insights into the 'true nature' of the thing represented.[18] Even relatively early on, advertising puffs commended shows to their prospective audiences on the basis of their verisimilitude and realism of effect. For example, a puff from 1785 assures us that the 'reality of the fox and hounds divests us of every idea of its being a fiction, and therefore we receive the same entertainment as we would receive were we to be spectators of a parcel of taylors in an actual fox chase'.[19] Given that the drama described here is the most familiar and constantly performed of all burlesque equestrian acts we must doubt whether an audience might have accepted it in the manner here suggested; however, the fact that the circus, in this case Astley's, thought to promote itself in these terms indicates the commercial value attached to reality of effect. Increasingly representational accuracy and detail became cherished values of the large-scale hippodramatic productions, especially battle re-enactments, which had gathered momentum at the turn of the century and carried on to the mid nineteenth century.

Although what appeared may be labelled realism of a sort, it was above all a spectacular realism which became increasingly dependent on elaboration, expense, luxury and, it claimed, accuracy of pain-stakingly researched detail. In this sense the circus anticipated the enthusiasm for luxury which crept into stage productions of the 1840s and which, as Michael Booth has observed, was shaping tastes in domestic interiors.[20] Astley certainly made much of his 'indefatigable' field work, actually travelling in one instance to Flanders in order to 'obtain a most correct knowledge of the places forming the feats of war, and arranging the most essential occurrences that happened, in or near each place, for the accurate information of the public'.[21] Saxon claims that during this era drama was often referred to as 'scientific' due to the 'ingenuity and complexity of their stage effects and tricks' and adds that, particularly historical productions, were put together 'with pedantic attention to historical accuracy' with the display of the de-signers' and machinists' craftsmanship being a priority and a boast in this project.[22] Indeed a puff of 1791 which describes Astley's 'Royal Fugitives' – a drama depicting the Royal flight from Paris – proclaims that the production proves 'that all verbal accounts of it are weak, indeed, to conveying any adequate idea of this remarkable event. Astley has, to a demonstration, proved that it could only justly be represented by the aid of scenes, characters and stage decoration.'[23] Though the circus, as we have seen already, may have been forced by legal injunc-tion to bypass 'verbal accounts', here its publicity is not only championing the superiority of its mute but spectacular mode of representation, which it seems to believe offers a more objectified reality through visual spectacle, but it is also making way for a new form of historical representation; the public representation of public events. Most poignantly in this case, the event which receives this theatrical treatment is the liberal Revolution in France and it is precisely because the so-called popular will is in action, expelling and supplanting the private rule of the Royal Family, that the arena in which this is played out must need be on such an enlarged scale and more widely accessible mode than printed or more confined theatrical accounts. The history of mass action is thus made available on a mass scale.

These reflections lead us to consider Peter Brooks's claim that the 'origins of melodrama can be accurately located in the French Revolution' and, furthermore, that this is the 'epistemological moment which it illustrates and to which it contributes'.[24] During this period (1789–99), he argues, Church and Monarch, the established forms of authority, or the 'traditional Sacred' as he calls them, are completely undermined along with the literary modes which accompanied them: tragedy and the comedy of manners. These two are replaced by melodrama, which thereby needs to be seen as 'a response to the loss of the tragic vision' because it exists 'in a world where the traditional imperatives of truth and ethics have been violently thrown into question'.[25] With the fall of the 'traditional Sacred', a new 'sacred' authority is sought in the Law, however the establishment of a new morality through the law leads to the pre-eminence of the melodramatic mode of articulating conflicts in which opposing positions are repeated 'over and over in clear language, it rehearses their conflicts and combats, it reënacts the menace of evil and the eventual triumph of morality made operative and evident'.[26] To this observation, however, should be added the qualification that it would be unlikely that Astley's newly popularised and accessible version of recent history would, in terms of its content, have necessarily lent political endorsement to the actions of the crowd, even though the hippodramatic form may have allowed for the representation of events on a scale which would not be matched again until the epic cinematic spectacles of the silent cinema such as *Birth of a Nation* (D. W. Griffith, 1915), *Napoléon* (Abel Gance, 1925), *The Crowd* (King Vidor, 1927) though, likewise, these did not necessarily couple their spectacular populism with radical politics. Astley was not the only proprietor whose populism was underscored by strong conservative and royalist leanings. Brooks maintains, however, that although melodrama may be classed as either 'revolutionary or conservative' in its content, the fact of its generosity of accessibility means that 'it is in all cases radically democratic'. Though Brooks doesn't explicitly use the term circus, he none the less traces the origins of this 'radical' drama to the pre-revolutionary upgrading of circus interludes such as Jean-Baptiste Nicolet's tightrope and acrobatics shows on the boulevard du Temple Theatre in 1764 to one of the future 'temples of melodrama', the Théâtre de la Gaîté.[27] Therefore, rather than see melodrama as something introduced to the circus at a certain early stage in its development which was somehow ousted by the American invasion, it is possible to see circus as one of, perhaps even the most important, of the progenitors of the melodramatic stage and its 'imagination', forging a language of gesture, music and visual spectacle in anticipation of the historical moment it would so fully and repeatedly articulate. It is also true that the American circus frequently played out its own histories within this epic format and the huge popularity of the wild west shows orchestrated by figures like Buffalo Bill suggests an obsessive drive to review, rework and relive the domination of the country and its native peoples that was as important to the establishment of a white American identity as the battle of Waterloo was in the continual need to form a British national identity and sense of citizenship. Paradoxically perhaps, the common and determining condition of both circus and theatre in the eighteenth and early nineteenth century, which must establish moral authority now in the law, is the legal injunction (in France pre-revolutionary) on the use of prose-based drama. The theatrical language which negotiates moral truths through the playing out of oppositional positions is itself born of a conflict and negotiation with the law itself.

The inclusiveness and populism of circus drama is also echoed in the circus parade, which was not only a supremely good way of drumming up business and attention, but also became a defining component of North American circus spectacle. In many ways it can be seen as a replacement for the lost Renaissance pageant of royal processions of power, in a place which has removed itself from royal influence, and, at the same time rejuvenates from this long antiquated tradition two key types of pleasure, as they have been identified by Roy Strong. Firstly, the pageants, and indeed the three-ring circus as a whole, returns its audience to a form of spectatorship in which the 'old-established means of décor in the form of scattered props and moveable pageant cars enabled everyone placed round three sides of a hall to take part in the visual experience'.[28] This stands in contrast to the development in the later part of the sixteenth century of indoor entertainments (specifically the masque) and proscenium arches which meant that the spectacle was 'viewable from one point only, for all the lines of perspective met in the eyes of the onlooking prince'.[29] Secondly, royal parades may have sought to impress the audience in the streets with the spectacular symbols of an authority which extended beyond the limits of the nation, but the purpose of the circus spectacle was at once to produce an awe-inspired audience and also, crucially, one which believed it could itself gain access to these exotic, marvellous, disparate worlds and peoples with the price of entry. So the circus extends the democracy of participation in world dominion whilst the circus performances themselves echo the court fête in which dramatic portrayals 'enabled the ruler and his court to assimilate themselves momentarily to their heroic exemplars'. Thus, Strong argues that it is in these court dramas that man's belief in his unchallenged authority over nature finds its 'most extreme assertion', and at the same time there are echoes of the circus in his characterisation of 'their astounding transformations, which defeat magic, defy time and gravity, evoke and dispel the seasons, banish darkness and summon light, draw down even the very influences of the stars from the heavens, they celebrate man's total comprehension of the law's of nature'.[30] The circus, in the terms in which I have so far attempted to characterise it, represents both the continuation of this transcendent impulse and its general democratisation beyond the confines of the court.

It is also significant that circus parades were accompanied not only by military-style marching bands but also by Apolonicon organs and, an instrument which would become synonymous with the circus in the United States, the steam calliope. Most obviously these organ-style instruments both invoke and undermine the religious associations of the organ with their piercingly high-pitched notes which must have sounded like some ghastly travesty of the sombre tones of the church organ, the centre-piece of their community, as they called their followers towards their tents of entertainment. It easy to see, therefore, why much of the objection to the American circus in the mid nineteenth century came from Christian groups made uneasy by this rival to the public's attention, where the concept of 'congregation' has always been fostered by an entertainment which directly addresses, 'educates', mystifies and encourages the participation of those it assembles within its tents.

One of the most important dimensions of circus aesthetics is the concept of anomaly. Of course most forms of art or entertainment, to differing degrees, may offer its audience anomalous objects, ideas or events. Yet rarely can they resist either sorting them out within a narrative or lending the anomaly some higher purpose, as for example in forms of avant-garde art such as surrealism which works to suggest unconscious connections between apparently anomalous objects. The circus, by contrast, finds a pure satisfaction in anomaly which is seen as a delight and an end in itself. Frequently these arise, as Kwint claims, from the performance of 'banal acts' in extraordinary positions. This could be something as simple as performing an act upside down, such as Ching Lau Lauro, an early example of an 'antipodean', dancing a Scottish hornpipe on his head, but may also equally arise from extraordinary performances in more banal positions such as when wild or domestic animals are trained to perform human skills.[31] Examples of this might include the bears riding motor cycles which I recently witnessed in an Indian circus or, perhaps most famously, the cult of the learned or even conjuring pig, horse or 'the wonderful Spelling or Academic Dog' in which an attempt is made to dupe the audience into attributing human levels of intelligence to brute animals.[32] It is perhaps the first example of such anomalous performance relationships between human and animals, however, which remains the most surreal-sounding in effect. A newspaper puff of 1792 advertises the 'celebrated Mr. Wildman's' exhibition of bees', clearly an act imported from the fairground, which consisted of his riding 'round the Riding Ground with a curious Swarm of Bees on his Arm' before coaxing them towards his head so that they cluster around it 'in imitation of a Bob wig'. Mrs Astley soon followed suit with the bees more appropriately forming no doubt a charming 'Lady's muff' on her arm.[33] Anomalies, therefore, although nearly always of a physical and spectacularly visual nature, also involved jolting the audience's received knowledge about mankind's relationship to the natural and civil world around them by subverting either social custom and/or the order of species. These subversions need not necessarily offer a profound challenge to general assumptions since the effect of the anomaly seems more often than not to be humorous, absurd or inviting of scepticism and almost always in the service of novelty, which, as discussed above, has always been one of the driving engines of circus aesthetics.

Much of what appears in circuses as anomaly would also fall within the category of the absurd. However, since this term refers now to some very specific theatrical and literary practices, mostly from the 1940s and 1950s, it is important to make some critical distinctions. As Martin Esslin has already pointed out, 'avant garde movements are hardly ever entirely novel and unprecedented' and the Theatre of the Absurd which emerged from writers such as Eugene Ionesco, Edward Albee, Jean Genet, Albert Camus and Samuel Beckett represents 'a return to old, even archaic traditions' which include circus and even pre-circus forms of entertainment such as mime, juggling, acrobatics and foolery or clowning.[34] Ionesco, in his polemical writing about theatrical practice however, makes it clear that the context into which such physical practices are inserted is informed by a very different agenda from the circus:

> People will say that my plays are musical turns or circus acts. So much the better – let's include the circus in the theatre! Let the playwright be accused of being arbitrary. *Yes*, the theatre is the place where one *can* be arbitrary. As a matter of fact, it is not arbitrary. The imagination is not arbitrary, it is revealing ...' [35]

Ionesco admires the dangerous and transgressive qualities of the circus as well as its apparently arbitrary combinations and sequences, yet for him, in common other absurdist dramatists, the arbitrary is always functional in the sense that it is intellectually 'revealing' in at least two important ways. Firstly, the Theatre of the Absurd represents a dramatic rendering of the philosophical concepts discussed by a group of existentialist French thinkers (including Camus and Sartre) which could communicate in dramatic and visual terms the absence of any overall logic governing the events of the world and therefore the final meaninglessness of existence. The difference between the theatre of the absurd and existentialist theatre is that, whereas the latter philosophises about this absurd predicament, the former '*presents* it in being – that is, in terms of concrete stage images'.[36] In other words, the structure of the plays (often very circular) and the forms of performance involved in them are an integral part of their expression. Ideally this should be both an 'intellectual exercise' and a 'therapeutic effect' in that, in the course of watching such a play, the spectator is disarmed of habitual anxieties about meaning in the world and no longer has to fabricate optimistic or illusory justifications born of these fears. As a result of this 'coming clean' about life's absurdity, a certain relief should be experienced in that from 'seeing anxieties formulated he can liberate himself from them. This is the nature of gallows humour and *humour noir* of world literature, of which the Theatre of the Absurd is the latest example.' [37] This, then, is a theatre which involves circus-related techniques and images: it is important to recognise, however, that the meaning and effect of these is reinflected by a very twentieth-century manifesto which has at its heart a depressive anxiety that it is no longer possible to believe in a supreme being which oversees the universe. Any humour which results, therefore, must first have touched the first base of despair. Thus while the circus clown, for example, and his frantic, nonsensical behaviour may be held within absurdist theatre as emblematic of a modern condition of existence, the circus itself has never been informed by or required any such philosophical framework in order to explain the enjoyment of absurd behaviour. In the Theatre of the Absurd, humour is a last resort, a positive gloss on what is at heart an admission of failure – failure to give the world meaning – whereas in the circus absurdity is not only an end in itself but frequently involves a much more cheerful celebration of skill and a demonstration of human mastery over the universe, in other words, quite the opposite of the absurdist project.

Secondly, the use of circus techniques and conventions fuels the absurdist foregrounding of non-verbal forms of theatre such as ritualised actions (in clown routines, for example), exaggerated gesture, manipulation of objects and mime so that ideas and character functions are expressed externally and visually or through music rather than the spoken word. Thus, for Esslin: 'The element of 'pure' abstract theatre in the Theatre of the Absurd is an aspect of its anti-literary attitude, its turning away from language as an instrument for expression of the deepest levels of feeling.' [38] The circus, however, has never been self-consciously anti-literary (Ducrow's most famous and exportable acts were based on adaptations, albeit loose ones, of Byron, Dickens and Shakespeare), nor has it encouraged its spectators to share in this suspicion over the efficacy of language as a mode of expression. As I have argued above, the absence of the spoken word in some elements of the circus and the development of acts which circumvent it has evolved partly out of the expediency of avoiding legal injunctions rather than any desire to offer an intellectual critique. So the circus's relationship to language is arguably a more innocent one in that it seeks merely to bypass the linguistic, not to traduce it. In distinguishing between these two mobilisations of similar techniques it is clear that circus skills and techniques may not in themselves constitute critical or avant-garde practices when performed in the circus; indeed they may seem reassuringly familiar. Yet when resituated and newly contextualised in the theatre before spectators more accustomed to narrative (if not necessarily realist narrative) drama it is argued that they acquire a certain novel and indeed shocking quality. Now of course the circus now has its own avant-garde practitioners, amongst whom we could count Que Cirque (French), Cirque Baroque (Canadian) and Legs on the Wall (Australian), yet these relatively recent practices are clearly not those which inspired the theorists of the absurd. Rather they are in many ways a later fusion: a return to circus via the avant-garde ideas on theatre which had percolated through western theatre and dance schools in the post-1968 period.

This is not to say that shock and sensation are not a very crucial part of the circus aesthetic in their own ways, but the application of these terms to the circus must be preceded by a process of definition and distinction. In this respect the debates in Britain around the so-called 'sensation novels' of the 1860s, which functioned to define and consolidate our modern use of this term, are suggestive of the ways in which this term acquired meaning within a particular social context. An examination of this debate provides signposts to some of the features of a general sensation aesthetic, whilst at the same time leading to the identification of the significant divergences which are particular to the circus. Quite obviously many of the features which led to the application of the term sensation to the novels of writers such as Wilkie Collins (*The Woman in White*, 1860 and *The Moonstone*, 1868) Mary Elizabeth Braddon (*Lady Audley's Secret*, 1862), Ouida (*Held in Bondage*, 1863) and Mrs Henry Wood (*East Lynne*, 1861), amongst others, relate to their various plot components which Lyn Pykett identifies as 'combinations of duplicity, deception, disguise, the persecution and/or seduction of a young woman, intrigue, jealousy, and adultery'.[39] Although these may well have been components of the melodramas performed on the circus stage, not only would the circus dramas have had a stronger tendency towards humour and burlesque, though as Gerrould points out these did have a limited place in melodrama, but it would also be more likely that their setting would be foreign, exotic and probably aristocratic rather than middle class and domestic, as was the rule in the sensation novel.[40] It is also the case that in the general use of this term in circus publicity of the period when, for example, the Royal Amphitheatre and Circus at High Holborn advertises 'More Great Engagements, More Novelties, More Star Artistes, More Sensations, More Equestrian Marvels' than others, it is not promoting itself in terms of moral dangers and seductions, but rather confines itself to the aesthetic (physical, spectacular and affective) dimensions of the sensational, or, to follow Ann Cvetkovich's distinction, to sensation rather than to the sensational.[41] However, these attributes of circus performances, dramatic or otherwise, quickly connect it to the more disreputable associations of sensation so that its displays of the exoticised or minimally dressed body (male and female) and its courting of physical danger saddle it with the kind of dubious morality which was more commonly the stuff of the sensation novel. Indeed Cvetkovich argues that any form of popular art, simply through its heavy reliance on 'affective power' rather than cerebral stimulation, is in danger of being regarded as either inferior or subversive since, she claims, its affectivity is seen as connecting audiences directly to their raw, uncultured emotions.[42] It is clear then that if sensation is to be a generally applicable term for the circus, it has to have significance beyond simply the consideration of its narrative themes since, as I have already established, circus is primarily a non-narrative art. Whereas debates about the phenomenon of sensation literature emerged and were consolidated through critical debates in review magazines of the 1860s, sensation had been a defining feature of the circus from the outset, though it did not begin to be named as such in circus publicity until the mid nineteenth century.[43]

An early incident at Astley's reported in the newspaper provides an interesting dramatic example of circus sensation:

> Last week as one of the horseman was exhibiting a performance, called sweeping the ground with his elbow, and leaping the bar in the same attitude, his horse fell in the leap flat on his side, which frighted all the company and particularly some ladies into fits. The ladies and the horsemen disappeared, and the company suspected he had broke his leg, or, at least, had bruised himself very much; but in a few minutes the ladies and the performer appeared, when he sprung on his horse, and went through the remainder of his performance seemingly unheard [sic].[44]

This sounds to have been an early accident, though of course it quickly became part of the trick to incorporate a feigned slip-up into a danger-ous act in order to remind the audience of the potential dangers involved. What is interesting is that the sensational effect is registered not so much through the details of the act but through its shocking effect on a female audience so overwhelmed by fear that it is reported to have become physically hysterical. At the same time it is highly likely that what is probably a newspaper puff is talking up the drama of the incident as a way of attracting audiences in search of morbid excitement. However, at the heart of this scene are a human and an animal body whose drama involving mortal danger appears to have a directly physical and traumatic effect on the female spectator's body. It is this feature of sensation which led to Margaret Oliphant's identification of its symptomatic qualities when she claimed that it was to be expected 'of an age that has turned out to be one of event, that art and literature should attempt a kindred depth of effect and shock of incident'.[45] In this sense the novels not only mirror what Bourne Taylor describes as 'the age of sensation', which, for *Blackwood's* middle-class readership 'encapsulated the experience of modernity itself – the sense of continuous and rapid change, of shocks, thrills, intensity, excitement', all of which are potentially attributable to the circus, but such brushes with modernity, it was believed, also left a dangerously contagious mark on those who experienced it.[46] Oliphant, for example, claims that the novels in question give voice to a 'prosaic and secularised culture' and represent a 'system which has paralysed all the wholesome wonders and nobler mysteries of human existence', so browbeaten is the age they depict by the onslaught of modernity. Here lies one of the key differences between the literary and the circus experiences of sensation. Panic about the dangerous influence of the novels was the result of a perception that public and private experiences of the modern world had provoked a crisis of morality. The circus on the other hand, represented a long-standing celebration of the shocks of modernity and of the strength and supremacy of the human body to transcend all difficulties thrown at it in a world that may be secular, but none the less is one in which wonder is still very much a presence. Though its source and inspiration is entirely the ingenuity, power and beauty of the human rather than any spiritual or metaphysical force, the wonder generated by the circus is always directed towards itself and not the world. Astley's horseman may have shocked his female audience into fits, but whether there was intention involved or not, it is the unspoken law of the circus that the performer always gets up again and leaves the ring a conqueror of animal, machinery or gravity. By contrast, the so-called 'morbid naturalism', as Bourne Taylor puts it, of novels such as *Lady Audley's Secret* leaves its morally ambiguous heroine crippled by hysteria, madness and an unsympathetic society.

Sensation in both these contexts can be defined as an aesthetic which anticipates and in some senses dramatises the secular experience of a society encountering novelty and modernity in both its shocking and exciting manifestations. In both contexts, to borrow Oliphant's terms, art is overtaken by event and, perhaps in the case of the circus, becomes an 'event'. It is therefore defined as a highly affective and, most importantly, involving drama, experienced through effects rather than moral, artistic or intellectual challenges. Central to both, however, is the body. Concern about the sensation novel's involvement with and perpetration of the social crises of the day was, as Bourne Taylor points out, partly confirmed by the fact that the novels foregrounded 'physiological metaphors' (revolving around nervous bodies of sorts) which were seen '*as* symptoms which themselves had, principally, physiological effects'. Thus, such figures of the body were not only assumed to be feminine because they were nervous, but were also held to be the 'product and metonymic model' of decline through their somatic playing out of 'a set of nervous responses that had become pathological by their very susceptibility to intense excitement and reaction'.[47] Sensation emerges here as a form of empathetic contagion through which the degeneration experienced by certain textual figures is transferred, through reading or watching, on to the bodies of the spectators or readers. The sensational affectivity of the performing circus body is entirely different. As we have already seen, far from generating a morbid excitement out of bodies which have lost control, the circus features exceptionally vigorous bodies which conquer rather than wither before the (always) physical challenges they encounter in the ring. Therefore the sensationalism of circus acts such as the horseman's described above, must derive from awe at the superiority of the body at the centre of the spectacle. If there is an empathetic dimension to circus sensation it is more life-affirming than it is morbid, although the possibility of serious injury or fatality is always a crucial ingredient of the excitement. Thus, in some ways circus and novelistic sensation in the nineteenth century can be seen as opposite sides of the same coin; both dramatise the frenetic, dangerous, spectacular and shocking energies of a modern secular world, yet while one plays out forms of panic and degeneration around 'real issues' the other, perhaps because it is without the baggage of moral and political dilemmas, not only celebrates the excitement of these energies, but also affirms the ability of human body and spirit to be enriched by such encounters, albeit in highly contrived and fantastical scenes.

Finally, it should be noted that a substantial part of the negative reaction to sensation novels derived from the high degree of commercialisation that marked their production. Both circus and sensation novel were highly commercialised forms of mass entertainment and, Cvetkovich argues, such genres were regarded as devalued forms of art 'through a process that often replicates nineteenth century discourses suspicious of working class readers, female audiences, and affectively powerful or non-realist literature'.[48] The moral panics about the circus had more or less died out by the 1840s with the passing of the Theatres Act and as the middle classes became a more substantial component of the audience in urban circuses. Though the circus was certainly not treated with any seriousness as 'art' at this time, it was perhaps its function as family entertainment which led to its being regarded (within utilitarian or functional views of industrial society) as an important part of modern industrial society in that it distracted people from their problems rather than spelled them out in lurid and harrowing detail. Also, since the circus had always been highly commercialised, this dimension of its sensational identity was not regarded as so threatening as it was for defenders of the novel who, as Bourne Taylor argues, saw the sensation novel as threatening a dangerous slippage between 'the "light reading" of a middle class and predominantly female public on the one hand' and the melodramatic ' "mass entertainment" of a relatively newly formed lower-middle and upper-working class readership on the other – and blurred any possible distinction between them'.[49] In fact, it is the circus's identity as commercial entertainment that allows such distinctions to be so clearly made in that the differential pricing and resulting hierarchy in seating arrangements marks out a spectator's relationship to the performance in fairly accurate class terms.

So the circus itself has rarely included overtly political dramas, aside from the displays of patriotism latent in the battle re-enactments of nineteenth-century hippodrama. However, this is not to say that there are not latent, and usually highly ambiguous, political implications, not only at the level of aesthetics, as we have seen, but in their content as well. Speaight reports that the first trick-riding act performed by Astley involved getting a horse to lie down on the ground as if dead before it miraculously rose again at Astley's word. This, however, was soon supplemented by a second act, 'The Taylor Riding to Brentford', which would go on to become one of the most frequently performed in the circus worldwide. What is interesting about this act is that it refers to a real political drama of 1768 involving the election of the political radical John Wilkes. Although Wilkes had previously been expelled from the House of Commons he none the less put himself forward for re-election to Parliament as a representative for Brentford in Middlesex. A great many people, inspired by this popular, renegade hero-figure transported themselves from London to poll their vote for him, with the result that he was returned to Parliament in great style. Astley's pastiche involved recycling an already popular narrative of a tailor called Billy Button whose abortive attempt to make his way to Brentford has him (often drunk) making several attempts to mount his horse, being unable to get his horse to move, and being thrown off a speeding horse which eventually chases him out of the ring.

There is much significance not only in the events of this scene but in its progress as a staple circus act. On the face of it this might seem a somewhat reactionary drama in which the supporters of the voice of political radicalism are satirised as useless buffoons over whom the audience is encouraged to feel superior.[50] Yet at the same time it must be remembered that it was for the very qualities of populism and direct action that Wilkes had become famous so in this sense the laughter at the tailor is in some sense also celebratory of irreverent, democratic and populist spirit over a Parliament perceived by a growing mercantile class (such as tailors) to be dominated still by aristocratic privilege.[51] Despite the aspirational claims made by Astley about the great popularity of his shows with the aristocracy, the audience at Astley's were far more likely to have been members of this growing middle class whose right to a voice in Parliament Wilkes championed.[52] Also important to the inherent political ambiguity of the scene is the fact that it is narratively twice-removed from history in the sense that the tailor-figure was the product of a piece of popular folklore which was then adapted for the circus so the historical and political dimensions of the narrative have already been partially obscured in their transformation into myth. When the piece was performed in other countries local adaptations were made to the title so that in 1773 in the States Jacob Bates performed 'The Taylor Humorously Riding to New York' and in France in 1795 'Rognolet et Passe-Carreau' was performed at Franconi's.[53] This suggests that the dramatic action, its physical dynamics, had meaning on a level over and above that of the political significance the scene may have had for its original London audience.

This example also furnishes us with a defining instance of clowning in the circus and, as such, suggests a way into understanding the dynamics of circus comedy. As we have already seen, the display of superior levels of discipline and control over the body is the foundation of circus sensationalism. The 'The Taylor Riding to Brentford' sketch suggests that circus clowning is nothing but the flip side to this coin in its staging of bodies which are made the object of laughter precisely for their physical ineptitude and failures of social and physical perception. In this sense Henri Bergson's 1911 essay on laughter offers some of the most useful terms with which to analyse circus comedy because both his theory of laughter as a form of social discipline and his conception of the human body in broadly mechanistic terms are consistent with circus's hunger to establish the human body's power and pre-eminence within a modern, secular and industrialised world.[54]

Contrary to Mikhail Bakhtin's account of medieval festive laughter, in which he stresses laughter's inclusiveness and the relative freedoms which it temporarily grants, Bergson, whilst he insists on laughter's 'strictly human' basis, also defines exclusion and distance as its necessary preconditions.[55] For him, though laughter always connects us to others – is always 'the laughter of a group' – it also depends on the emotional separation of that group from the object of their laughter. Emotions such as pity, affection and sympathy must needs be absent from the comic which, he argues, 'demands something like a momentary anaesthesia of the heart. Its appeal is to the intelligence, pure and simple.'[56] Whilst for Bakhtin laughter had been the moment of release from a restrictive and hierarchical medieval social order in which a temporary inversion takes place, Bergson's terms assume a modern world in which all subjects are engaged in large-scale organised labour and in which 'society will therefore be suspicious of all *inelasticity* of character, of mind and even of body, because it is the possible sign of a slumbering activity as well as of an activity with separatist tendencies' (his emphasis).[57] Laughter, then, comes close to being ridicule in that it is seen as a way of curbing both disruptive 'eccentric' behaviour and mental and physical petrifaction through the threat of humiliating exposure (laughing *at*) and thus, for Bergson, has the happy 'utilitarian aim of general improvement'.[58]

As this suggests, Bergson's thesis on laughter is shot through with early twentieth-century modernist anxieties about the automating effect of industrialisation on the human body and soul with his stress on the necessity of imagination, elasticity and the facility of adaption as the positive terms which are none the less defined against an underlying negative assumption that the *'attitudes, gestures, and movements of the human body are laughable in exact proportion as that body reminds us of a mere machine'* (his emphasis).[59] Mechanisation may be a necessary condition for efficient production, speed and surplus-value, yet laughter also performs the (at times) dangerously contradictory task of not only jolting humans out of 'mere' automatism, rigidity and, possibly, 'inertia', but also of working to maintain their continuing observation of socially approved rather than 'eccentric' forms of behaviour. However, whilst we may observe the historical specificity and limitation of Bergson's terms, when we look at the following analysis of what he sees as the perpetual human conflict between 'reason' and 'imagination', 'matter' and 'grace', it is precisely these terms which are in tune with the specific dynamics of the circus, itself a product of the industrial revolution:

> whatever be the doctrine to which our reason assents, our imagination has a very clear-cut philosophy of its own: in every human form it sees the effort of a soul which is shaping matter, a soul which is infinitely supple and perpetually in motion, subject to no law of gravitation, for it is not the earth that attracts it. This soul imparts a portion of its winged lightness to the body it animates: the immateriality which thus passes into matter is what is called gracefulness. Matter, however, is obstinate and resists.[60]

Though Bergson never mentions the circus, it is hard to imagine a more keen-sighted summary of the contrary energies which it has traditionally offered across its variety of acts. Equestrian performers and, as we will see in the final chapter, aerialists, have conventionally been surrounded by a rhetoric which has precisely emphasised 'winged lightness' and physical gracefulness and which has served to fuel the fantasy that they are endowed with the facility of defying or resisting gravity. In this sense they are both figures *for* the imagination, as Bergson suggests, and figures *of* imagination, in that they seem capable of fantastic physical acts. At the same time, by interspersing these moments of grace with clown routines, the circus reminds us of the 'matter' which is 'obstinate and resists' as the clumsy, preposterously big-footed auguste clowns are bound to an earth to which they constantly fall and are defeated both by the tyrannical wit of the white-faced clown and the pieces of everyday objects and machinery (bicycles, cars, hose pipes) which inevitably get the better of them.

Of course one of the dangers into which the circus risked falling, even from its earliest days, was to be seen itself as an entertainment of routine and mechanical performances rather than an incitement to wonder and imagination. A generically limited repertoire of acts in the circus has resulted in the constant revamping and restaging of familiar figures and scenes in order to proliferate novelty. Spectacle, on an ever-increasing scale, was the first weapon of the urban circus which, by the early part of the nineteenth century, was distinguished from many of the travelling circuses which brought smaller-scale productions to country fairs and towns. In the latter, as Kwint points out, the very presence of the circus was a novelty in itself, whereas in the city, the permanently based companies resorted to manufacturing novelty and variety in their publicity.[61] For example, in 1796 a puff from Astley's boasts that 'the change of performance every week is certainly more amusing than a repetition of fulsome, stale entertainments ... It is to variety that Astley may attribute his present success'.[62] Yet in 1798 he was severely criticised by a writer, probably in the service of one of the minor theatres, who visited the Royal Grove 'with the expectation of meeting some novelty or other' but in this respect declared himself 'disappointed', the entertainment on offer displaying 'motley exhibitions', a 'total want of genius, and an error in judgement'.[63] The danger for any circus of being thought to be offering a 'motley' rather than a varied entertainment was an ongoing cause for concern, and one way to counter such accusations was to incorporate highly publicised levels of exoticism into the acts.[64] It was in this way that orientalism and imperialism quickly became significant dimensions of the circus aesthetic when, as Kwint claims, 'novelty became more geographical than temporal in emphasis'.[65] However, the circus did manage to incorporate a level of acceptable repetition into its productions in the sense that, as Kwint argues of Astley's, it had become a 'highly ritualistic form ... commercialising ritual and ritualising commerce' which chimed with the seasons of the year (always opening on Easter Monday and being associated with other public holidays). In becoming a traditional family entertainment it had, by the mid nineteenth century, become 'seasonal and regenerative' as well as 'a seemingly inevitable part of growing up and getting old'.[66] Thus whereas, as Cvetkovich claims, sensation novels were regarded with suspicion since they were 'read and then discarded, replaced by the next season's fad', the value of properly edifying art was partly measured by its durability and timelessness.[67] Yet by the mid-nineteenth century we see that the circus had managed to combine its promotion of fascinating novelty and an engagement with the speed, spectacle and danger of the modern world with assurances of timelessness, universality and family tradition.

The role of the circus in the consolidation of orientalist discourses in the late eighteenth and early nineteenth century has rarely been mentioned, and yet the circus's involvement, not only in the representation and dramatisation of so-called oriental cultures, but also in the accumulation of (human and animal) performers from the East is extensive and complex. First of all there are the coincidences of time and place. As Edward Said has argued, the key period during which the seeds of orientalism were sown were the years following the Napoleonic invasion of Egypt in 1798 and the 'period of immense advance in the institutions and content of Orientalism coincides exactly with the period of unparalleled European expansion; from 1815 to 1914 European direct colonial dominion expanded from about 35 percent of the earth's surface to about 85 percent of it'.[68] Not only, does the first of these dates almost exactly coincide with the birth of the equestrian spectacle in the eighteenth-century amphitheatre, but these dramas frequently drew on oriental themes, and the battle re-enactments re-played colonial victories in India, Africa and China as well as equestrian dramatisations of Romantic literary orientalism.[69] Easily the most popular example of the latter was the dramatisation of Lord Byron's poem 'Mazeppa', in which (see figure 5) Adah Isaacs Menken's cross-dressed performance further fuelled its celebrity reputation by lacing an exoticism of character and place with some well-publicised eroticism.[70]

This is not to say that the circus as an institution is necessarily or essentially in the service of orientalism since its separate parts have long preceded the historical moment of orientalism. The modern circus may have its roots in eighteenth-century Europe but its various generic components have long since been adopted and adapted into very different forms by most of the countries which were the subjects of the colonial expansion described by Said. For example, although the modern Egyptian circus only began at the beginning of this century, it was able to draw on a long tradition of acrobats, contortionists and clowns going back to 2,500 BC.[71] Said himself suggests a certain congruence between the language with which orientalist discourse depicts the orient and the characteristic modes of circus language when he claims that orientalism's 'representative figures' and 'tropes ... are to the actual Orient ... as stylised costumes are to characters in a play; they are like, for example, the cross that Everyman will carry, or the particolored costume worn by Harlequin in a *commedia dell'arte* play'.[72] Circus with, as we have seen, its long-standing reliance on caricature, the pantomimic, *commedia dell'arte* and pastiche, like orientalism, works through a 'language [which] is inaccurate ... because it is not even trying to be accurate', and perhaps this is the very reason that the circus's orientalist discourses have been so flexible and open to reclamation.[73] The fact that one of Ducrow's critics commented on 'the delightful degree of obscurity which envelops the entire arrangement of the spectacle' is testimony to the fact that the circus has always been able to combine performances which encompass specific local references with vagueness or confusion and performative structures of expression which, like the broad symbolic types to which Said refers, are open to constant obscural and renewal across time, space and culture, whilst at the same time, being firmly rooted in western dramatic structures.[74]

Just as the European hippodramas had an orientalist tendency to look to the eastern cultures for subject matter, as well as to fairy tale and momentous historical events and battles, so too did the spectacles, or 'specs', which opened and/or closed the three-ring circuses in the United States, reinvent and mix together the categories of history, myth and culture, most often guided by an energetic combination of exoticism and patriotism. For example, the Ringling Brothers Barnum and Bailey spectacle of 1954 (directed by Richard Barstow with aerial choreography by Barbette) consisted of four separate displays, the first of which was called 'Rocket to the Moon' which was a vehicle for introducing the Spanish trapeze artist Pinito Del Oro whose entry, sitting astride a space rocket, was perhaps intended to echo her own weightless flights. The second display, 'Dreamland', consisted of a variety of fairy-tale characters such as Cinderella, Little Red Riding Hood and Humpty Dumpty as well as many of the circus animals, and this was followed by a display called 'Fiesta', a Mexican-style ensemble which introduced Alexander Konyot (a dressage rider) alongside Guadeloupe Partida and his 'congress of wild-riding Charro rope spinners'. The climactic display, entitled 'U.N.', paraded all the flags of the United Nations together with sportingly mobile globes, an internationalism which finally gave way to patriotism as a tripartite flag portraying Eisenhower as cadet, general and President was finally raised in the centre ring.[75]

In many ways it is the contemporary or 'new' circuses such as Cirque du Soleil and Cirque Baroque who represent a return to a circus tradition (of narrative-based, orientalist/mythical dramatic spectacle) as much as they offer deviation or innovation (no animals, ring master and so on).[76] Both, then, invest in a model of social anthropology which sells cultural otherness as visual spectacle.[77] In the case of Ringling Brothers Barnum and Bailey, its mission to entertain is couched in the Barnum-style rhetoric of education and cultural investigation whilst at the same time consolidating long-standing western stereotypes, mostly seeming to draw upon the cultures from which the largest ethnic groups in the United States are descended. For example the 1989 *Ringling Brothers Barnum and Bailey Program* boasts of the painstaking fieldwork performed by Kenneth Feld as he 'travels the globe' to Mexico, the People's Republic of China and the 'shores of Europe'. On this occasion the spectacular has an African theme which, on the one hand, genuinely seeks to present some of the rituals of the Natal Province through the dances of several Bantu warriors, but, on the other hand, it would be hard to find a more dense concentration of colonialist myth. There are constant references to the 'Dark Continent of Africa', the 'jungles of Africa', the 'hidden African continent' and the 'uncivilised territory', as well as the mobilisation of a rhetoric of astonishment ('astonishing Tribal war dance'), incredulity (the 'Incredible Tahar!') and fantasy ('fantastic once-in-a-lifetime adventure'). The central fig-ure, Tahar, is every inch the 'noble savage' as he appears from the 'mist ... a man of mystery, his past cloaked in myth', thus apparently demonstrating that a 'mystical bond links man and beast'.[78]

This rhetoric resonates with the language of nineteenth-century colonialism and there seems to be little difference between this and the advertising of nineteenth-century European pantomimes with a colonial theme. Yet not only is this show playing before contemporary and, we can assume, mixed-race audiences, it also seems appropriate to question the seriousness with which such shows might ever have been received. Both Cirque du Soleil and Ringling Brothers Barnum and Bailey's The Greatest Show on Earth have regular Las Vegas venues and the combination of earnestness and mimicry, which for many cultural critics are the primary characteristics of kitsch (rather than camp), suggests that, rather than the circus conforming to the

Figure 5 Advertising bill poster of 1864 featuring Adah Isaacs Menken

conventions of Vegas spectacle, it is the Vegas spectacle which is a descendant of the circus spectacular. In the example of the Tahar show, whilst the circus demonstrates the earnest intention of presenting 'authentic' African rituals and people, the very process of transporting and restaging such rituals within state of the art sound and lighting techniques works to fetishise their gaudy artificiality and, by the same turn, empty them of realism, history and authenticity.[79] Indeed, it seems that in the process of performing 'Africanness' for a North American audience, the performance itself can only be read as a pastiche identity, circumscribed as we have already seen by the rhetoric of nineteenth-century fantasies about ethnic origins and identities. These spectacles, therefore, cannot be argued to be undermining or subverting such discourses in any way, and yet their effectiveness in shaping an audience's view of Africanness has to be offset against the alternative experience, knowledges and images which shape the perceptions of a contemporary audience.

In summary, this sketch of some of the key features of the circus's institutional and aesthetic developments since the late eighteenth century suggests that as an entertainment form it has continued to tread a peculiarly slippery line with regard to legitimacy and its aesthetic dimensions, many of which, as we have seen, have been an offshoot of the latter, have produced a form with a unique relationship to the issue of representation. It is this issue of representation which is to be investigated in the second half of the book by focusing on the ways in which three key artists of the nineteenth and twentieth century (Charles Dickens, Federico Fellini and Wim Wenders) have attempted to represent the circus. Each has done so in ways which signal their attraction to a form which facilitates a certain thematic licence to consider comic, subversive or dangerous figures (the clown, the aerialist, the vagabond player) in entanglements with legitimacy and order. At the same time each, very differently, works to draw our attention to certain representational and intellectual instabilities. In other words, the texts discussed in the next three chapters demonstrate the ways in which many of those elements which we can now see as defining the circus (its liveness, immediacy, danger, dramatic sensationalism, the privileging of the bodily over the linguistic, the absence of intellectual critique or justification, its sense of event) are precisely those which render it resistant to narration, representation and philosophical/political/artistic discourses; in other words, all those things which have come to constitute the foundations of modern forms of western literary and film art. It follows also that those same markers of resistance caused by the uneasy inclusion of the circus in forms of art defined by their mechanical reproduction and inscription have a tendency to indicate a vacancy in the representational forms they may occupy temporarily, leaving behind dead or empty figures which send an unsettling echo throughout the text as a whole.

Notes

1 Coxe, *A Seat at the Circus*, pp. 24–5.
2 Coxe, 'Equestrian drama', p. 109.
3 See Erving Goffman, *Frame Analysis* (Garden City, New York, Doubleday, 1974).
4 Goffman, *Frame Analysis*, p. 157.
5 Paul Bouissac's study is exceptional in this respect in that it attempts to provide a thorough technical account of the physical dynamics involved in all the central circus acts and to describe their individual internal languages without recourse to metaphor or psychology. see Paul Bouissac, *Circus and Culture: A Semiotic Approach* (Bloomington, Indiana University Press [1974], 1976).
6 Raymond Williams, *Keywords* (London, Fontana Paperbacks [1976], 1984), p. 42.
7 Williams, *Keywords*, p. 42.
8 See, for example, Colin McCabe (ed.), *High Theory/Low Culture: Analysing Popular Television and Film* (Manchester, Manchester University Press, 1986).
9 As Marvin Carlson points out, cabaret, music hall, fairground and circus forms were a central source of theatrical and musical inspiration both for Brecht and for the innovators of the Russian theatre at the beginning of the century such as Vsevolod Meyerhold and Sergei Radlov. He also suggests that these popular forms were valued, not just for their association with the popular, but because they brought conciseness and profundity, clarity and vigour to stage drama. *Performance: A Critical Introduction* (London, Routledge, 1996), pp. 87–8. see also, Meyerhold's writings on popular forms, especially 'The fairground', in Edward Braun (ed.), *Meyerhold on Theatre* (New York, Hill & Wang, 1969) and, for an overview of Soviet and pre-Soviet theatrical practice see Konstantin Rudnitsky, *Russian and Soviet Theatre, 1905–1932*, trans. Roxane Permar (New York, Harry N. Abrams, 1988).
10 Bertolt Brecht, 'Short description of a new technique of acting which produces an alienation effect' (1951), in John Willett (ed.), *Brecht on Theatre*, trans. John Willett (London, Methuen [1964], 1986), pp. 143–4.

11 The Marxist critic, James S. Moy, however, has sought to defend circus and variety acts against such views by arguing that circus spectators experience a radical dislocation and (Brechtian) alienation from the content of the performance because of the way acts either displace one another or are presented simultaneously. see 'Subverting/alienating performance structures', in James Redmond (ed.), *Themes in Drama*, vol. 9 (Cambridge, Cambridge University Press, 1987).

12 Antonin Artaud, 'Oriental and Western theatre' (1935) trans. Victor Corti in Victor Corti (ed.), *Collected Works of Antonin Artaud*, vol. 4 (London, Calder & Boyars, 1974), p. 51.

13 Antonin Artaud, 'On the Balinese theatre' (1937) trans. Victor Corti in Victor Corti (ed.) *Collected Works of Antonin Artaud*, vol. 4 (London, Calder & Boyars, 1974), pp. 38–9.

14 Artaud, 'On the Balinese theatre', p. 39. See also p. 44 and p. 47. 'The theatre of cruelty (first manifesto)' (1932) trans. Victor Corti, in Victor Corti (ed.), *Collected Works of Antonin Artaud*, vol. 4 (London, Calder & Boyars, 1974), p. 68, p. 72 and p. 75. In the latter, Artaud includes an section titled 'Interpretation' in which he asserts that 'the show will be coded from start to finish, like a language' (p. 75).

15 'We intend to do away with the stage and auditorium, replacing them by a kind of single, undivided locale without any partitions of any kind and this will become the very scene of action', Artaud, 'The theatre of cruelty', p. 73. Contemporary Catalan-based theatre companies such as Fura dels Baus and Els Joglars are excellent examples of theatre which is much more in the Artaudian tradition than the circus one.

16 The play, together with a series of contemporary critiques of it compiled by Victoria Nes Kirkby, has been translated by Helen Wilga and Ewa Bartos and reproduced in *The Drama Review*, 17:1 (1973), pp. 64–89.

17 Eisenstein, in turn, acknowledges the aesthetic value of the circus in an essay 'Montage of attractions; for Enough Stupidity in Every Wiseman' when he he claims that 'film and above all the music hall and the circus constitute the school for the montage-maker, since, properly speaking, putting on a good show (from the formal point of view) means building a strong music hall-circus program', trans. Daniel Gerould, *Drama Review*, 18 (1970), p. 79.

18 Williams quotes Samuel Johnson's definition of realisation as 'an Act of the Imagination, that realises the Event however fictitious' and its modern use as a term refering to 'the *means* and *effect* of bringing something to life', *Keywords*, p. 260.

19 April 1785, *Astley's Cuttings*, vol. 1, item 656.

20 Though Booth doesn't discuss the circus in his study of the history of Victorian spectacle, it belongs more than any other form of performance to the nineteenth-century history and consumption of urban spectacle, in London and Paris, of which much has been written elsewhere. see Michael

Booth, *Victorian Spectacular Theatre 1850–1910* (London, Routledge & Kegan Paul, 1981), p. 4, and Rachel Bowlby, *Just Looking: Consumer Culture in Dreiser, Gissing and Zola* (London, Methuen, 1985), pp. 1–18.

21 6 March 1794, *Astley's Cuttings*, vol. 2, item 92A.

22 Saxon, *Enter Foot and Horse*, p. 55.

23 29 July 1791, *Astley's Cuttings* vol. 2, items 33c, 34a, 34c, 34d.

24 Peter Brooks, *The Melodramatic Imagination: Balzac, Henry James and the Mode of Excess* (New Haven and London, Yale University Press [1976], 1995), pp. 14–15.

25 Brooks, *The Melodramatic Imagination*, p. 15.

26 Brooks, *The Melodramatic Imagination*, p. 15.

27 Brooks, *The Melodramatic Imagination*, p. 84.

28 Roy Strong, *Splendour at Court* (London, Weidenfeld & Nicholson, 1972), p. 73.

29 Strong, *Splendour at Court*, p. 73.

30 Strong, *Splendour at Court*, p. 74.

31 Kwint, 'Astley's amphitheatre', p. 246. see *Circus Programmes*, vol. 1, benefit poster of 1831, item 32.

32 May 1792, *Astley's Cuttings*, vol.1, item 47c.

33 April 1772, *Astley's Cuttings*, vol.1, items 62 and 64.

34 Martin Esslin, *The Theatre of the Absurd* (Harmondsworth, Penguin Books [1961], 1991), p. 327. see also Arnold P. Hinchcliffe, *The Absurd* (London, Methuen, 1969).

35 Eugene Ionesco, *World Theatre*, 8:3 (1959), p. 47.

36 Esslin, *The Theatre of the Absurd*, p. 25.

37 Esslin, *The Theatre of the Absurd*, p. 414.

38 Esslin, *The Theatre of the Absurd*, p. 328.

39 Lyn Pykett, *The Sensation Novel from 'The Woman in White' to 'The Moonstone'* (Plymouth, Northcote House Publishers, 1994). p. 4.

40 For some early examples of these see J. C. Cross, *Circusiana*, 2 vols (London, Lackington, Allen & Company, 1809).

41 Whitsun 1868, *Townsend Walsh Scrapbook*, 3C40, Hertzberg Collection. Cvetkovich argues that the 'appearance of the Victorian sensation novel in the 1860s marks the moment at which sensations became sensational. Whereas the use of the term "sensation" to refer to perceptions originates in the 1600s as part of the ideology of empiricism, the sensation novel prompted less neutral use of the term to refer to literature … The "sensational" became an aesthetically, morally and politically loaded term used to dismiss both particular kinds of representations and the affective responses they produce', *Mixed Feelings: Feminism, Mass Culture and Victorian Sensationalism* (Brunswick, NJ, Rutgers University Press, 1992), p. 13.

42 Cvetkovich, *Mixed Feelings*, pp. 22–3.

43 See Henry Mansel, 'Sensation Novels', *Quarterly Review*, 133 (1863),

p. 512 and Margaret Oliphant, 'Sensation novels', *Blackwood's*, 91 (1862), pp. 564–9, and 'Novels', *Blackwood's*, 102 (1867), p. 209. See also poster for Franconi's Cirque Imperial, Music Hall Dublin, May 1853 which boasts the ENTHUSIASTIC SUCCESS & EXTRAORDINARY SENSATION, created by the ASTOUNDING PERFORMANCE, of THE THREE PARISIAN BROTHERS!, *Townsend Walsh Scrapbook*, item 3C40, Hertzberg Collection.

44 April 1768 *Astley's Cuttings* vol. 1, item 6.

45 Oliphant, 'Sensation novels', p. 565.

46 Jenny Bourne Taylor, *In the Secret Theatre* (London, Longman, 1988), p. 3.

47 Bourne Taylor, *In the Secret Theatre*, p. 4.

48 Cvetkovich, *Mixed Feelings*, p. 15.

49 Bourne Taylor, *In the Secret Theatre*, p. 4. see also Cvetkovich, *Mixed feelings*, p. 15.

50 This position is neatly summarised by a contemporary critic quoted in G. Rudé who describes London as a 'great Bedlam under the dominion of a beggarly, idle and intoxicated mob without keepers, actuated solely by the word *Wilkes …*', *Wilkes and Liberty* (Oxford, Clarendon Press, 1962), p. 50 and p. 173.

51 Edward Royle argues that although Wilkes was only a 'symptom of a groundswell of radical opinion', none the less he 'received suppport from across the social spectrum'. This 'appeal to the middle ranks of society was most important, for their support was founded on sound commercial and economic interests which were ill-represented under the existing political system', *Modern Britain: A Social History, 1750–1985* (London, Edward Arnold, 1987), p. 117 and p. 118.

52 As Kwint observes, 'audience descriptions, neighbouring artforms and the main protagonists of the stage and ring (tailors, sailors, sergeants and cobblers) suggests that Astley's was primarily and most consistently the province of the artisan and yeoman classes', 'Astley's amphitheatre', p. 79. In any case, E. P. Thompson qualifies Wilkes's radicalism by suggesting that he was in the pocket of 'wealthy tradesmen, merchants and manufacturers of the City who were Wilkes's most influential supporters' and that he himself maintained a certain contempt for his own mass following. see *The Making of the English Working Class* (London, Penguin Books, 1963), p. 76.

53 George Speaight, 'Some comic circus entrées', *Theatre Notebook*, 32 (1978), pp. 24–7.

54 Henri Bergson, *Laughter: An essay on the Meaning of the Comic*, trans. Cloudesley Brereton and Fred Rothwell (London, Macmillan [1911], 1935).

55 Mikhail Bahktin, *Rabelais and His World*, trans. Hélène Iswolsky (Bloomington, Indiana University Press [1965], 1984), pp. 59–144. Bergson, *Laughter*, pp. 3–5.

56 Bergson, *Laughter*, p. 5.

57 Bergson, *Laughter*, p. 19. At the same time Bergson stresses the way in which laughter is connected to the possibility of luxury and surplus in that it is enjoyed only when people have been 'freed from the worry of self-preservation' and may then 'regard themselves as works of art', p. 20.

58 Bergson, *Laughter*, p. 20. This tyrannical and sadistic dimension in laughter is emphasised by Angela Carter, in her short essay on clown dynamics in *Nights at the Circus*, when Buffo the clown claims that the 'child's laughter is pure until he first laughs at a clown' because 'the mirth the clown creates is in direct proportion to the humiliation he is forced to endure' *Nights at the Circus* (London, Vintage [1984], 1994), p. 119. Norman Manea makes a similar point in his essay on the connection between political tyranny and the control of laughter when he asserts that '(r)idicule has its own secret power, that of amusement, and it is vengeful', 'On clowns: the dictator and the artist (notes to a text by Fellini) (1990), in *On Clowns: The Dictator and the Artist* (London, Faber & Faber, 1994), p. 39.

59 Bergson, *Laughter*, p. 29.

60 Bergson, *Laughter*, p. 29.

61 See Kwint, 'Astley's amphitheatre', pp. 235–44.

62 August 1796, *Astley's Cuttings*, vol. 2, item 140c.

63 June 1798, *Astley's Cuttings*, vol. 2, item 165e.

64 As Kwint points out, publicity stunts were important in order for Astley's in particular, a basically static institution, to 'project an image of itself as a kaleidescope of change and exoticism', 'Astley's amphitheatre', p. 90.

65 Kwint, 'Astley's amphitheatre', p. 235.

66 Kwint, 'Astley's amphitheatre', p. 237 and p. 243.

67 Cvetkovich, *Mixed Feelings*, p. 19.

68 Edward Said, *Orientalism* (Harmondsworth, Penguin Books [1978], 1995), p. 41.

69 Interestingly, however, as Kwint points out, the 'incipient nationalisms provoked by Napoleon's expansionism were none the less ideal subjects for melodramatic sympathy towards the underdog', for example, 'British Valour and Indian Tomahawks' (1800), 'The British Glory in Egypt' (1801), 'The Burmese War; or, the Treacherous Esquimaux' (1826), 'The Bombardment and Capture of Canton' (1858). see Kwint, 'Astley's amphitheatre', table 6.2.

70 Adah Isaacs Menken, originally an American, later found great fame on the London stage through both her apparently naked performances (though she wore pink leggings) and her famous literary acquaintances (Alexandre Dumas snr, Dante Gabriel Rossetti and Algernon Swinburne). see Bernard Falk, *The Naked Lady: A Biography of Adah Isaacs Meuken* (London, Hutchinson, 1952).

71 'Several of the acts performed now may be identical to even more ancient Egyptian traditions. The lady contortionist or Kowitshouk, is as favorite a spectacle today as, according to carvings found at the temple at Thebes,

it was 3,000 years ago. And acrobats, equilibrists, and even a clown, are depicted in wall paintings in the Nile Valley dating to 2,500 B.C.', Hugh Leach, 'The Egyptian circus remembered and revisited', *King Pole*, 103, June 1994, p. 45.

72 Said, *Orientalism*, p. 71.
73 Said, *Orientalism*, p. 71.
74 August 1832, *Astley's Cuttings*, vol. 3, item 1331.
75 *Ringling Brothers Barnum and Bailey Program*, 1954, Special Collections, Milner Library, State University of Illinois.
76 Recent productions have included 'Saltimbanco' (1992/3), 'Alegria' (1994/5) and 'Mystere' (1993–), all using fairy-tale settings with hazy mythical and multi-cultural references.
77 Cirque du Soleil designers, one newspaper report claims, are encouraged to draw inspiration from '*National Geographic* and other magazines', 'Mystery, not clowns or animals, from new age circus', *New York Times*, 6 April 1998. In line with this, they have signed a twelve-year deal with Walt Disney World in Florida to stage a permanent show there.
78 *Ringling Brothers Barnum and Bailey Program*, 1989, Harry Hertzberg Collection.
79 The circus has a long-standing tradition of 'exhibiting' representatives of African, Asian and South American cultures, though frequently their ethnic difference has been accompanied by some defining oddness or strange ability. Astley presented the 'Three Monstrous Craws, Wild Born Human Beings' as inhabitants of an obscure South American tribe, when in fact they were later discovered to be Italian village dwellers suffering from severe gout. See 13 August 1787, *Astley's Cuttings*, vol. 1, items 975–7. Between 1935 and 1940 the 'Brass-Necked Ladies of Padaung' or the 'Giraffe Women' were exhibited at the Olympia Circus in the United States at around the same time as Franz Taaibosch, a South African bushman or Khoisan, otherwise known as 'Clicko' (for his distinctive language – generically known as 'khoikoi'), was presented in Europe and the United States. see Robert Bogdan, 'Circassian beauties: authentic sideshow fabrications', *Bandwagon*, 30:3, May/June 1986, pp. 22–3, Bernth Linfors, 'Circus Africans', *Journal of American Culture*, 6:2, 1983, pp. 3–19, and Neil Parsons, '"Clicko" or Franz Taaibosch: South African bushman entertainer in Britain, France, Jamaica and the USA: his life from 1908–1940', African Studies Association Conference Paper, 21 November 1992.

II

Representing the circus

6

'. . . crammed with all sorts of dry bones and sawdust': Dickens's disruptive circus

Dickens's interest in all forms of popular entertainment has been well documented.[1] His fascination with the circus in particular led to its explicit inclusion in many of his works (fiction and non-fiction) as a figure of thematic, narrative and figurative significance. The circus furnishes Dickens not only with a series of exceptional bodily perform-ances and dramatic character-types similar to those he has often turned out himself, but he also recognised that, as a form of live, predominantly mute, body-centred entertainment, it issues a radical challenge to literary representation itself. Other writers, both of his and later periods, may have glossed over this constituitive difference be-tween the languages of live circus and literary representations of them and have deflected the problem of representation by concentrating instead either on discussions of the moral or political status of circus and its performers or on the retelling of the romantic and often con-tradictory myths about the circus (as exotic, tawdry, dangerously 'vagabondish', childishly tame, kind-hearted, cruel, respectable, demonic and so on). Some of this mythology has been generated by the circus itself, as we have seen, but rival entertainers, moral reformers or over-fastidious critics have also played a part in the consolidation of both the idealisation and demonising of the circus.[2] Though Dickens may at times have casually confirmed such romantic constructions, on another level, the circus is visible in his work in the form of an invasion or disruption of coherent literary embodiment and, through this, his writings suggest to us the ways in which the circus is not only commercially and culturally modern, but also that its language

115

of performance constitutes a special challenge to formal modes of inscription.

As we saw in part I, the Theatre Licensing Act of 1737 established and preserved the dominance of the patented royal theatres and this had the side-effect of producing the strategically mute art form of the circus, as well as other related popular forms which were also constituted through music, animal acts, dance and mime performance. These new entertainments, having established both a regular audience and familiar infrastructures (physical and financial), lasted well beyond the Theatres Act in 1843 which lifted licensing restrictions. By this date the generic identity of the circus as a mute, musical or pantomimic dramatic form had been firmly established and fully exported around the world and, if anything, the narrative components of circus shows declined as the century progressed. From the 1820s onwards, the circus generally (most especially the permanent city circuses) began to be less suspected of inciting dangerous or immoral behaviour and increasingly sanctioned by celebrities, people of fashion and royalty. At the same time, its softened, less notorious reputation and ever-increasing popularity meant that the circus was more frequently held up as an example of debased mass culture. By the 1820s, the circus had transformed itself from being an object of social control to being a successful and highly competitive form of commerce, indeed, as Schlicke points out, '[of] all forms of amusement in the nineteenth century, the circus is the one which best illustrates the growing commercialisation of leisure'.[3]

Disher claims that Astley's in particular, 'however firm its foothold over the emotions of the masses, was to be a stock joke. Journalists, all its life long, laughed at it. Poets made game of it. Novelists sent their most simple-minded characters to it ... Gaudy, inglorious Astley's.'[4] As Kwint argues, Astley's, by the time of Ducrow, 'was able to maintain its own appeal until the late nineteenth cenury because only superficial changes were needed to refresh a highly ritualistic form that had successfully marked the stages and cycles of many people's lives' and, as such, it had 'become a seemingly inevitable part of growing up and getting old'.[5] Astley's newfound respectability had to be offset against the fact that it was increasingly seen as a childish and ritualistic entertainment whose shocks, dare-devilry and ribaldry had by this stage been well rehearsed before their adult audiences.

This is the impression conveyed by Dickens in his sketch, 'Astley's', as he gives an account of the way he is now 'far more delighted and amused with the audience' than 'with the pageantry we once appreciated' (p. 107).[6] Yet what is most interesting about his portrait of Astley's is the way the adult's ability to recollect childhood and childishness is set up in relationship to forms of language mastery. Before Dickens turns to Astley, he offers a brief preamble on the tendency for 'black Roman capitals, in a book, or shop window, or placarded on a wall' to call forth 'an indistinct and confused recollection of the time when we were first initiated into the mysteries of the alphabet'. Whilst many other adult experiences, may produce this 'same kind of feeling', there is, Dickens suggests, 'no place which recalls so strongly our recollections of childhood as Astley's' (p. 106). On one level a similarity is set up between going to Astley's and alphabet learning. Firstly, not only is the lettering given deliberately mimic qualities in that they are described as mute 'staring' capitals, but it was precisely Roman lettering which was often used in circus-poster advertising, a fact we are reminded of in *Hard Times*.[7] Secondly, both letter learning and Astley's belong to childhood and, by implication, Astley's is to circus entertainment what the alphabet is to language: Astley's established the constituent figures of the circus in the same way that the alphabet constitutes the foundational figures of written language. The difference between the two is that although learning the characters of the alphabet is a process of difficulty for a child whose mind is 'bewildered' by the process and whose ideas are in 'confusion', they grow into a better mastery of the language in adulthood. Appreciation of Astley's, however, which communicates through pageant and gesture, belongs to childhood and fades for the adult. At this stage, for Dickens, the circus seems to represent the possibility of a dyadic, perhaps regressive, relationship within non-literary signs.

This dependency on pure visual spectacle means that the performances at the circus are not so much interesting in themselves, but for the way they allow Dickens the journalist access to the past and to human behaviour, as exemplified both by the audience and the hangers-on at the stage-door entrance. Yet those who attend Astley's turn out to demonstrate all the qualities which have led Dickens to become bored of the stage performers: repetition (they are a 'regular Astley's party'), histrionics and pageant (displayed by most members of the family and certainly the men who 'swagger' at the stage door). Dickens undoes the separation between audience and performer in this way only to draw the curtain between them again at the end of the sketch with his mock disbelief ('Impossible! We – cannot – we will not – believe it' [p. 111]). In avoiding describing the show at Astley's, Dickens turns to the audience but knowingly transforms them into a parallel Astley's show in an attempt to make a point similar to the one made in 'The Pantomime of Life'; that life offers an equally, if not more, rich array of comic characters as the pantomime, therefore, when seen through the caricaturist's eye, 'we are all actors in The Pantomime of Life'.[8] Yet these final impressions are ultimately belied both by their obvious irony and also by the opening comparison of the sketch which makes it clear that the language of the literary caricaturist and the language of the circus are fundamentally and constituitively different. It is this problem, this recognition of the failure of one form of performance to flow into another, that will reappear in Dickens's subsequent work with increasingly interesting effects and implications.

Astley's reliance on 'pageantry' and 'histrionic taste' naturally points to one of the circus's commercial advantages in that, as a form of generally, but of course not entirely, mute entertainment which was also essentially opportunistic and adaptable, it had cultivated an international language of performing figures which could potentially be redrawn and specifically reinflected in almost any country. In *Pictures from Italy*, Dickens demonstrates that the language of the circus, though verbally mute, is conventional rather than universal. He gives an account of 'an equestrian company from Paris' which he comes across in Modena, advertising a performance of Ducrow's famous act, *Mazeppa*, by means of a street procession.[9] Through a typical act of circus multiple cultural reprocessing, Dickens witnesses a drama based on the work of an English writer, Byron, whose dramatic poem itself takes its cue from a section of voltaire's narrative about Charles XII of Sweden, whose officer Mazeppa tells him of an early adventure in the Ukraine. Ducrow's version has presumably been customised here by a French company and is now to be offered to the Italian audience (the 'tame population of Modena' [p. 69]). The circus appears from nowhere and seems entirely anomalous in the medieval streets of Modena as Dickens describes being 'suddenly scared to death by a blast from the shrillest trumpet that was ever blown'. Yet, paradoxically, it is precisely from this disruption and the fake exotic qualities of the 'stately nobleman with a great deal of hair', the 'Mexican chief, with a great pear-shaped club on his shoulder like Hercules' and the women in 'extremely short petticoats' and 'unnaturally pink tights' (p. 68) that Dickens almost appears to find a comforting familiarity and a relief. A dramatic contrast is set up between the two previous theatrical arenas he has encountered, the old and now long-abandoned theatre of the Farnese Palace and the Cathedral, and the physically unrestrained circus parade with the former two emerging as 'one of the dreariest spectacles of decay that was ever seen – a grand old gloomy theatre, mouldering away' and a 'subterranean church' filled with 'crowds of phantom-looking men and women' (p. 67). The church mass is led by 'officiating priests' who 'were crooning the usual chant, in the usual, low, dull, drawling melancholy tone' (p. 67). The rotten, ghost-inhabited structure of the theatre and the cathedral which are deadening the spirit with habitual practices, are suddenly overtaken as the Farnese's 'lost sunbeam' is dramatically eclipsed by the 'beaming looks' of the performers whose speeding entourage, full of colour, 'tearing' energy, and danger, negotiates the 'uneven pavement' (68) in upright positions whilst on horseback.

Kate Flint points out that the Roman carnival envelops Dickens in, as he puts it, its 'contagious' and 'irresistible' (p. 125) energies to the point that he can no longer separate himself off as 'observer and judge' of the Italians with whom he temporarily identifies.[10] On the contrary, here the circus parade has the opposite effect. A division already exists between the performers and the onlookers who have 'come out of the church to stare', but on whose faces is 'a latent expression of discomposure and anxiety' (p. 69), when Dickens adds a further division of onlookers between himself and an old lady he sees kneeling in church who

> had seen it all, and had been immensely interested, without getting up; and this old lady's eye, at that juncture, I happened to catch: to our mutual confusion. She cut our embarrassment very short, however, by crossing herself devoutly, and going down, at full length, on her face, before a figure in a fancy petticoat and a gilt crown; which was so like one of the procession-figures, that perhaps at this hour she may think the whole appearance a celestial vision. (p. 69)

Together, perhaps, with a typically English amusement at the theatrics of Catholicism, Dickens's cultural familiarity with the circus as a form (over and above the apparent foreignness of the individuals in the procession) lends him a superiority over the old lady who, he believes, has no context but a religious one within which to (mis)understand what she has just witnessed in her own town. None the less it is not difficult to read in Dickens's series of explicit echoes a conception of the circus as a force which raises the ghosts of theatre from the dead, animates the stilled wild animals, the 'horses' heels, the griffins, lions, tigers and other monsters in stone and marble' (p. 68) depicted on the walls of the cathedral and reimagines the religious figure 'in a fancy petticoat' (p. 69). This connection is rounded off in the penultimate sentence of the account when Dickens speculates that the old lady watching the procession from a kneeling position in the church may explain away her experience of the 'procession-figures' as a 'celestial vision', so much does the lady in tights on horseback resemble the 'figure in a fancy petticoat and a gilt crown' whom she worships (p. 69).

John Schad has used this example of the cathedral in Modena, with its untidy arrangement of kneeling humans inside, to argue that Dickens's urban churches are a place where the city is subverted (rather than the conventional view that it is vice versa). However, the trumpet blast which signals the circus's arrival provides precisely the 'kind of thundering cannon, or rebellious noise' which Schad attributes to the work of church bells elsewhere in Dickens and which he suggests places such noises 'within an oral subculture that in relation to the period's newly dominant literate culture is a subversive or a subterranean force'.[11] In this respect it is easy to see why Dickens responds so warmly to the circus's storming arrival since it delivers a blast of modern urban (Parisian) spectacle, mockery, secularised ritual and qualified eroticism into a landscape which for him is too dominated by a past fast driving him into melancholy. Dickens is marked out, not so much as Flint has argued of other moments, for his Englishness, but for his membership of a contemporary, cosmopolitan, urban, secular, mass culture for which knowledge of circus conventions is the transient marker.

At first glance, Dickens seems in these echoings to construct the circus as a temporary and bewildering continuity between past and present and offers Modena's inhabitants a replacement for all these now atrophied elements of their cultural and spiritual life through something which is given the appearance of being a natural successor. At the same time, the 'subversive' and 'subterranean' potential of the circus, which my reference to Schad's reading might imply, requires qualification since the circus appears to subvert very little here. Firstly, whilst the circus during this period may undoubtedly have been a powerful contributor to the oral subcultures of the day, as we have already seen, by this stage it has already begun to cut across categories of class and culture and was certainly no longer much of a 'subterranean' form in its relationship to the law. Secondly, although, as I've indicated above, Dickens sets in place clear continuities within his use of metaphor in his accounts of the church and theatre on the one hand and the circus on the other, the relationship seems less one of either continuity of subversion but rather one of mimicry, parody and shadowing. The procession is described as having a 'flouting' attitude towards the 'monsters in stone and marble' depicted on the church walls; the implication of mockery working to empty these symbols of any former religious seriousness they may have possessed. Though for a short amount of time the circus spectacle is capable of taunting the dead icons with its intensity of spirit and energy, the forms which this taunting inhabits, through the same move that they mimic the ghostly symbols, also resemble them. The exotic and spectacular forms which the circus parade turns out differ from the theatre and church only in that all its physical qualities are ephemeral and are absorbed and expire during the moment of performance so that no symbolic edifice or statuary is left behind and no lasting effect is left on those it resembles. Dickens is left in a state of mourning (they 'left a new and greatly increased sense of dullness behind') following the circus's passing. It leaves no palpable trace or mark, but rather can be accommodated into a comparable religious image, though this 'celestial vision' has an essentially parodic function in relation to the church image it mirrors and mimicks. Clearly Dickens enjoys the parody while it lasts but, leaving nothing behind, far from injecting the town with new spirit, its spectacle merely serves to illustrate to Dickens the absence of life in the first place. The circus may leave behind the mental imprint of an impressive vision, but not only does it avoid any physical commemoration of itself as an event (except of course a few advertising bills), it appears in fact to mock and parody other forms of symbolic spectacle which rely on such testimony.

Both of these sketches are valuable illustrations of the circus of the period in that Dickens, the social commentator, demonstrates its important role in the transformation of popular culture into formations which have been adapted to a well-regulated urban, commercial and industrial society whilst, within this, it continued to present performances more frenetically energetic, spectacular and dangerous than rival popular forms. At the same time, both of them also register the circus's difference from and resistance to literary language and other forms of commemoration; these are pictures of a circus perpetually vanishing from the present.

Hard Times[12] also needs to be understood for the way in which it documents the cultural and political discourses which had begun to surround the circus by the mid-century. As Kwint has argued, by the beginning of the reformist second half of the nineteenth century, an 'altogether more liberal and indeed functionalist view of entertainment as a necessary safety valve had prevailed over the ideology of unrelenting labour'.[13] *Hard Times*, alongside Wilkie Collins's *Hide and Seek*, was part of this debate about the social significance of popular amusements. Conventionally critics have read the role of the circus in *Hard Times* in exactly these terms: as an escapist alternative to the labours of industrial society, rather than as a symptom or product of it. Thus critics of the left such as Raymond Williams have been moved to use this reading as a way of critiquing what they see as Dickens's 'denial' of the 'real basis ... of the hard times' and his subsequent championing of the 'instinctive, unintellectual, unorganised life' of the circus (representing 'genuine feeling') over the route of unionisation, which is dismissed as callous and bullying in the Stephen Blackpool plot.[14] However, the terms and limits of Dickens's metaphorical mobilisation of the circus, as Catherine Gallagher has demonstrated, are more complex, unstable and confused than such readings allow; readings which perhaps themselves distinguish too readily between fact and fancy in their polar opposition of industrial society and the circus.[15]

For a figure to work textually as a metaphor for something else we must first understand something of what it is in itself. The circus does not make its first physical appearance until chapter 3 of *Hard Times*, yet the question of defining the circus is at the heart of the novel's opening drama. At stake in the first chapter is a conflict of definitions, between the school-board triumvirate (Gradgrind, M'Choakumchild and Bounderby) and Sissy Jupe, which not only sets utilitarianism against circus values, but involves questioning the very possibility of definition at all:

> 'Bitzer,' said Thomas Gradgrind. 'Your definition of a horse.'
> 'Quadruped. Graminivorous. Forty teeth, namely twenty-four

grinders, four eye-teeth, and twelve incisive. Sheds coat in the spring; in marshy countries, sheds hoofs, too. Hoofs hard, but requiring to be shod with iron. Age known by marks in mouth.' Thus (and much more) Bitzer.

'Now girl number twenty,' said Mr Gradgrind.'You know what a horse is.'

(Charles Dickens, *Hard Times*, pp. 5–6)

Sissy Jupe, 'girl number twenty', has been taken into Gradgrind's 'monotonous vault of a schoolroom' (p. 1) after being abandoned by her father, a failed circus performer. Here, at the opening of the novel she is brought up short by Gradgrind for being unable to define a horse. The scene sets up an opposition which is to propel the drama of the rest of the novel whilst at the same time it undermines, through political satire, any straightforward polarity within the terms of this opposition. Clearly Gradgrind, wedded to his 'facts and calculations' (p. 3), is the satirical vehicle for Benthamite utilitarianism; a mechanistic, calculating and hard-headed view of nature which is continually opposed and interrupted even as it is articulated. The horse, which is the contested object of definition, is temporarily pinned down by Gradgrind and Bitzer, even though previously Gradgrind has been guilty himself of fictionalising definitions in his account of Sissy's father's occupation (a circus horse-rider) by insisting on his being labelled as 'a veterinary surgeon, a farrier, and horse-breaker' (p. 4). His is a translation of entertainment into function and of occupation into profession which simultaneously works to expose Gradgrind's middle-class snobbery; itself manifested as a desire to turn the circus into something 'respectable'. The horse, therefore, is available both as a symbol of labour and industry as well as of the circus, within which it constitutes the founding entertainment and to which, here, it has a synecdochic relationship. However, Gradgrind's insistence on the primacy of the symbolism of the former over the latter, of the horse as 'fact' as opposed to 'wonder', is continually undermined in the course of the novel, until finally he must rely on a circus 'pony gig' (p. 386) to remove his own delinquent son Tom abroad in order to escape capture by the police, an act which is both practical and designed to delude. It is at this point that the punning implications of 'Jupe' as 'dupe' come into play, indeed perhaps with this name Dickens makes reference to Oxberry's account of Grimaldi's use of 'chuckles' and facial gestures which he added 'to the dupe of his artifice'.[16] The circus here both entertains and benevolently deceives and this naturally overlaps with the English translation of 'jupe' as dress and therefore, in the context of the circus, costume, which is the clown's disguise and Tom's means of refuge. Finally, there is irony in the fact that the more intractable obstacle to Tom's escape in the end proves to be the now grown-up Bitzer who, determined to turn Tom in to the police, has become a consummate product of the heartless and inflexible former Gradgrind 'catechism' (p. 383).

What is instructive in all this is both the struggle between definition and entertainment on the one hand, and, on the other, the failure of the circus representative to define, or rather to be allowed to define, its two central figures: the horse and the clown (Signor Jupe's main occupation as a clown is covered up here even by Sissy). Gradgrind's inadequate and pragmatic definition which erases all colour, shadows the subsequent events of the book in that Signor Jupe is evoked thereafter but never appears in the book and the horses are absent until the show at the end.

The circus book-ends and, we could say, encircles the novel; it is factually absent from the central part of the plot, though, as I will show, it percolates through some of the novel's most important metaphors. As Paul Schlicke puts it, 'the circus in *Hard Times* matters far more for what it means than for what it is.'[17] Perhaps the most important line here, then, follows Sissy's reference to the practice of breaking horses 'in the ring' when Gradgrind admonishes her with 'You mustn't tell us about the ring, here' (p. 4). Dickens, too, will shortly banish the factual ring from his narrative until its conclusion, pushing it to the margins of his narrative just as, as Schlicke points out, the circus was conventionally banished to the physical margins of the town's outskirts.[18] Yet this leaves a gaping hole, or rather a series of holes, gaps and absences which, like Louisa as she is later described by Tom, are 'crammed' with 'sawdust' (p. 179). Through these holes it seems as though Dickens rarely ceases to 'tell us about the ring', yet we must ask why it is that he seems unable to represent what the circus *is*, even whilst he is able to discuss what the circus *means*. Strange metaphorical references to it litter the narrative and concoct a complex but, as Gallagher argues, tellingly inconsistent set of relationships between industrialisation and the new mass leisure culture.

One of the most striking ways in which the circus is included in *Hard Times* is, as I have suggested, through metaphor when its figures are mobilised imaginatively in order to refigure. Hazlitt, in his essay 'The Indian jugglers' represents an interesting precedent for this in his use of the Indian Juggler as a metaphor for a certain kind of physical achievement and dexterity. Yet his celebration of those qualities is disingenuous since, even as he praises the juggler's precision and his 'lightening' movements, he abstracts him into a series of similes ('like planets in their spheres', 'like sparkles of fire', 'like flowers' or meteors', 'like ribbons or like serpents').[19] Thus, whilst Hazlitt appears to humble himself before the awesome skills of the juggler, the transformation of physical technique into telling metaphor finally works to champion the intellectual and creative skills of the abstractionist who bestows added layers of beauty and meaning on the performer; a reading which squares with Hazlitt's final Romantic celebration of the man of 'genius' over the merely 'talented'. Though it was written only ten years before 'Astley's', Hazlitt's encounter seems a much more Romantic account than Dickens's: Hazlitt presents a single street performer for whom he believes he is the only (important) spectator, whereas Dickens is always part of the commercial context of a paying audience of consumers.

None the less, Dickens, whilst he uses the circus as a key plot device in the novel, also constitutes it both as a figure through which to explore the social purpose of writing (as entertainment, diversion, education, reform), as well as a way of complicating the figurative. As Catherine Gallagher has already claimed, *Hard Times* is a 'book *about* metaphors' in which 'the circus ... is both a metaphor in itself and the novel's major symbol of fancy, the metaphor-making faculty'.[20] Yet she also argues that 'the circus and its illusions are ambiguously presented' and that this tendency towards ambiguity and illusion results in a suspicion over the value and motivation behind metaphor-making in general. Razak Dahmane argues that we should see the crucial division in *Hard Times* as being that between literal and figurative language, rather than between 'fact' and 'fancy', as has often been the case.[21] However, this reading depends on the ability to make clear distinctions between characters and institutions which partake in the figurative, and those bound by the literal, and the circus is precisely the figure which makes any such division impossible. Not only does the example above demonstrate that Gradgrind's speeches in favour of utilitarianism fictionalise as they prescribe, but Bounderby, in a process Gallagher has already described as 'inverted similarity', is the most tyrannical, hard-headed and fiscally minded as well as the most absurd, entertaining, clown-like, opportunistic and quite obviously self-fictionalising figure in the novel.[22] His name itself, whilst it evokes 'bounder' and 'bound' or 'bounded', is also very close to 'boundary' which, while it suggests his controlling nature, also calls forth the defining structure of the circus itself in which the performance space of the ring is separated off from the audience by a boundary perimeter. Of course it is also suggestive for this reason of the ideas of limit, liminal and threshold; of boundaries which are also challenges to transgression. His apparent counterpart, Mr Sleary, may be most well known as the genial proponent of amusement, yet when he assures Sissy that her father will always be able to find her through Sleary because he is a well-known figure who 'alwayth paythe ith way', we are told that he 'worked out the whole matter like a sum' (p. 51). Just as Dickens's industrial images and figures are infiltrated by the circus, in turn the latter is coloured by the metaphorical language of finance.

Finally, the most striking and recurrent circus images of the book are contained in the descriptions of the industrial landscape of Coketown in which the mills are 'Fairy palaces', their smoke takes the form of 'monstrous serpents' and the workers in them are 'melancholy mad elephants' (p. 91). At the level of metaphor then, Dickens collapses the boundary with which critics such as Williams have argued he separates the circus from the economic realities of industrial Britain, and which thereby render the solution he offers essentially idealistic. These metaphors are as evocative of the corruptions and labours of the circus as they are of an industrial society of which, as I have suggested above, this entertainment is the product. Through these images of elephants and serpents the circus in turn may be seen to bear the imprint of industrialisation's domestic and colonial distortions and therefore cannot, as Paul Schlicke has suggested, be read as the symbol of 'untainted' positive value.[23] Far from removing the circus from the implications of industrialisation through its metaphorical rendering, Dickens makes these all the more visible but at the same time reversible with 'fancy' and imagination so that, as Steven Connor has suggested, the novel's 'inconsistency in the use of metaphor and metonymy' reflects 'an uncertainty about language, and particularly about the kind of language to be used in representing such strict binary oppositions as the one between Fact and Fancy'.[24]

The uncertainty identified above over the possibility of representing binary opposition relates also to Dickens's ongoing anxiety about the possibility of separating audience and performer; categories which are both reversible and substituent. Whereas in both 'Astley's' and the encounter with the French circus in *Pictures from Italy* Dickens concentrates his focus on the audience dynamics at the expense of a detailed account of the performers and performances, in *Hard Times* the real audience for the circus is banished and we have in its place only people who are forced to watch performances as interlopers. In the first such case, Louisa and Tom are forced to 'peep' at the show from outside the tent through a 'loophole' and, in the second, Louisa and Sissy must sneak in to the ring unrecognised; when they are, Sleary separates them from the rest of the audience and again forces them to 'peep at the ring' through a 'thpy-hole' which is a 'chink in the boards' (p. 375). In the second example the rest of the audience is mentioned only as it vacates the ring and a peculiar reversal of parts then takes place in which Gradgrind, the principal voice against the circus, moves straight from condemning it from the outside to sitting down 'forlorn, on the Clown's performing chair in the middle of the ring' whilst his son Tom, now forced into performance as a clown in order to escape the law, watches him from 'one of the back benches, remote in the subdued light and the strangeness of the place' (p. 377). Tom wears the 'comic livery' of a 'black thervanth' clown which involves a series of 'exaggerated' and ill-fitting garments, the poverty of which clearly symbolises his bankrupt moral position. Yet we are also given a description of the 'seams in his black face, where fear and heat had started through the greasy composition daubed all over it'. The double reference here to both industrialisation (with the invocation of the black 'seams' of a coal mine where the individual faces are blackened and concealed) and to Empire (the black slave), is a sort of reversal of earlier descriptions of Coketown's industrial landscape in which the picture of the factories is interrupted by striking circus metaphors.

The fact that the clown is everywhere in this scene, in the sense that both the space of entertainment and of the world which surrounds and is marked off by it are occupied by clowns is, perhaps paradoxically, a further example of Dickens's failure to represent the clown. After all, at no point is either of these clowns engaged in any sort of entertainment; rather they are still, drained figures who are 'sullen' and 'forlorn' respectively. Their inability to interact with each other is not determined by the 'limits' of the circus ring but by the psychological barriers between them which the 'verge' of the circle merely symbolises. In other words, the real circus clown is dead in this scene, none of his energies are present, yet his ghost is present in the form of his borrowed clothes and masking make-up, as well as in the form of a disturbing extended metaphor which touches on familial and economic alienation, industrial labour and colonial expansion.

So, whereas in previous texts Dickens had avoided offering his readership a direct and sustained account of circus performances by concentrating instead on its effects as they are experienced by its audiences, in *Hard Times* he evacuates the paying circus audience from his drama. Though we get the briefest of reports of the acts which Sissy and Louisa witness while they are still inside the ring, strangely this description is mainly confined to facts: these even occasionally distanced by irony. Sissy watches the 'Emperor of Japan' whilst he rides round the ring on his 'old white horse stencilled with black spots' and 'twirling five wash-hand basins at once, as it is the favourite recreation of that monarch to do' (p. 372). We are told, again with irony, of Sissy's interest in the performer's heritage ('though well acquainted with his Royal line, had no personal knowledge of the present Emperor'), but are given few details of what he does or how he does it and, when Sleary's daughter Josephine appears to perform her Tyrolean Flower Act, her act is overtaken by the clowns who lead her in and who, rather than entertain Louisa and Sissy, rather worry and slightly bore them as their 'performance seemed a little long' and 'consumed time'. They, after all, are in 'in great suspense' (p. 373) over the events taking place outside, rather than inside, the ring.

It is as though *Hard Times*, which would seem to be the text by Dickens which is most about the circus, provides his most indirect presentation of circus performance and, like *Nicholas Nickleby* (1839) in the realm of popular theatre and *The Old Curiosity Shop* (1841) in travelling menageries, offers the reader a portrait of the characters behind the scenes of such entertainments instead. Yet, as my comments above on the scene between Tom and his father as well as my examination of the use of metaphor in the novel indicate, the circus moves like a ghost through the novel, haunting the depictions of many of the other characters and settings, offering unsettling, distorted visions and, in its circumvention of embodiment, constitutes a radical commentary on the evident resistance between circus performance and literary narration.

Above all circus figures, Dickens is interested in the clown yet, as we have seen, the clown is also associated continuously with death, shadows and absence. Dickens's name has most closely been associated with Joseph Grimaldi who, though his father was a choreographer at Charles Hughes's Royal Circus, worked exclusively as a theatrical rather than a circus clown. Dickens is credited with editing Grimaldi's memoirs and composing its introduction. It is clear that his father also had a hand in editing the volume, though Dickens biographers disagree over the extent of his contribution.[25] The association is none the less interesting in a number of ways. Firstly, not only is Grimaldi already dead by the time Dickens receives the memoirs, but he had retired from the stage years before when Dickens was twelve years old (a famously significant point in his own life; about the same age, we can calculate, as Sissy Jupe when Signor Jupe abandons her). Dickens's introduction to Grimaldi's memoirs follows his description of a clown act with a lamentation for Grimaldi:

> We have lost that clown now; – he is still alive though, for we saw him only the day before last Bartholomew Fair, eating a real saveloy, and we are sorry to say that he had deserted to the illegitimate drama for he was seated on one of 'Clarke's Circus' waggons: – we have lost that Clown and that pantomime, but our relish for the entertainment still remains unimpaired.[26]

Here, again, the clown, who is no clown in particular but the pantomime clown in general, is a lost figure who leaves only his animated ghost behind. However, he is a ghost, paradoxically, because he is too much associated with real life (he eats a 'real saveloy' rather than a prop) and has moved to what would have been Alfred Clarke's circus. The prejudice Dickens demonstrates here for pantomime over circus is not substantiated elsewhere, rather this view facilitates his framing of the clown as an always-already 'lost' figure who, perhaps most importantly, possesses an appreciative audience who must necessarily, therefore, always both 'relish' him intensely and be saddened by what is now missing from his performance.

Dickens was not alone in this nostalgic championing of the pantomime. In an essay of 1817, Leigh Hunt enthusiastically asserts, 'Yes, there is something *real* in Pantomime: there is animal spirit in it'.[27] At the same time he constructs the clown's energies as being parallel to the positive aspects of the modern world in 'its bustle, its variety, and its sudden changes'.[28] Yet by 1831 this tendency towards reflecting the

Zeitgeist seems to have become a detrimental tendency for Hunt when he declares that 'It is agreed on all hands that Pantomimes are not what they were' because they 'have become partakers of the serious spirit of the age' and therefore appear 'to be waiting for the settlement of certain great questions and heavy national accounts, to know when they are to laugh and be merry again'.[29] The rhetoric of accountancy in Hunt's terms is of course evocative of Gradgrindism, but it is difficult to separate, in both Dickens and Hunt, weariness with the performance of clowning and of pantomime in general which, since the retirement of Grimaldi in 1824 has lost its leading light, and weariness with the growing political influence of utilitarianism which *Hard Times* satirises so sharply. Certainly there is little evidence to suggest that circus pantomime lacked 'bustle' in the late 1820s and 1830s; on the contrary, as we have seen (Part I), with Ducrow at the height of his popularity, pantomimic performance was at its most exciting, fast-moving, popular and celebratory, even in its engagement with politically topical material. Rather, it seems more plausible that what saddens Hunt and Dickens is the loss, or at least the transformation, of the sort of clown pantomime which provided a continuity between the modern theatre and the long-standing clown performances in the *commedia dell'arte* tradition going back to the town square and fair shows of the Renaissance period throughout Europe. The small-scale space of the theatrical facilitated a close focus on the skill of individual actors whereas in the already highly commercialised circus the individual skills of the performer are transformed by the necessity of capturing the attention of increasingly vast audiences and competing for this with elaborate music and sets as well as, often, other performers.[30] In some ways, Dickens's and Hunt's mourning over the pantomime clown is also a mourning over the loss of artisanship to industrialisation and of human to commercial values.

Edwin Eigner suggests biographical reasons for the absence of the clown and his mournful and evasively indirect presence at this point in Dickens's career; reasons which are entirely consistent with this argument in that Eigner argues that Dickens's father, John, was the model for Wilkins Micawber in *David Copperfield* (1850) and that, following Dickens's witnessing of his father's harrowing death from unsuccessful, bloody and anaesthetic-free surgery in 1851, Dickens's portraiture of clown-like figures who had previously been positive and regenerative, was thereafter either mournful or corrupted by the remembrance of the grotesque conditions in which Dickens last saw his father.[31] Yet such a reading can only account for the absence of positive depictions of the clown after 1851 and not the negative ones which precede this since Dickens's earliest clown portrait, Dismal Jem Hutley's tale in *The Pickwick Papers* (1837), is surely his grimmest.[32] Here the pantomime clown's mute performance occurs, not on stage, but on the streets of London and on his deathbed, with each step of his decline being accompanied in Hutley's narration by the uncomfortable juxtaposition of laughter ('the roar of laughter which followed his first tumble onto the stage' (p. 34), 'the clown's shrill laugh' (p. 36) and the physical contortions of his 'withered limbs' in death are described as though 'he was acting-he was at the theatre' (p. 37). The closer the clown comes to death the more he is characterised as a successful clown; his final moment, full of convulsion, gesture and muteness seems to be his most spectacular performance. Yet his mute gestures are an inadequate substitute for speech. In fact, failing to make himself understood, gesturing becomes a terrible block to expression as he clearly struggles to express himself finally in words but cannot do so.

This association of the clown with death and morbid speechlessness helps us makes sense of the fact that it is the absence of the clown, his departure from the circus and from his family, which triggers the opening event of *Hard Times*: Sissy's presence in the schoolroom. It is the clown's absence which is generative of narrative. Signor Jupe has indeed exiled himself from Sleary's circus, but this does not seem to be because his skills are out of place in Sleary's, which is a far cry from Astley's in scale and revenue, indeed is mostly a small-town and rural circus. Rather, whatever skills Jupe possessed now seem to have disappeared and we are told he is 'missing his tip' and 'loose in his ponging' (pp. 39–40). Although he might become a 'cackler', E. W. B. Childers assures Gradgrind and Bounderby that there is no living to be made in this occupation and it is of great importance that the cackler is defined as a talking clown who engaged in verbal quips with the ringmaster. However, whilst Dickens may, in his introduction to the Grimaldi memoirs, have exhibited a certain nostalgia for a lost, in some way more authentic, form of clowning, in *Hard Times* the function of the clown figure throughout the text is considerably more radical and complex.

Contemporary accounts of Grimaldi's pantomime offer crucial insights into the difficult relationship with which Dickens must grapple between the physical movement of the mute clown performance and language itself: the language of performance and the language of representing performance:

> It always appeared to us that Grimaldi *moved his ears*; and this, anatomically speaking is not an impossibility. Be it as it may, the way in which he drew down his lower jaw on any sudden surprise gave this effect to the auricular organs. Speech would have been thrown away on this performance of Clown: every limb of him had a language.

> An attempt to describe Mr Grimaldi's Clown has always proved a failure: his humour could not be tied down to pen, ink and paper: it was an essence too subtle to yield to phraseology ...[33]

> The face of Grimaldi is a source of laughter, night after night, to many hundreds of people; it is a living jest-book, in which may be read all the whimsical notions which owe their birth to his prolific fancy. There is not, perhaps, a more perfect *figure of fun* to be found in existence ...[34] (author's emphasis)

Ducrow, in Oxberry's memoir of the same era, is celebrated as representing the zenith of pantomime achievement: whilst 'in the air', Ducrow 'reminds us of that celebrated eulogy on the memes of old. Their very nods speak – their hands talk, their fingers have voices'.[35] Each of these accounts establish that the pantomimists' use of their body, whether as clowns or equestrians, constitutes an effective language in itself; not only is Grimaldi's face a 'jest-book', but 'every limb of him had a language'. Most importantly, the second quotation suggests the critic's awareness of a fundamental incongruity between this essentially mute language of the body and any attempt on the part of writers to capture this 'essence' which resists and refuses to 'yield' to the abstractions of 'phraseology'. As Eve Sedgwick has already pointed out in the context of her discussion of Gothic fiction, this tension between embodiment and abstraction is one which is constituitive of all fiction, though it is perhaps most overtly dramatised within the Gothic.[36] Yet the clown issues a very different kind of fictional challenge in that, far from a being a hysterical body, one in which spoken language is blocked and rerouted into a body which consequently suffers physical debilitation (a body essentially talking to itself), it is one which, on the contrary, performs with beauty, ease and humour and which, far from being frustrated by the spoken word, seems instead to bypass it.

Although Jacques Derrida, in his essay 'The double session', does not explicitly discuss the representational terms of the circus, he comes very close to it in his engagement with Mallarmé's figure of the Pierrot clown (in *Mimique*) which he examines in conjunction with Plato's discourse on mimesis in his *Philebus* dialogue.[37] Derrida explicitly addresses the relationship of the mimed performance to writing or, more specifically, to what Derrida calls the 'play of literature and truth' which constitute the post-Platonic understanding of mimesis:

> In the beginning of this mime was neither the deed nor the word. It is prescribed ... to the Mime that he not let anything be prescribed to him but his own writing, that he not reproduce by imitation any action (*pragma*: affair, thing, act) or any speech (*logos*: word, voice, discourse). The Mime ought only to write himself on the white page he is; he must *himself* inscribe *himself* through gestures and plays of facial expressions. At once page and quill, Pierrot is both passive and active, matter and form, the author, the means, and the raw material of his mimodrama.[38]

As the previous accounts of Grimaldi's performance suggest, the mime (and other circus acts) may be by definition mute, but within this the movements of the body form a 'gestural writing' which bypasses any mimetic purpose in that, rather than mirroring or imitating something which precedes or follows it, his performance is a 'textual labyrinth panelled with mirrors' which are facing inwards rather than outwards, backwards or fowards.[39] Thus the clown writes himself, is his own 'page', 'quill', 'author' and 'raw material', and cannot, therefore, be 'subjected to the authority of any book'. The 'truth' of the clown has nothing to do with verisimilitude 'but truth as the present unveiling of the present' which contains a 'lustre which is itself nothing beyond its own fragmented light'.[40] In this way Mallarmé, in his description of *Pierrot Murderer of His Wife* as 'a mute soliloquy that the phantom, white as a yet unwritten page, holds in both face and gesture', also allows us to account for the ghostliness and emptiness which so frequently underpins representations of clowns and other mute performances.[41] The performance generates its own 'lustre' but not one which can reach 'beyond the looking glass' to the world. As such it constitutes a 'reference without a referent, without any first or last unit, a ghost that is the phantom of no flesh, wandering about without a past, without any death, birth or presence.'[42] Almost, paradoxically, the performance which is most firmly founded in bodily gestures, physical skills and athleticism is the one which, referentially, is the most ghostly since, embodying nothing but its present self, it is always, representationally, a white 'unwritten page'.

Looking again at *Hard Times* in the light of this discourse, we can view the disappearance of the clown differently: as the event which initiates the narrative but which is absent from it. The clown is not only absent as a character but also as a performance since, as Derrida has claimed, he may only represent himself. Yet the account of the clown as his own 'page', author' and 'raw material' suggests the potential for an impossible identification between author and figure, between Dickens and Jupe, both of whom who are figures absent from the narrative but who are, at the same time, the ghostly father-figures and absent clowns who shadow it. This reading would be reinforced by the fact that, as I suggest above, one of the things most obvious in *Hard Times* is its almost complete evasion of the direct presentation of any circus performance and its redirecting of circus images into metaphors which not only describe other things (failed family relationships, grotesque industrial landscapes, colonial exploitation), but do so using language within which loss, emptiness and melancholia are implicit and which often at the same time register a loss of faith in the authority of literary language. Yet there are two further ways in which the circus marks *Hard Times*, though the mark which it leaves in both cases also takes the form of noticeable absences, holes or, what Steven Connor refers to as 'blind spots'.[43]

Firstly, the novel follows Gradgrind's opening expostulations about the primacy of facts with a detailed account of the performative dimensions of these words:

> The scene was a plain, bare, monotonous vault of a schoolroom, and the speaker's square forefinger emphasised his observations by underscoring every sentence with a line on the schoolmaster's sleeve. The emphasis was helped by the square wall of a forehead, which had his eyebrows fore its base, while his eyes found commodious cellarage in two dark caves, overshadowed by the wall. The emphasis was helped by the speaker's mouth, which was wide, thin and hard set. The emphasis was helped by the speaker's voice,

which was inflexible, dry and dictatorial. The emphasis was helped by the speaker's hair, which bristled on the skirts of his bald head, a plantation of firs to keep the wind from its shining surface, all covered with knobs, like the crust of a plum pie, as if the head had scarcely warehouse-room for the hard facts stored inside. The speaker's obstinate carriage, square coat, square legs, square shoulders, – nay, his very neckcloth, trained to take him by the throat with an unaccommodating grasp, like a stubborn fact, as it was, – all helped the emphasis. (pp. 1–2)

The metaphorical work of this portrait, like so many of Dickens's most famous comic portraits, constructs Gradgrind's character in terms of a series of absurd juxtapositions of incongruous physical objects (the 'plantation of firs' on Gradgrind's head surrounded by 'the crust of a plum pie') and by transforming personal physical appearance through the use of surreal and inappropriate adjectives (in this case the exact squareness of Gradgrind's every dimension). These, as William F. Axton observes, are all examples of the way in which Dickens's prose at times resembles 'the popular theatre of the day' in which there were 'inventions of unlikely beings and objects tumbling about amid incompatible juxtapositions of everyday things' and facilitates the 'sprightly transposition of animate and inanimate worlds where pantomime clowns became animals, vegetables, and objects, and where machinery, inanimate things, and vegetable life turned into people or took on some extraordinary activity of their own.'[44] This makes an excellent summary of Bakhtin's *carnivalistic mésalliances* in which things which had previously belonged to different and discrete categories 'are drawn into carnivalistic contacts and combinations'.[45] But it is also much more than this, since it describes what Dickens will do throughout the book with his use of circus metaphors, such as the account of the industrial landscape, in which inanimate (factory machinery) is allied with animate life (the 'mad melancholy elephants'). The absurd *mésalliances* which, in the circus, take place between physically present things (a clown with a bladder on his head or a man riding round the ring with a beehive on his hand), take place in Dickens between language (metaphor) and object; between, in Saussurian terms, the signifier (the metaphor) and the signified (that which it represents).

What is most interesting in this paragraph then, is the way that the very physical gestures which make Gradgrind a clown (his square finger, bristling hair and so on) work to contain and even undermine an investment in the language of his body. This account is placed entirely in relation to the written word by the insistent use of the term 'emphasise'. Gradgrind's body is not emphatic in itself, it does not underscore its own meaning, does not constitute a reliable language in itself but rather is illustrative *in relation to* the words which precede it. These words communicate Gradgrind's belief in the centrality of written language (the letter and the number), even while Dickens mocks him through a series of metaphors which portray him as a ridiculous clown and, with the metaphor of the strangulating square neckcloth, finally suggest that Gradgrind's uncompromising squareness will result in his self-destruction. With every gesture Gradgrind makes to emphasise his words, it is not the gesture that makes him ridiculous but the way in which the gesture is freighted with absurdity as it is transformed into a grotesque or inappropriate shape precisely through the use of metaphorical language.

The second way in which the circus marks the language of *Hard Times* is through an ongoing depiction of gaps and vacancies, a rhetoric which produces some of the novel's oddest and most striking moments. Steven Connor has already provided an invaluable and exhaustive deconstructive reading of Sissy's misnaming of statistics as 'stutterings' (p. 75) in her discussion with Louisa about her failure to grasp M'Choakumchild's systematic teachings. He argues that the structure of this joke depends on reading Sissy's 'stutterings' as a reference to Mr Sleary's lisp, and as such it 'bring[s] forward the materiality of signifiers, which delays or prevents the simple substitution of words for things'. By highlighting the signifier's lack of transparency 'the joke reveals the structure of difference which constitutes authority of meaning'.[46] But Susan Stewart's account of the relationship between the spoken and written word suggests a greater prominence be given to the role of the body in the physical performance of a 'stutter':

> The space between letters, the space between words, bears no relation to the stutters and pauses of speech. Writing has none of the hesitation of the body; it has only the hesitation of knowing, the hesitations which arise from its place outside history – transcendent yet lacking the substantiating power of context.[47]

By accidentally but insistently identifying stutterings in the statistical 'facts' she is taught, Sissy draws attention to the difference between the speech which is bodily mediated *before* and whilst it becomes the physical performance of enunciation and the regulation of written figures. Like M'Choakumchild's method (itself representative of a utilitarian capitalist method) written language and its coherent oral delivery may only operate at the cost of suspending hesitation by placing itself above and beyond history and, with this, discourse. Again, however, we have the illustration of a gap between a physically performed language and the possibility of registering this in a written inscription, since the tendency of the latter is always to regulate or erase the 'stutter'.

Many of the gaps which surround this scene may likewise be identified as 'stutters' within the system. The incident which lends chapter 3 its title, 'A Loophole', has Louisa and Tom 'peeping' into the circus through a hole in the 'deal board' which make up the circus's walls. The trope, as we have already seen, is repeated when Louisa and Sissy return to see the circus when it is giving temporary shelter to Tom. As Schlicke points out, this is both a literal and a metaphorical loophole, yet is hard to decide whether, as a metaphorical loophole, it exists within Sleary's or Gradgrind's system since, although it is a dimension of Sleary's property, it opens up a space between the two worlds which facilitates a temporary respite for the two 'models' (p. 11) to escape their place of production.[48] Given that a loophole is the place within any system which offers an escape from or evasion of it through some form of internal contradiction or oversight, and since it is Tom and Louisa rather than any members of the circus for whom it represents an escape, it makes sense to see the loophole, not as a gap within the circus system, but as a doubled image of the circus ring which itself was formed in response to a legal loophole in theatrical legislation (with regard to horses) which was spotted by Astley and others. Thus this loophole becomes the figure which precisely represents the circus as a 'necessary safety valve' which, as Kwint suggests, constituted the 'functionalist view of entertainment' that by the 1850s 'had prevailed over the ideology of unrelenting labour'.[49] In these terms the circus, and other forms of popular entertainment, were a product of and attachment to industrial society, blocking off from which caused both enervation (Louisa) and pent-up frustrations (Tom). This reading of the loophole is substantiated by the evidence of the end of the novel where Sleary, in contrast to Gradgrind's blindness to the possibility of a loophole and his subsequent hurry to block his children's access to it, is not only fully aware of the 'dodgeth' people play on him, but actively directs Sissy and Louisa to 'take a peep at the ring' through the 'thpy-hole' (p. 375).

Yet such a reading sees the circus providing the metaphor of the loophole which stands for the circus itself, or at least a realist reading of its social function. In other examples the gaps Dickens opens up in his text seem to introduce more intangible and troubling meanings. One such moment occurs early on when Bounderby has persuaded Louisa to allow him to kiss her on the cheek. But the circumstances leading up to the kiss colour the encounter with the terms of economic exchange as Bounderby, claiming to have smoothed things over with their father for them after the peeping incident, tries to persuade Louisa that 'that's worth a kiss', to which she is forced to reply 'You can take one, Mr Bounderby.' So much does she resent his taking of a kiss, however, that she stands fixed to the spot 'rubbing the cheek he had kissed, with her handkerchief, until it was burning red'. Tom cautions her that she will 'rub a hole in your face' to which her determined response is, 'you may cut the piece out with your penknife if you like, Tom. I wouldn't cry!' (p. 27). The meaning of burning fire will again be metaphorically significant and ambiguous slightly later on when the fire in her room becomes both the only space in which her 'unmanageable thoughts' are given free reign to 'wonder' (Tom asks whether she sees a circus in it), but the short-lived energy of its sparks finally inspire her only to conclude, 'how short my life would be, and how little I could hope to do with it' (pp. 70–1). Thus the fire implies resistance (to Bounderby and to Gradgrind's regime) and self-destruction and it is this metaphorical double-edgedness which is significant in relation to the narrator's earlier description of her as 'a fire with nothing to burn' (p. 16) and Tom's later description of her as 'crammed' with 'sawdust' (p. 179). Later she describes her life to Tom as lying 'through all the night of my decay, until I am dust' (p. 252). The former suggests the waste and potential danger of undirected energy and the latter metaphor implies that her desire to fight off Bounderby is gone and that indulging any desire to do so might only be self-destructive.

Of course the mark on her face is also a further example of what Peter Brooks refers to as the text of muteness which permeated melodramatic and pantomimic stage theatre of the nineteenth century and which found its way into the novel in the second half of the century.[50] This circular burning ring on Louisa's face is the mute figure which represents what cannot be spoken by her, feelings so violent that she threatens to intensify their physical manifestation into a permanent physical scarring by gouging a hole in her own cheek. In this sense the mark on Louisa's cheek represents a continuity between her and the industrial workers over whom Bounderby also has economic control and who are forced to yield up to him their bodily labour under the mask of the free exchange of labour.[51] The problem for the novel is that, paradoxically, in order to represent muteness it must use language. Yet so excessive is the image of the burning circle on her face that it becomes a kind of emblem of muteness itself, far exceeding its own literal meaning and, in this sense, it is another displaced figure of the circus: a circular figure, mutely expressive, visibly and spectacularly emblazoned. This use of fire as the place of the most brightly significant but indecipherable or inaccessible meanings is used again when an uncertain Louisa looks to 'her own fire within the house' and the 'fiery haze without' in search of some clue to her own fate. Her search, however, is fruitless, since not only does 'Old Time' not speak, but even 'his Hands are mutes' (p. 126).[52] Entirely metaphorically then, the circus is present in the narrative as the figurative link between a complex chain of interconnections between circularity, fire, sawdust, imagination and muteness which serve equally to fuel the novel's ongoing thematic antagonisms and as well suggesting the limitations of its representational scope and of literary language in general.

Perhaps the best example of this occurs towards the end of the second book when Louisa is involved in another painful encounter, this time involving her mother whom she finds on her deathbed. Mrs Gradgrind seems to have become increasingly confused and weakened; indeed we are told that 'the sound of another voice addressing her seemed to take such a long time in getting down to her ears, that she might have been lying at the bottom of a well'. Yet, in finding herself in this place which, again, the narrative likens to a darkened hole, we are told that she is 'nearer Truth than she ever had been' (p. 264). She appears to have lost contact with her own physical senses; when Louisa asks her if she is in pain she replies, 'I think there's a pain somewhere in the room ... but I couldn't positively say that I have got it' (p. 264). It is as though her body is a figure now also emptied like the well. This sense is reinforced by her urgent and increasingly desperate need to communicate something to Louisa:

But there is something-not an Ology at all-that your father has missed, or forgotten, Louisa. I don't know what it is. I have often sat with Sissy near me, and thought about it. I shall never get its name now. But your father may. It makes me restless. I want to write to him, to find out for God's sake, what it is. Give me a pen, give me a pen. (p. 266)

Not only is this something itself another absence, something her father has missed, but it cannot be spoken. As in the previous scene, Mrs Gradgrind's final unintelligible scribblings ('what figures of wonderful no-meaning she began to trace upon her wrappers' [p. 267]) are meaningful only insofar as they signify absence, the inadequacy of the signs of communication (written and verbal), and the gaps in Gradgrind's 'system', all of which concepts have been figuratively tied to the circus in the novel.

The description of Mrs Gradgrind's disappearing voice is also a clear anticipation of the situation in which Stephen Blackpool is to find himself in book 3 when, fleeing the law which has wrongfully charged him with the bank robbery, he fatally falls down an abandoned mine shaft. He too, therefore, carries with him to the bottom of the shaft a suppressed and unspoken truth which at this stage is socially proscribed and physically swamped. It is also significant that the drama of his final hours is quite specifically likened to a macabre and inverted circus spectacle. Bounderby draws attention to the search by printing up the details of the crime and of Stephen's appearance 'in great black letters on a staring broadsheet' as he goes about stirring up a crowd which will finally assemble itself around the top of the 'Old Hell Shaft' into which Stephen, now both outlawed and on the run, has fallen. The crowd, who have brought with them 'windlasses, ropes, poles, candles, lanterns' (p. 356) form 'a large ring round' (p. 357) the shaft, full of hushed expectation and united by morbid voyeurism who look on 'attentively' with 'all eyes were fastened on the pit' (p. 358) and in 'rapt suspense' (p. 359) as the candlelit operation of wynching up and down by ropes, which disappear into the hole 'ring by ring', is enacted before them with only one 'interval' (p. 358). With the spectacular death of Stephen Blackpool, in which his body is reduced to 'the figure of a poor, crushed, human creature' (p. 361), Dickens reverses the circus's celebration of the body which, as I have suggested in my discussion of circus aesthetics, idealistically dramatises the human potential to withstand and conquer all the challenges of the modern industrial world (speed, height, other cultures and creatures). In doing so, he foregrounds the destructive and overwhelming capacity of both industrialisation's substructures and of the social formations it engenders. At the same time, this scene makes it harder to read Sleary's claim that people 'must be amuthed' (p. 53) as a call for the preservation of circus as an innocent distraction from industrial labour. The fact that Dickens so precisely mirrors the dynamics of spectator/circus relations in Stephen's hounding-out and exhumation makes it clear that the circus is not an alternative to labour but, rather, is industrialism's own diversion, sharing but inverting its language. Both of these scenes (Stephen's and Mrs Gradgrind's death), although they involve characters who have not previously been seen as having any connection to the circus plot in the novel, work to connect the circus, through a series of displaced rhetorical figures, with a premature morbidity, like Dickens's clowns discussed above, which has its root in supressed speech or knowledge.[53]

It is worth noting the use of the adjective 'wonderful' here in the description of these 'figures' of 'no-meaning' since it belongs to the novel's deliberate and ongoing misapplication of a rhetoric of astonishment. This involves the continual use of terms such as 'wonder', 'astonishment' and 'amazement' which imply mute appreciation. Though they are common enough rhetorical terms, especially in the nineteenth-century novel, here they are specifically associated with the circus, therefore their ironic use to describe facts or events which are usually utterly mundane is significant. Gradgrind's redirection of wonderment follows his appropriation and perversion of the terms of wonderment ('In the name of wonder, idleness and folly!' [p. 15]) and what we learn has been an earlier injunction, 'Louisa, never wonder!' (p. 64). Thereafter, Bounderby warns Mrs Sparsit 'I am going to astonish you' (p. 139) with the news of his marriage to Louisa, but he is disconcerted by his lack of effect since this is news she has been fully prepared for. In a description of the landscape of Coketown in which it is presented as a 'dense, formless jumble' which 'showed nothing but masses of darkness', the narrator tells us that 'The wonder was, it was there at all' (p. 146). James Harthouse, still 'a stranger', on learning from Mrs Sparsit that Louisa married Bounderby when she was 'Not twenty', replies, 'I was never so astonished in my life!' (p. 162). Later the narrator tells us that Harthouse, although it is 'much against the precepts of his school to wonder', in the face of Tom's increasingly desperate behaviour he managed to raise 'his eyelids a little more, as if they were touched by a feeble touch of wonder' (p. 235). Slackridge, on telling the assembly of workers of Stephen Blackpool's refusal to strike, addresses them with, 'I do not wonder that you, the prostrate sons of labour, are incredulous of the existence of such a man' (p. 185) and is subsequently described as being in possession of 'a wonderful moral power' (pp. 189–90). In each case wonder and astonishment have been hijacked by a character who is demonstrated to be manipulative in his use of illusion (as deceit) for false or calculating ends. In the case of the landscape, its use is ironically inappropriate in that we are drawn to wonder, not at the indistinct, illusory presence of the town, but at the fact of its continuing existence. By contrast, Sissy qualifies her reaction to Louisa's change of behaviour towards her after her marriage with, 'Not that I wondered at it' (p. 300). Wonderment and astonishment, in being banished from industrial Coketown and the Gradgrind regime (which holds that everything can be explained and defined), are corrupted in the same way that the circus images of the Fairy palaces, elephants and serpents become ugly and threatening when they metaphorically represent Coketown. They have become not aspects of the performance but rhetorical devices, part of the performance of Dickens's writing, the terms of which, as I have suggested, cannot directly accommodate the object it describes (the circus) and which therefore draws attention to its own processes of abstraction and illusion by misplacing and inverting the rhetorical terms and the generic figures of the entertainment it represents.

The circus, either as a whole or in the form of its individual performers, consistently appears in Dickens's writings as something either already beyond his text or as an unstable or excessive metaphor, a gap, an absence or a ghostly presence within it. Far from constituting a focus for sentimental or nostalgic feeling, as has sometimes been claimed of Dickens's circuses, *Hard Times*, in common with several other works by Dickens, harbours an implicit recognition of the circus's resistance to, in Derrida's terms, the 'play of literature and truth' which has been the discursive basis of forms of mimetic representation (including the novel). The result is a novel which evades, complicates and honours the challenge which the mute, gestural, athletic and noisy circus issues to modes of representation which might seek to commemorate or inscribe it. In *Hard Times* the circus is abstracted into a series of spectral metaphors which complicate hackneyed idealising clichés of the circus by weaving circus figures into an industrial landscape which is touched by references to Empire. Yet it is also legible as a series of 'loopholes' in the text through which the form or rhetoric of the circus interrupts the textual performances of literary emodiment which the novel parades.

Notes

1 See Paul Schlicke, *Dickens and Popular Entertainment* (London, George Allen & Unwin, 1985), 'Dickens in the Circus', *Theatre Notebook*, 47:1 (1993), pp. 3–19, and Schlicke's 'Theatre and Theatricality' and 'Circus' entries in Paul Schlicke (ed.), *Oxford Reader's Companion to Dickens* (Oxford, Oxford University Press, 1999), pp. 102–4 and pp. 559–64.

2 For examples of both tendencies in nineteenth-century literature see Wilkie Collins, *Hide and Seek* (Oxford, Oxford University Press [1854], 1993), Amy Reade, *Ruby; a Novel, Founded on the Life of a Circus Girl* (London, Writer's Co-operative Publishing Co., 1889) and *Slaves of the Sawdust* (London, F. V. White & Co., 1892). *Ruby* contains an explicit demonisation of Sleary when a sadistic circus manager, Signor Enrico, defends his brutal methods for training young girls with the line, 'The public must be amused; they have a right to demand what they can pay for ...', p. 414.

3 Paul Schlicke, 'Introduction', *Hard Times* (Oxford, Oxford University Press [1854], 1989), p. xx.

4 Willson Disher, *Greatest Show on Earth* (London, Bell, 1937), p. 91.

5 Marius Kwint, 'Astley's amphitheatre and the early circus in England, 1768–1830' (D.Phil thesis, Oxford, 1994), p. 243.

6 Charles Dickens, 'Astley's', *Dickens' Journalism: Sketches by Boz and Other Early Papers, 1833–39*, ed. Michael Slater (London, J. M. Dent, 1994), pp. 106–11.

7 This reference to Roman lettering also makes us think of the sign outside the Pegasus Arms in *Hard Times* in which Steven Connor reads a process of 'metonymic accretion' through which the sign continually deflects connections between itself, the figure of Pegasus, the circus poster and the circus, thereby making it 'difficult to see the bar as stable and self-contained' whilst at the same time drawing 'close attention to the signifiers themselves, in their material shape and texture', *Charles Dickens* (Oxford, Oxford University Press, 1985), p. 93.

8 Charles Dickens, 'The Pantomime of Life', in *Dickens' Journalism* (pp. 500–7), p. 507. Though this view of pantomime as mimetic is contradicted elsewhere by Dickens when he suggests that the pleasure of the pantomime for 'an audience of vulnerable spectators, liable to pain and sorrow' may find itself 'superior to all the accidents of life, though encountering them

at every turn', 'A Strange Dance Round a Strange Tree', *Household Words*, 17 January (1852), p. 386.

9 Charles Dickens, *Pictures from Italy* (Harmondsworth, Penguin Books [1846], 1998), pp. 67–9.

10 Kate Flint, Introduction, *Pictures from Italy*, p. xxiii.

11 John Schad, 'Dickens's cryptic Church: drawing on *Pictures from Italy*', in John Schad (ed.), *Dickens Re-Figured: Bodies, Desires and Other Histories* (Manchester: Manchester University Press, 1996), p. 8.

12 Charles Dickens, *Hard Times*, ed. Paul Schlicke (Oxford, Oxford University Press, [1854] 1989).

13 Kwint, 'Astley's amphitheatre', p. 155.

14 Raymond Williams, *Culture and Society 1780–1950* (Harmondsworth, Penguin Books [1958], 1984), p. 106. see also, Robert E. Lougy 'Dickens's *Hard Times*: the romance as radical literature', in Harold Bloom (ed.), *Charles Dickens's Hard Times* (New York, Chelsea House, 1987), pp. 12–15.

15 Catherine Gallagher, *The Industrial Reformation of English Fiction: Social Discourse and Narrative Form 1832–1867* (Chicago, Chicago University Press, 1985), pp. 149–66.

16 *Oxberry's Dramatic Biography; Or, The Green-Room Spy*, vol. 1 (London, G. Virtue, 1827), p. 119.

17 Schlicke, *Dickens and Popular Entertainment*, p. 156.

18 Schlicke, *Dickens and Popular Entertainment*, p. 168.

19 William Hazlitt, 'The Indian Jugglers' (1825), *Selected Writings* (Oxford, Oxford University Press, 1991), p. 128.

20 Gallagher, *The Industrial Reformation of English Fiction*, pp. 160–1.

21 Razak Dahmane, ' "A Mere Question of Figures": measures, mystery, and metaphor in *Hard Times*', *Dickens Studies Annual*, 23 (1994) pp. 137–61.

22 Gallagher, *The Industrial Reformation of English Fiction*, p. 162.

23 Schlicke, *Dickens and Popular Entertainment*, pp. 152–3.

24 Connor, *Charles Dickens*, p. 165.

25 Richard Findlater claims that the young Dickens was too much preoccupied at this time with establishing his name in journalism and that his father completed the bulk of the editorial work, whilst Peter Ackroyd says that 'Dickens's method was to cut an already abridged account and then dictate the results to his father'. See Richard Findlater, Introduction, - *Memoirs of Joseph Grimaldi* (London, Macgibbon & Kee [1838], 1968), p. 11, and Peter Ackroyd, *Dickens* (London, Sinclair-Stevenson, 1990), p. 241.

26 Charles Dickens, *Grimaldi; the Clown* (London, George Routledge & Sons [1838], 1884), p. 12.

27 Leigh Hunt, 'On pantomime', 5 January 1817, reprinted in *Leigh Hunt's Dramatic Criticism; 1801–1831*, ed. Lawrence Huston Houtchens and Carolyn Washburn Houtchens (New York, Columbia University Press, 1949) (pp. 140–3), p. 140.

28 Leigh Hunt 'On pantomime, continued from a late paper', 26 January 1817, reprinted as a footnote to 'On pantomime', in *Leigh Hunt's Dramatic Criticism*, pp. 312–3.

29 Leigh Hunt, *The Tatler*, 28 December 1831, reprinted in *Leigh Hunt's Dramatic Criticism*, p. 330.

30 In his introduction to the Grimaldi memoirs Dickens asks 'What mattered it that the stage was 3 yards wide, and four deep? *We* never saw it. We had no eyes, ears, or coporeal senses, but for the pantomime.' *Grimaldi; the Clown*, p. 10.

31 Edwin M. Eigner, *The Dickens Pantomime* (Berkeley, California University Press, 1989) pp. 169–71.

32 Charles Dickens, *The Pickwick Papers*, ed. James Kinsley (Oxford, Oxford University Press [1837], 1988).

33 Quoted in Findlater, *Grimaldi: King of Clowns* (p. 151). Reference given as *New Monthly Magazine*, July 1839, but I have not been able to locate the reference in this source.

34 *The Champion*, 29 December 1816, p. 132.

35 'Memoir of Andrew Ducrow', *Oxberry's Dramatic Biography*, vol. 2 (pp. 1–15), p. 14.

36 Eve Sedgwick, *The Coherence of Gothic Conventions* (London, Methuen, 1986).

37 Jacques Derrida, *Dissemination*, trans. Barbara Johnson (London, Athlone Press [1972], 1997), pp. 173–286.

38 Derrida, *Dissemination*, p. 198.

39 Derrida, *Dissemination*, p. 195.

40 Derrida, *Dissemination*, p. 206 and p. 208.

41 Derrida, *Dissemination*, p. 175.

42 Derrida, *Dissemination*, p. 206.

43 Connor, *Charles Dickens*, p. 168.

44 As William F. Axton, *Circle of Fire: Dickens' Vision and Style and the Popular Theater* (Lexington, Kentucky University Press, 1966), p. 29.

45 Mikhail Bakhtin, *Problems of Dostoevsky's Poetics* (Manchester, Manchester University Press [1973], 1984), p. 123.

46 Connor, *Charles Dickens*, pp. 166–7.

47 Susan Stewart, *On Longing: Narratives of the Miniature, the Gigantic the Souvenir, the Collection* (Durham, NC, and London, Duke University Press [1984], 1993), p. 31.

48 Paul Schlicke, Introduction to *Hard Times*, p. vii.

49 Kwint, 'Astley's amphitheatre', p. 116.

50 Peter Brooks, *The Melodramatic Imagination: Balzac, Henry James, Melodrama, and the Mode of Excess* (New Haven and London, Yale University Press [1976], 1995), pp. 56–80.

51 Catherine Gallagher has already suggested that, within a system of metaphorical connections which move and change in the novel, Louisa and

Tom are amongst the schoolchildren who are collectively and metaphorically (but temporarily) linked to industrial workers in the first chapters of
the book and also that, for the first half of the novel, Louisa and Stephen
are directly connected in that their 'stories proceed on independent but
parallel courses' until the second half of the novel when their interests
come into direct conflict over the figure of Tom. In the first half, their
stories may, as Gallagher argues, 'intersect only through their common
inclusion of Mr Bounderby', but, as this scene shows, they are both
physically exploited by him, even at this stage. See *The Industrial Reformation of British Fiction*, p. 150.

52 As a novel of the same period which is dedicated and critically connected
to Dickens's, Wilkie Collins's *Hide and Seek* provides a valuable contrast to
Hard Times in terms of its contrasting representation of circus muteness.
Unlike Dickens, for whom muteness constitutes an ongoing figure for the
problem of representation in the novel, Collins directly embodies it in the
single figure of Madonna. Her muteness, however, far from being a performance to be admired and wondered at, is an irreversible affliction which
turns her into an object of pathos and concern. Although Madonna's
muteness disrupts the novel at the level of plot, since the relationship of
Madonna and her mother to all the other characters is its central enigma,
these issues are finally resolved. Dickens, on the other hand fills his text
with mute moments, often cloaked in dramatic metaphor, and these open
up substantial questions and problems within the text which remain
unanswered.

53 Again, see Steven Connor's similar reading of these 'blind spots' in *Charles
Dickens*, p. 168.

7

Subtle, wasted traces:
Fellini and the circus

The Cinema is very much like the circus.[1]

The cinema is also circus, carnival, funfair, a game for acrobats.[2]

It is an art form and at the same time a circus, a funfair, a voyage aboard a kind of 'Ship of Fools', an adventure, an illusion, a mirage. It is an art form which has nothing to do with other arts, least of all with literature.[3]

The special characteristic of the circus is that one is creating and living at the same time, without having to keep inside fixed bounds, as one has to do with painting and with literature − one is constantly involved in action. It's an entertainment that's got force, courage − and I think the cinema is just the same.[4]

Even until very recently critical assessments of Fellini's films have continued to be couched in the terms of old-style auteur criticism. Fellini's status as a remarkable 'artist' of the cinema whose ' "personal" cinema contains a strong autobiographical element'[5] and whose preoccupations are consistently 'expressed' in his films is confirmed through readings which search out the traces of a distinct narrative and visual 'manner' across his work and through elevating comparisons to 'a short story writer or a lyric poet'.[6] In beginning this discussion with these quotations from him about the circus and the cinema, however, I do not wish to consolidate this approach. On the contrary, I want to demonstrate that these much-cited auteurial statements about the connection between the two art forms voice a desire for their impossible convergence; a desire played out in several of his films but which is also inevitably frustrated. The circus, then, is not just another of Fellini the auteur's 'personal obsessions', rather his cinematic renderings of the circus point up a failure, or at least a gap, between his reported declarations about the relationship between the two forms and what is possible. This is because, most especially in *The Clowns*, Fellini's films demonstrate a more complex and subtle under-standing of the difficulties of translating a live art into a mechanically reproduced one than is evident in the much-cited statements above. At stake in this argument is not only the validity of approaches to Fellini's work which have insistently depended on situating him as an auteur, but also the broader issue of the relationship of the cinema to forms of live art, most particularly the circus.

Returning now to the four quotations with which I began, I want to interrogate them for evidence of how Fellini claims to regard what he sees as the close relationship between circus and cinema. He begins with a loose analogy ('the cinema *is very much like* the circus') with which we might indeed concur and subsequently set to compiling a list of overlapping possibilities and characteristics. In the next two state-ments, however, the two forms are placed in a relationship of semi-convergence. Whilst the cinema is a unique art form, Fellini claims, at other times it is capable, not just of resembling, but of *being* another ('The cinema *is also* circus'). Finally, a common essence is identified within each, that of 'creating and living at the same time', which not only allows Fellini to celebrate what he sees as the dual superiority which these two share over all other art forms from which they are decidedly distinct, but also leads him to deliver the claim that they are 'just the *same*'.

It is acceptable to think that the cinema in some respects resembles, or 'is very much like', the circus and I will outline here some suggestions about those resemblances, especially insofar as they relate to four of Fellini's films, *La Strada* (1954), *8½* (1963), *Juliet of the Spirits* (1965) and *The Clowns* (1970). However, whilst several auteur-based critics cited above, have taken their cue from these quotations, none has gone any further than being able to demonstrate that the circus has thematic significance in Fellini films. They have consequently neglected to examine the cultural and formal relationship of the two forms of entertainment, presuming that the cinema is quite definitely *not* the circus and that when Fellini's films contain a circus topos they do not *become* the circus but merely represent it. We can none the less pose a number of productive questions, the answers to which may have significance beyond Fellini's films. Given that the circus is not the cinema, then why would Fellini want to believe that it is? What happens to this desire for convergence in the films themselves? What is at stake in this connection both for Fellini's films and, by extension, for other kinds of cinema?

All this is not to say that it is not important to examine how the circus figures in Fellini's films since it is an indisputably pervasive thematic – from his first solo feature film, *The White Sheik* (1952) during which Ivan Cavelli is entertained in a market square by a juggler at the lowest moment of his apparently hopeless search for his wife, to Marcello Mastroianni's appearance as a ringmaster in *Intervista* (1987). They are even present in unrealised projects such as *The Actor*.[7] Yet beyond this the mobilisation of the circus as a metaphor, and more plainly as a dramatic context, bears on the formal and cultural questions I would like to address subsequently. For example in *La Strada*, though the dominant metaphor of the film appears to be 'the road of life', it is one complicated by all three of the circus players who dominate the film's drama (Il Matto, Gelsomina and Zampanò) whose acts don't so much reflect the linear progression implied by the image of the road, but rather an insistent circularity of movement, especially during performance. Their psychic development is fuelled by returns to familiar physical environments along what becomes a kind of circular road.[8] Most obviously, Zampanò both begins at the edge of the sea, where he buys Gelsomina from her mother, and finally ends up prostrating himself through grief and guilt on the beach where, André Bazin argues, after Gelsomina and Il Matto's deaths he acquires a soul thus completing a circle which demonstrates the 'interdependence of salvation'.[9] For Bazin then, the circus is an interesting metaphor within the film insofar as it offers Fellini the opportunity to dramatise characters who possess 'an aura of the marvellous' within a world which Bazin elevates to the grand level of the 'quasi-Shakespearean'.[10] Thus, though Bazin is interested in the circus to the extent that it provides a means of securing Fellini's status as a serious auteur (itself a move within the larger project of securing the status of film as a serious art form), he remains uninterested in the specificity of the metaphor, something which I would like to explore here.

There is an important distinction to be made between Fellini's metaphorical use of the circus and those figures in *La Strada* whom Fellini allows to *become* the circus. Zampanò is part of the general metaphor which encourages us to compare the journey of life with a travelling show and yet, though he owns his own small show, it is as though he doesn't really belong to the greater world of the circus and cannot participate in its ethos; he is ejected from the circus troupe almost as soon as he arrives. However, whilst he and others *perform* circus acts, thus implying a distance between character and routine, Gelsomina *is* the circus, or rather she is a fantasy of what the circus might be. In this sense she is very much like Chaplin's tramp. Naomi Ritter has already noted the resemblance of style and appearance; but a deeper connection is visible bewteen *La Strada* and Chaplin's only film about the circus, *The Circus* (1928), a film in which the tramp unwittingly becomes part of the clowns' performance when he strays into the circus ring as he attempts to escape from the police.[11] His impromptu antics generate far more excitement and laughter than the professional clowns could ever have hoped to do and he is promptly hired by the manager. As in Gelsomina's training session with Zampanò however, because both figures are natural clowns or life's clowns, training and the introduction of 'technique' or routine only serves to corrupt their facility for entertaining. Both fail miserably in the exercise and, whilst this in itself may be funny in both cases it is only Gelsomina's suffering as a result of her apparent incompetence which jarringly interrupts the comedy. So here Fellini consolidates what Slavoj Žižek has identified as Chaplin's 'wild theory of comedy' which is based on the blindness of a diegetic audience to the scene in front of them.[12] In *The Circus*, Žižek claims, 'the audience laughs and applauds, mistaking his desperate struggle for survival for a comedian's virtuosity – the origin of comedy is to be sought precisely in such cruel blindness, unaware of the tragic reality of a situation', a blindness which is also present in the scene following Zampanò's cruelty to Gelsomina when they perform for an audience in a public square.[13] Žižek's account of Chaplin's construction of dramatic irony is pertinent here because it draws attention to the multiplication of audience points of view available in the cinema but not in the circus; the cinema spectator moves between Gelsomina's, the audience's and their own removed point of view shots and are able to place the spectacle within the context of a narrative, something always unavailable to the circus spectator.

In *8 ½*, after being presented with at least the possibility of Guido shooting himself in the head rather than face critical ridicule and accusation, he is led by Maurice the magician to the circus ring where the circus band of clowns play. Little Guido ushers in all the figures from his life who are all the figures who constitute *8 ½*. As I suggest above in relation to *La Strada*, the construction of visual spectacle in the circus is a relatively simple process compared to what is available in the cinema. The main distinctions are that in the circus characters rarely belie any interiority (they are pure spectacle) and the relations of looking are more direct (the spectator has only one point of view and his or her gaze may be returned by the performer). When Guido turns his world into a circus therefore, it obtains an order and a structure which he was unable to lend it as a film-maker. Yet he has none the less done so on film and this means that the circus is inevitably framed as an impossible and fantastic one because, up to this point, it has been a film in which the distinction between life and performance has been nearly impossible to make and in which distinctions between subjective vision and external reality are constantly undermined or blurred.

In *Juliet of the Spirits* it is Fanny the circus dancer, with whom Giulietta's grandfather absconds, who is the circus in the film, though this function is also shared by Iris and Suzy since they are all played by the same actress and carry some of the same meanings for Giulietta. Like Il Matto, Fanny first appears both on a circus contraption (Il Matto on the high-wire and Fanny on a trapeze swing) and suspended in the air, though at this stage Fanny exists only as an internal diegetic image in Giulietta's head and in this sense is a uniquely cinematic figure from the outset. Shortly after this, as Giulietta retells some significant incidents from her youth we see how Fanny's trapeze may be counterpoised with the blazing grill to which Giulietta is tied as she plays the part of a religious martyr who is hoisted up to the sky, apparently towards God. The two images could not be more different; Fanny is literally alive and kicking as she guides the flower-draped trapeze back and forward, laughing and showily dressed, whilst Giulietta is utterly passive, tied down, draped rather than clothed, suffering a martyrdom, moved by religious authorities and surrounded by deadly flames rather than blooming flowers. Her grandfather proves to be the intermediary figure between the two and it is he who becomes Fanny's lover. Fanny then becomes the symbol of everything that the circus stands for in the film – life, pleasure, autonomy, physical and sexual freedom – and it is her grandfather, or rather Giulietta's memory of him, which finally leads her to liberate herself symbolically and psychologically from the martyrdom which has dominated her life since childhood. She mentally replays the scene of her liberation from the grill, but this time it is Giulietta in the active role of (self) liberator as she takes over from her grandfather and eventually runs to join him in the circus plane with Fanny. Suzy too is connected to this repertoire of airborne creatures through the butterfly on her back, her indoor chute and her outdoor treehouse. Giulietta cannot become Suzy just as she does not belong in the circus, yet her encounters with these figures are the most significant in the film since it is through them that she is able to return to her life anew.

In each of these three cases, then, the circus at times goes beyond simply acting as a metaphor for something else as it enters the film in the form of an impossible figure or a fantasy – Gelsomina, the fool, Fanny the circus dancer, the ring of life. All these figures provide instruction, inspiration, solace and an impetus for positive change, yet with this also inevitably comes a sense of loss and sadness; in itself an acknowledgement of the fact that they are precisely fantastic figures. Each is an unearthly form through whom and from whom the main protagonists move on. This fantastic status is also signalled through the fact that each is also connected to childhood states and dramas – Gelsomina's naïvity, sexual innocence and physical androgyny, Giulietta's childhood trip to the circus and Guido's circus ring at the centre of which is himself as a young boy. The circus is tied up with a nostalgia for childhood,[14] which always fuels action in the present for an adult self; a fantasy which enters the real and which is involved in reconstituting social relationships. At the same time the function and meaning of all three is dependent on their cinematic constitution and, as such, whilst thematically they may point to the connections between the circus and 'creating and living', finally they do more to undermine than illustrate Fellini's assertion that the cinema and the circus are 'just the same'.

What is also evident through this analysis is that there is always a particular kind of ambivalence (fantastic but influential, life-giving but lost and so on) about Fellini's use of circus figures. This ambivalence not only structures aspects of these films but, in doing so, leads us to an investigation of the presence of the carnivalesque within them, for which exercise it is useful to have recourse to Bakhtin.[15] For Bakhtin, there is necessarily an ambivalence and a dualism in all carnival acts which automatically somehow imply an inseparable opposite. Just as 'crowning already contains the idea of immanent de-crowning' and all symbols are 'two-leveled', so carnival expressions such as laughter are also ambivalent.[16] This is because carnival rituals, and especially those which mobilise ritual laughter, '[deal] with the very process of change, with *crisis* itself'. In 'funeral laughter', Bahktin writes, 'ridicule was fused with rejoicing' and this is exactly the confusion of emotion embodied in the clowns' frantic but exhilarating funeral in the last scenes of *The Clowns* .[17] The laughter here links death with rebirth, yet the two are never separable, just as Fellini's circus figures are always both temporary and eternal, past and present, fantastic and real. All of them also provide ways of accommodating crisis, change and renewal.

The circus as discussed above becomes like, or rather overlaps with, the carnival in the sense that it becomes 'the place for working out, in a concretely sensuous, half-real and half-play-acted form, a *new mode of inter-relationship between* individuals, counterpoised to the all-powerful socio-hierarchical relationships of non-carnival life'.[18] In the course of this 'working out' the carnivalistic impulse 'brings together, unifies, weds and combines the sacred and the profane, the lofty with the low, the great with the insignificant, the wise with the stupid'.[19] Undoubtedly it is precisely these two categories of carnival which are at work in Guido's circus ring and are perhaps typified in his gesture of kissing the Cardinal's ring before he joins the circle; a gesture which is potentially one of mockery and as such involves both the removal, possibly ridicule, of the Cardinal's social superiority at the same time as it signals his acceptance into the newly established community and familiarity between individuals.

The cultural significance of Fellini's circuses also comes into focus a little more clearly when the contextual connections with Bakhtin are pursued a little further. In his account of Bakhtin's *Rabelais and his World*,[20] Simon Dentith writes:

> the whole book is best read as a coded attack on the cultural situation of Russia in the 1930s under Stalin – or, to use a more Bakhtinian vocabulary, the book is to be read as a hidden polemic against the regime's cultural politics ... The regime's grip on cultural policy tightened significantly after 1934 when 'socialist realism' was officially promulgated as the only permissible

aesthetic for the novel; much of Bakhtin's account of grotesque realism may be seen as an implicit rejoinder to this.[21]

The comparison with Fellini's position as a film-maker is a complex and incomplete one since he both deals with the humourless and rigid tyranny of Italian fascism in his films and can also be seen as rebelling against a dominant but confining artistic aesthetic of social realism (neo-realism). However, in Fellini's case the former is not responsible for the promotion of the latter; neo-realism was of course part of a leftist reaction against Italian cinema under fascism which had been dominated by inane middle-class studio comedies and propaganda.[22] Yet because neo-realism was unpopular with the Christian Democratic government, especially Giulio Andreotti, but also later attacked by the communist film professor Umberto Barbaro, it fell between two stools.[23] In this light neo-realism may be seen as one of the most popular, but certainly not a universal or officially enforced aesthetic.[24] None the less, in his championing of *La Strada*, André Bazin draws attention to Fellini's problematic relationship to (and Roberto Rossellini's falling foul of) the 'critical guardians of neo-realist orthodoxy', a practice he sees as having been redefined and policed by the Marxist *Cinema Nuovo* critics (Chiarini and Aristarco) and which, for Bazin, can now be labelled 'socialist realism'.[25] If *La Strada* marked a limit of acceptability in neo-realism for the Marxists with its 'neo-realism of the person', it is easy to see how Fellini's later films such as *8 ½* and *Juliet of the Spirits* would have strongly offended Bazin's preference 'that nothing is ever revealed to us from the interior of the character' since both these films rely heavily on subjective visions, flashbacks and dream sequences.[26]

So both Fellini and Bakhtin, as film-maker and critical theorist respectively, can be seen as differently embracing carnivalesque conventions and rituals in their work as a response, if only indirectly, to a confining and politicised aesthetic which has been labelled 'socialist realism'. For both men, it could be argued, it becomes important to look to the past to rejuvenate and, in doing so, venerate a long-standing popular and festive practice which, as an anti-authoritarian form, has now been marginalised or transformed. Bakhtin discovers the medieval carnival and believes that many of its anti-authoritarian features have survived the 'bourgeoisification' of literature to be transposed into the writing of Dostoevsky and Rabelais. As I have already suggested, Fellini's work also demonstrates evidence of this popular legacy, but also of another connected one, that of the *commedia dell'arte*. This form of popular theatre which dates back to the sixteenth century and was performed primarily in the marketplace or public square (a key setting in so many Fellini films), was, in the same way as the carnival, 'progressively monopolised by well-to-do "society"' during the eighteenth century.[27] Where Bakhtin finds a continuity between the carnival (as the carnivalesque) and Dostoevsky and Rabelais, Fellini establishes a continuity with *commedia dell'arte* in his work through the figure of the clown.[28]

In the circus clown, therefore, Fellini finds not only the legacy of of a popular and satirical dramatic form, but also what he sees as at least a potentially anti-authoritarian figure. Clowns, he believes, are both 'solemn' and authoritarian as well as 'the first and most ancient anti-establishment figure(s) and it's a pity that they are destined to disappear under the feet of technological progress'.[29] Whilst Fellini concedes the duality and ambiguity of the clown in this statement, he goes on to describe a kind of utopian nostalgia for clowning; a nostalgia which has very specific implications for Fellini's own art form of cinema which of course is part of the detrimental 'technological progress' to which Fellini refers.[30] These tensions come into focus most explicitly in *The Clowns* where the clowns' ambiguities, and the kinds of tensions these may cause with the filmic form through which they are represented and reproduced, constitute the drama of the film.

In the opening sequences of the film in which Fellini remembers his first encounter with the circus he dramatises the dual potential of the clown. Not only does the violent energy of the show make the young Fellini feel frightened and endangered as well as fascinated, but the fact that the circus is set up in such close proximity to the local mental asylum with its barred, prison-like windows is a telling one; it is a connection reinforced later when we are given a flashback of the Fratellini brothers when they are forced by economic circumstance to play in trenches and in insane asylums run by nuns.[31] As the tent is erected next to Fellini's house, hellish groaning noises accompany its movement upwards. The circus, and especially the clowns, mirror the loss of order and limitation that define the mental asylum's inhabitants and yet, in Fellini's terms, the circus has licence not to have to 'keep inside fixed bounds' and in fact to celebrate those same deficiencies for which the asylum patients have been confined. The clowns perform the insanity which those in the asylum experience; the potency of their performance may indeed then lie, as Fellini claims, in their 'creating and living at the same time' in their performance. This may explain why, whilst the performance is unremarkable to those already in the asylum (because it is more life than art), the spectacular immediacy of this performance is too much for young Fellini. No longer able to differentiate between reality and performance, he is taken away in tears. This of course raises the question of what happens to the clowns' performance when committed to film if it is indeed the case that its force is derived from its potential to cross the limit which marks performance off from life – an issue also implicit in my earlier account of the circus figures in *La Strada*, *8 ½* and *Juliet of the Spirits* who go beyond representing or performing the circus to *becoming* it.

The subsequent sequence in *The Clowns* however, within which Fellini provides examples of the 'other strange and troubled characters' in his childhood of whom the circus performers remind him, functions to qualify this question. Half of the characters who appear could be labelled Auguste clowns (Big John the tramp, the midget nun, the diminutive drunken husband) and the other three (the station-master, the injured war veteran and the military officer) are white clowns. However, the military officer, brought in by the self-important station-master to enforce decorum on the train full of schoolboys, is also exceptional among these. His deathly white complexion and blackened eyes mark him out as an authoritarian white clown. Yet there is nothing about his interaction with either the station-master or the young boys which could generate laughter; rather his presence commands a fearful silence and a wave of fascist salutes. Again, this seems to suggest that, although Fellini has himself characterised Hitler and Mussolini as white and Auguste clowns respectively, in a way these characterisations are merely metaphorical accounts of the two figures whereas, as the appearance of the fascist demonstrates, there are some forms of authority in the real world which cannot easily be substituted through metaphor or undermined through laughter.[32] There is then, a limit to the extent to which circus paradigms may be mapped on to or equated with lived experience and a limit also on their potential to exert cultural or political influence.

So it is perhaps not so much the characteristics and dramatic or political potential of the clown for which Fellini is nostalgic since these are not qualities which he presents in an especially unproblematic or utopian light. Rather the clown in this film represents to Fellini a form of entertainment, more than that of an art, which not only does he feel is lost to him, but which draws attention to the painful limitations of his own art form, the cinema. I am thinking particularly of the implications to be drawn from two scenes in the film which both involve the failure of film technology to capture and reproduce a clown act. The first of these occurs on Fellini's visit to the Fratellini family when Pierre Fratellini decides to show him some rare documentary film footage of the Fratellini's performance in 1924. The projector, which Pierre explains is 'old like me', breaks down twice and on the second occasion the film burns up on screen before anyone gets a chance to see anything. The second scene takes place in some French television studios where Fellini has booked himself in for a special screening of some footage of a performance by the French clowns Rhum and Pipo. As the camera captures the grey soulless building in which the film is housed, Fellini's voice-over describes how a 'vast funereal atmosphere underlies our search for a lost world'. The assistants there are hostile and ignorant (he is addressed as M. Bellini) and to them the films are merely numbers for which they display no feeling. Rhum appears halfway through the film which lasts only about thirty seconds in total. Again Fellini's voice-over accompanying the image conveys his anti-climactic emotions – 'We felt disappointed, as if an undertaking had failed, as if our journey had led us nowhere. Maybe the clown really is dead.' This conclusion is a premature answer to the questioning discourse with which Fellini had initially framed his quest to find the clowns:

> Where are the clowns of my childhood? Where are they today; that terrifying comic violence, that noisy exhilaration? Can the circus still entertain? The world which it belonged to no longer exists. Theatres transformed into runways. Glowing ingenuous sets, the childish naïvité of the public; they no longer exist. What remains of the old circuses? Subtle, wasted traces.

It is not just that the film and the film equipment in these instances are old. There is evidence in these scenes of a more fundamental incompatibility between the circus and a film apparatus which could capture it.

At the heart of Fellini's enterprise in this film is the recovery of the circus as a live art form, a recovery which is driven and facilitated by the process of making a film. Yet the evidence of the two dramas I have described above indicates a failure of film to capture the life and essence of the circus which, when reproduced on film, only appears as the 'subtle, wasted traces' with which Fellini had initially been so dissatisfied. It is as though Fellini then becomes caught up in what Noël Burch has described, with reference to early cinema, as the 'pursuit of a class phantasy, ultimately that of a culture: to conclude the conquest of nature by triumphing over death through a substitute for life itself'.[33] He is referring here to the nineteenth-century middle-class fantasy that the cinema would become the ultimate form of representation which would not just scientifically reproduce a 'reality' before a spectator, but which would be devoted to 'restoring "beauty" to photography' in pursuit of what he refers to as the bourgeoisie's 'Frankenstein ideology' within which men would attain immortality by recreating life through the cinematic apparatus and thus symbolically abolish death, the 'supreme phantasm'.[34] When Fellini describes the cinema and the circus as having a common facility for 'creating and living at the same time' he is attempting to transpose the immediacy and live presence which defines the circus on to the cinema. Yet what the filmic reconstructions of the clowns clearly demonstrate is the impossibility of this; on film the clowns are, at best, visual two-dimensional traces of a live performance which lead Fellini to lament and confirm their disappearance rather than enable him to recover them.

In this respect his encounters with these early films confirm Siegfried Kracauer, Susan Sontag, Roland Barthes and Walter Benjamin's identification of the correlation between photographic and film reproduction and the reduction of 'aura' or 'authenticity' in art. Kracauer describes how what photographic images 'by their sheer accumulation attempt to banish is the recollection of death', none the less what they reproduce in their images is 'not the person who appears in his or her photograph, but the sum of what can be deducted from him or her'.[35] Thus the figure in the photographic image both stands as a disavowal of death and, since it constitutes only a series of traces of the life represented, it confirms the disappearance of both the moment and the person as they are represented. Likewise when Susan Sontag claims that photography is 'the inventory of mortality', she echoes Kracauer to the extent that she has also identified this implication of the photographic image in the evocation of death.[36] However, she also acknowledges the 'posthumous irony' which accompanies the act of viewing old photographs in her suggestion that the viewer's witnessing of the presence of the figures ('people being so irrefutably *there*') in the picture is at the same time always informed by the inescapable knowledge of the history that has since overtaken the figures represented.

In much the same terms Roland Barthes picks up on this inevitable and painful interruption of history within the contemplation of old photographs during his account (in *Camera Lucida*) of his discovering old photographs of his mother following her death.[37] With one important exception, he laments the pictures' failure to satisfy him either as 'photographic performance(s)' or as 'a living resurrection of the beloved face'.[38] Like Sontag's subjects, Barthes's mother appears in her photographs to be 'caught in a history (of tastes fashions fabrics)' which leaves him 'distracted' from her towards the 'accessories which have perished'.[39] Thus, as he claims later in his essay, the effect of the photograph is 'not to restore what has been abolished (by time, by distance)', since, like Sontag he accepts that history always acts as a 'division', but rather it works to 'attest that what I see has indeed existed' and to work as a 'certificate of presence', but, crucially, a presence in the past.[40] However, it is also important to acknowledge the distinction which Barthes draws between photography and film in this respect:

> Because the photograph, taken in flux, is impelled, ceaselessly drawn toward other views; in the cinema, no doubt, there is always a photographic referent, but this referent shifts, it does not make a claim in favour of its reality, it does not protest its former existence; it does not cling to me; it is not a *specter*. Like the real world the filmic world is sustained by the presumption that, as Husserl says, the experience will constantly continue to flow by in the same constitutive style. (emphasis in original)[41]

For Barthes the power and meaning of still photographs cannot reach from the past into the present except through a form of haunting because they are always circumscribed by death. At the same time, unlike stills, in motion pictures each image offers the next so that an expectancy of the future is somehow built into its impellent dynamic. This distinction is interesting in terms of *The Clowns* because of the way Fellini appears to be discontented with the still photographs and memories he has of the clowns and seeks to supplement, perhaps to make complete, through the addition of film – the archive/family film and his own. However, his encounters with old (documentary) film footage both challenge Barthes's Husserlian characterisation of film aesthetics since they are both in different ways abortive and seem only to attest further to the irretrievability of the clowns' energy.

Fellini, then, is engaged in constructing a cinema of his own which, in Barthes's terms, does not just 'resurrect' the clowns and their particular comic tradition but rather gives them life in the present. Yet Walter Benjamin's account of the representational problems involved in the processes of recording images, figures and events is particularly pertinent for this argument since he is most interested in the specific capacity of film to wither 'tradition':

> One might subsume the eliminated element in the term 'aura' and go on to say: that which withers in the age of mechanical reproduction is the aura of the work of art … the technique of reproduction detaches the reproduced object from the domain of tradition. By making many reproductions it substitutes a plurality of copies for a unique existence. And in permitting the reproduction to meet the beholder or listener in his own particular situation, it reactivates the object reproduced. These two processes lead to a tremendous shattering of tradition which is the obverse of the contemporary crisis and renewal of mankind. Both processes are intimately connected with the contemporary mass movements. Their most powerful agent is the film.[42]

Not only is the art object removed from tradition once it is involved in processes of mechanical reproduction such as film, but, Benjamin claims, this process 'emancipates the work of art from its parasitical dependence on ritual'.[43] Of course now we can see that in many cases, for example the *Mona Lisa*, reproduction has worked, quite conversely, to intensify the aura of the original rather than to erode it. None the less, when Fellini mourns the disappearance of the clown 'under the feet of technological progress' he must of course acknowledge his own complicity in this since it is the mass media of cinema and television which have superseded the circus in popularity and dominance. In trying to recover the clown on film, *The Clowns* may succeed insofar as it is a documentary history of significant clowns but, as I am suggesting above, the film also dramatises its own painful but fundamental incompatibility with the dynamics of clowning. As a (pseudo-) documentary the film sets out to describe and record clowning as a tradition, tracing its roots through various significant contributions to the Pierrot and Auguste figures. Yet paradoxically *The Clowns*, which sets out to recover a tradition, ends by confirming its disappearance since film, in Benjamin's terms, by its very nature removes the unique art object, the one-off performance, 'from the domain of tradition' by reproducing and multiplying it. It is in the nature of the photographic image that in appearing to banish death by preserving the image of an object for ever, the reproduced image becomes a haunting trace of a now irrecoverable dead moment. This situation is exacerbated through the clowns since culturally clowning is not only a popular tradition into which the film attempts to breathe new life. It is also one which insistently revolves around rituals (which are by definition live), albeit carnivalesque ones, through which mechanical reproduction, according to Benjamin, has apparently wrested art from a 'parasitical dependence'.

It is no coincidence, then, that the ritual chosen for the spectacular finale in *The Clowns* in which Fellini attempts to make the cinema finally do justice to the clowns' talent and energy, is a funeral. The funeral is of course both carnivalesque and ambivalent. Aesthetically it offers the most dizzying, mobile and colourful cinematography of the film and as well as dramatically the most diverse and entertaining range of clown acts and characters seen so far. Yet it is, above all, a funeral for the clowns in which the laughter that is reborn in their chaotic and obscene performance is inevitably also attached to an acknowledgement of the death of the whole tradition. Not only is this underlined by a couple of the ageing, out-of-breath clowns who discharge themselves from the increasingly frenetic circular procession, but also the film crew's last words over the image of the final clown (who had previously played the late Jim Guillon), 'Turn it off. It's over.' The words indicate that the live performance is over, but perhaps also the clown tradition itself. Now the clowns have been committed to film and so, like Guillon's partner Fru-Fru, can be summoned up again, but, as this final scene suggests, the figure which appears magically from nowhere and similarly disappears into thin air is a 'wasted trace', an imaginary, ghost-like figure called back from the dead.

Questioning of Fellini's most notable circus films, then, reveals the circus figures within them to be involved in more ambiguous and more critically challenging dramas than much previous criticism has been able to uncover. Fellini's assertion that the cinema could *be* the circus may indeed be the symptom of a 'great European art' director's desire that his highly personal cinematic vision could be a personally influential one, since it is clear that thematically the circus in his films is defined and valued for its consistent ability to cross the boundaries which inhibit other forms of art and entertainment from entering life and transforming (individual) lives. None the less, all these circus figures are involved in an impossible relationship with the objects of their influence, an impossibility frequently signalled by their cinematic constitution which in itself formally places them at one remove from the circus. The ambiguous quality of these circus figures encourages a reading of their carnivalistic potential, yet whereas Bakhtin was concerned with art which dramatised social change and crisis, Fellini's is concerned more narrowly with particular lives. The more telling connection between Fellini and Bakhtin lies in their mutual embracing of long-standing but vanishing popular cultural forms (the circus and the carnival respectively) which may be taken to be indicative of a nostalgic desire in each. In Fellini's case, however, his desire to revitalise and preserve the live performance of the circus clowns is profoundly revealing for film criticism in general. Not only does it dramatise explicitly an irreconcilable dysjuncture between circus and film aesthetics (as live and mechanical arts), but in doing so operates as a register of the fundamental ambivalence of the film image itself which both reinvents life and marks its passing.

Notes

1 *Entretiens avec Federico Fellini: Les Cahiers RTB Series Télécinéma* (1962), repr. in Suzanne Budgen, *Fellini* (London, BFI Education, 1966), p. 52.
2 Costanzo Costantini (ed.), *Fellini on Fellini* (London, Faber & Faber, 1994), p. 30.
3 Costantini, *Fellini on Fellini*, p. 176.
4 Budgen, *Fellini*, p. 90.
5 Pam Cook, 'Authorship and cinema', in *The Cinema Book* (London, BFI Publishing, 1986), p. 118.
6 John C. Stubbs, 'The Fellini manner: open form and visual excess', *Cinema Journal*, 32:4, summer 1993, p. 51. See also the following examples which accept Fellini's declarations about the relationship between circus and cinema on face value: Budgen, *Fellini*, p. 52, Donald P. Costello, *Fellini's Road* (Notre Dame and London, University of Notre Dame Press, 1983), p. 146, and Naomi Ritter, *Art as Spectacle: Images of the Entertainer since Romanticism* (Columbia and London, University of Missouri Press, 1989), p. 276.

7 For an outline of this project see Lietta Tornbuoni (ed.), *Federico Fellini* (New York, Rizzoli International Publications, 1995), pp. 23–55.

8 Ritter points to the resonance of the chain with which Zampanò encircles his chest and sees it as a metaphor for his learning to 'burst the circle of his animal self' (p. 301). Whilst it is certainly an important image of circularity in the film, this would seem an odd reading since it is his 'animal self' which struggles against the chain. It is part of Zampanò's reformation that that he accepts the image of the chain and that he can indeed be part of a series of connections between people rather than a destroyer of them.

9 André Bazin, 'La Strada' (1956), trans. Joseph E. Cunneen, repr. in Peter Bondanella (ed.), *Federico Fellini: Essays in Criticism* (Oxford, Oxford University Press, 1978), p. 58.

10 Bazin, 'La Strada', p. 58.

11 Ritter, *Art as Spectacle*, p. 295.

12 The term 'diegetic' is used in film theory to refer to everything that is included in the world of the film. Thus, the 'diegetic audience' here simply refers to the audience which is represented within the film as opposed to the spectators of the film itself. see David Bordwell and Kristin Thompson, *Film Art: An Introduction* (New York, McGraw-Hill, 1990), p. 56.

13 Slavoj Zizek, *Enjoy your Symptom!: Jacques Lacan in Hollywood and Out* (London, Routledge, 1992), p. 4.

14 Ritter similarly identifies in Fellini's use of the circus a 'nostalgia for innocence' which he projects on to 'various clown figures', *Art as Spectacle*, p. 312.

15 Such a reference, however, needs be qualified by two of Bakhtin's own acknowledgements; firstly that 'Carnival itself ... is not, of course, a literary phenomenon. It is *syncretic pageantry* of a ritualistic sort', and secondly, that 'carnival knows no footlights'. Thus, we need to hold on to the distinction in Bakhtin between carnival and *carnivalised* or *carnivalesque* forms which are those which, in Bakhtin's terms, may have been 'transposed' into art, though he is concerned only with literature. Yet, despite these clearly stated distinctions, there do indeed seem to be similarities between Bakhtin's desire for literature to *become* carnival and Fellini's for film to become circus. Mikhail Bakhtin, *Problems of Dostoevsky's Poetics*, trans. and ed. Caryl Emerson (Manchester, Manchester University Press, 1984), p. 122.

16 Bakhtin, *Problems of Dostoevsky's Poetics*, p. 124.

17 Bakhtin, *Problems of Dostoevsky's Poetics*, p. 127.

18 Bakhtin, *Problems of Dostoevsky's Poetics*, p. 123.

19 Bakhtin, *Problems of Dostoevsky's Poetics*, p. 123.

20 Mikhail Bakhtin, *Rabelais and his World*, trans. Helene Iswolsky (Cambridge, MA, and London: Massachussetts Institute of Technology Press, 1968).

21 Bakhtin, *Rabelais and his World*, Simon Dentith, *Bakhtinian Thought: An Introductory Reader* (London, Routledge, 1995), p. 71.

22 See Frank Burke, *Federico Fellini: Variety Lights to La Dolce Vita* (Boston, Twayne Publishing, 1984), pp. 1–2.

23 For a more detailed discussion of these debates see Mira Liehm, *Passion and Defiance: Film in Italy From 1942 to the Present* (Berkeley and Los Angeles, University of California Press, 1984), pp. 99–102.

24 ' ... throughout the political upheaval, the explosion of neo-realism, and the aesthetic revolution, the Italian cinema did not once cease to pursue what was at that time condemned with particular savagery by the critics, namely the big spectacular, mythology, opera, melodrama', Pierre Leprohon, *The Italian Cinema* (London: Secker & Warburg, 1972), p. 96.

25 Bazin, 'La Strada', p. 56.

26 Liehm, *Passion and Defiance*, p. 57 and p. 58.

27 John Rudlin, *Commedia dell'Arte: An Actor's Handbook* (London, Routledge, 1994), p. 4.

28 Like Fellini in *I Clowns*, André Gide visited the Cirque Medrano in Paris, but unlike Fellini he did get to see the Fratellini brothers perform live and was so impressed that he urged them not to 'hesitate to remain simply clowns, the heirs to the divine commedia dell'arte', André Gide quoted in Rudlin, *Commedia dell'Arte*, p. 181.

29 Quoted in Costantini, *Fellini on Fellini*, p. 74.

30 Bakhtin too has been charged with providing a utopian account of carnival. see Peter Stallybrass and Allon White, *The Politics and Poetics of Transgression* (London, Methuen, 1986).

31 For a psychological interpretation of this split see Frank Burke, 'Three phase clown process and the white clown–Auguste relationship in Fellini's *The Clowns*', *Film Studies Annual*, 1977 (pp. 124–42), pp. 125–6.

32 Anna Keel and Christian Strich (eds), *Fellini on Fellini*, trans. Isabel Quigley (London, Eyre Methuen), 1976, p. 130.

33 Noël Burch, 'Charles Baudelaire v. Dr. Frankenstein', *Afterimage*, 8/9, spring 1981, p. 6.

34 Burch, 'Charles Baudelaire ...', p. 21.

35 Siegfried Kracauer, 'Photography' (1927), trans. Thomas Y. Levin, repr. in *Critical Inquiry*, no. 3, spring 1993, p. 432.

36 Susan Sontag, *On Photography* (Harmondsworth, Penguin Books, 1979), p. 70.

37 Roland Barthes, *Camera Lucida* (London, Flamingo, 1984), pp. 63–71.

38 Barthes borrows Proust's words to describe the way the 'Winter Garden Photograph' allows him to experience 'for the first time, an involuntary and complete memory' of his mother and thereby to achieve for himself, at least 'utopically', what he describes as '*the impossible science of the unique being*' (emphasis in original), pp. 70–1 and p. 64.

39 Barthes, *Camera Lucida*, p. 64.

40 Barthes, *Camera Lucida*, p. 82 and p. 87.
41 Barthes, *Camera Lucida*, pp. 89–90.
42 Walter Benjamin, 'The work of art in the age of mechanical reproduction' (1935), repr. in Gerald Mast and Marshall Cohen (eds), *Film Theory and Criticism* (Oxford, Oxford University Press, 1982), p. 852.
43 Benjamin, 'The work of art ...', p. 854.

8

Flights of fantasy: representing the female aerialist

As I demonstrated in part I, the capacity of the human body to perform beyond its normal or even imagined limitations in forms which are entertaining, astonishing and beautiful has always constituted the very core of the circus. In the acrobatic, equestrian and aerialist acts which demonstrate human transcendence in the natural world (over animals) and the natural elements (defying gravity and fire), over machinery (wires, bicycles, cannons) and over the possibility of death itself, this power is partially signified in surrounding discourses by what might at first seem an incongruous set of attributes describing the powerful bodies involved as light, often weightless, flying or even transcendent of the physical body. Kwint has identified the way this 'vague but recurrent quality' in such performances can be linked to the construction of eighteenth- and early-nineteenth century circus spectacle as a whole: the circus itself was designed to appear light and 'airy' – a summer rather than winter entertainment like the theatre – with its '[t]ransparent paintings, pastoralism, pantomime fantasy and gossamer air balloons' making it 'generally consistent with the "frothy" Rococo style of the 1780s, which left its mark in Regency elegance'.[1] Of course these manifestations of, as one critic put it, 'tinsel gorgeousness', still need to be offset against the domination, albeit temporary, of the stage and ring by equestrian hippodramas, 'those thrilling plays of blood, thunder and love'.[2] These, though they celebrated a great variety of heroic conquests, involved their players in direct confrontation or battle with some threatening force, as a result of which they emerge a tested but victorious Wellington, Blood Red Knight or Mazeppa.[3] The circus performer, however, does not have to prove his/her prowess or moral authority in competition with others because this superiority is taken

166

for granted in the ring and perhaps has already been established elsewhere in myth or history by the well-known figures whose deeds are enacted. It need not be tested, therefore, but merely displayed. The fact that this trend for melodramatic and militaristic hippodrama was a temporary one tells us as much about the nature of the circus which accommodated these dramas. On the gravity-defying bodies which will be considered in this chapter, therefore, are legible not only the ambitions and fantasies of the circus as a whole. Such bodies are frequently reinscribed within subsequent texts about the circus with further more specific meanings which may have little or nothing to do with circuses. In this respect, Wim Wenders's *Wings of Desire* (1986) represents an important exploration of the contradictions and challenges inherent in the aerialist's performance. Whilst the aerialist in the film, Marion, functions to deconstruct certain of the (at times contradictory) myths which have surrounded the female aerialist since the mid nineteenth century, as she becomes more symbolically central and radical as a figure within the film, she becomes more familiar and conventional in terms of the history of circus representations.

Kwint cites a number of examples of early usages of metaphors of flight in eighteenth-century newspaper puffs to describe the glory of a performance; the most significant of which may be the account of John Astley who, in 1784, was championed over the lamentably poor Mme Vestris and Mademoiselle Constance the famous opera performers who were judged to be suffering from a 'trifling inferiority' in comparison with young Astley's ability 'to engage two elements in his service – the earth and the air, while the opera is obliged to content itself with only one, and that the most gross, humble, and subordinate – the earth'.[4] What is significant here is not only the implication of a weightlessness, superior to that even of a ballet dancer, but also the implied mastery over the body, the horse and the very elements themselves. The most famous of all equestrians, Andrew Ducrow, is likewise lauded in very similar terms in the course of an article in *The Theatrical Journal* of 1849 which recalls Ducrow's horsemanship in the *Carnival of Venice* at Astley's.[5] As Ducrow circles the ring, whilst standing on his horse, the critic marvels as a 'change comes o'er the spirit of his dream' so that in the time it takes to look away and look back

the peasant has disappeared, and in this place – behold! – Harlequin! Harlequin on horseback! The mere abstract idea of it puts quicksilver in the feet and fingers of the fancy, and sends one's spirits careering among the stars. But we must call them home again to the scarcely less unearthly realities before us.[6]

An inversion of physical properties appears to have taken place as abstraction of thought lends 'feet and fingers' to the imagination whilst at the same time bodies are transformed into air as the 'seeming' harlequin

still moving round in his endless path, like the wind round the 'earth globose' transforms himself into a symbol of that wind itself, and flies before us like a winged Zephyr pursuing, with the speed of light, the invisible Flora of whom he is enamoured.[7]

Doubly abstracted now from once being the wind to now a mere 'symbol' of it, Ducrow none the less seems to acquire, almost paradoxically, greater strength of force in the process of these bodily diminutions:

The mingled grace and gusto of his movements, as he flew after the flying object of his fairy love – the lightening speed to which he urged the motion of his steed, as the imaginary object of his pursuit fled before him – the miraculous skill with which he took advantage of the centrifugal and centripetal forces that were counteracting each other, to give his course the semblance of a flight through the air, by merely touching the horse with the tip of one foot – his whole frame literally hanging pendent in the supporting air; all this must have been seen to be duly admired and wondered at; and even then it was one of those cases ... in which 'seeing is not believing'.[8]

Apparently god-like in his control over his horse, in his 'miraculous' marshalling over the 'forces' of physics, we are told, he maintains the appearance of an unearthly, dreamlike being. Unlike the accounts of Astley's horse-riding, discussed in part I, in which audience disbelief moved to discomfort and then to light-hearted rhetoric suggesting nefarious intervention, here, over fifty years later, it is a sign of the circus audience's growing aesthetic sophistication and articulacy that Astley's successor performs before spectators who delight in the seductions he performs on their sense of the reality of the body and its limits. Indeed, an almost Gothic fear of demonic bodily possession appears to have been replaced, even in the early nineteenth century, by a classically Victorian sense of 'self possession' which is exercised at the level of the body. Circus acts, with their origins in Astley's military-style exercises and self-teaching manuals, exemplify the myth that the limitations of the physical body exist only when the will to transcend them is absent.

By the mid nineteenth century metaphors of flight became attached more exclusively to equilibrists and trapeze artists than equestrians as the former replaced the latter as the sensational focus of the circus. The first person to master the flying trapeze is usually cited as Jules Léotard.[9] In 1859, and at the age of twenty-one, Léotard perfected the technique of swinging off one trapeze and launching himself into flight through the air to catch the bar of another. Speaight draws attention to contemporary accounts of Léotard's performances in the Cirque d'Hiver in Paris and the Alhambra theatre in London which described him as resembling a 'tropical bird leaping from branch to branch and leaving in the dazzled eyes of the spectators a brilliant but confused impression of its bright plumage'.[10] A review of his 1868 New York performance in the *New York Clipper* contrasts his body 'swaying through the air backwards and forwards ... as lightly as a bird' with the 'iron frame' which carried him.[11] This image of Léotard as a dazzling, plumed bird (with echoes here already of Angela Carter's fictional conceit of the doubtfully winged female trapeze artist Fevvers in *Nights at the Circus*) was partly due to a technique which involved taking off from one trapeze just before it had reached the lowest point of its downward swing (rather than the highest point of its upward swing as you might expect) and from this point seeming to 'fly' slightly downwards before appearing magically to rise and catch the second trapeze as it was swung towards him. Other trapeze artists sought alternative means of flight by attaching their trapeze to the bottom of a balloon carriage and performing tricks as they ascended to great and often fatal heights.[12]

However, the birdlike impression given by Léotard, quite obviously and predictably soon had implications (in the mind of the circus audiences and of the performers themselves) for the classification of the trapeze act in terms of gender. Whilst the fact that Léotard was able to achieve this spectacular flight from one trapeze to another because of his superior strength and gymnastic skill, his subsequent analogy with a bird and the highly aestheticised nature of Léotard's brightly coloured performance (which, like Ducrow's *appeared* to privilege physical weightlessness and beauty over strength) meant that the act was very quickly surrounded by a rhetoric more conventionally associated with the feminine.

This tension in the flying trapeze act between a great physical labour which must be masked in the interests of an *impression* of effortlessness and grace was one of which it seems performers of the period quite quickly became aware. Hugues Le Roux and Jules Garnier's book, *Acrobats and Mountebanks* (1890), which doubles as a kind of manual for the acts, includes a chapter on equilibrists of whom they write:

> The equilibrists, are the most artistic acrobats, the true Olympians. The gymnast excites our admiration by the development of his thorax and limbs, and by the epic relief of his muscles. The equilibrist does not require the same effort in his work. The beauty of the performance lies in the delicacy, variety, facility, and grace of the artist's movements, and on this account women excel as equilibrists, for men cannot reconcile themselves to the suppression of their strength in the feats they achieve, and therefore take a second rank in equilibrium. They prefer special branches of the art and are usually jugglers, bicyclists or antipodeans.[13]

There is something slightly disingenuous about this account. The flying trapeze and high-wire acts, to this day, are generally regarded as the most difficult and dangerous, and indeed Le Roux and Garnier themselves acknowledge the equilibrists in general to be the 'Olympians' of the circus. However, in their gendering of the act they play down the physical strength and danger to privilege its aesthetics. So, while the (male) gymnast is admired for his corporeal and muscular strength (the 'epic relief of his muscles'), the body of the female disappears in their prettifying account of her image in which bodily strength is replaced by an impression of 'delicacy, variety, facility, grace'.

This sense that the gravity-defying female performer must somehow be relieved of the burden of her body is bizarrely consolidated in Le Roux and Garnier's subsequent claim that 'love destroys the centre of gravity of tightrope dancers, and, as a rule, equilibrists, that is to say the true artists ... might rank with the Roman vestals ... It is not just a question of averting the danger of maternity, which ends the artistic career of an equilibrist' but it is also so that 'those who are particular on these points can enjoy the performance of an equilibrist without any uneasiness about her private life.'[14] So the audience must be able to trust that the trapeze artist's body is untouched, consecrated, a 'vestal virgin', and even if we might not believe this were actually the case in practice, it is nevertheless important to note that such great stock was placed in the myth of this female figure who appears to transcend both the social space and her own body. These two attributes (social and sexual/physical transcendence) which are consolidated in Le Roux and Garnier's account, continue to mark representational accounts of the aerialist to the present day as we will see in Wenders's rendering of the aerialist Marion.

As Le Roux and Garnier rightly indicate, women did begin to pre-dominate in the performance of the static trapeze and to have a considerable and surprisingly high-profile role in flying trapeze troupes from the late 1850s onwards. The first woman flying trapeze artist is usually cited as being Mlle Azella who performed her act in Holborn in 1868 (nearly ten years after Léotard).[15] Some indication of the nature of these performances, frequently set up in theatres rather than in the circus, can be gleaned from the famously perverse nineteenth-century diarist Arthur J. Munby. In his diaries the female aerialists' bodies are surrounded by the language of his own highly sexualised curiosity. This was also a curiosity about gender ambiguity, since within these accounts it is possible to see how both the gender and the sexuality of the aerialist have frequently been conceived in ambiguous and at times quite contradictory terms. During 1868 the female acrobats of the London stage and circus became rivals in Munby's imagination to the milkwomen and working women whom he had previously sought out, and he began not only to describe the acrobats in detail but also to collect photographs and make sketches of them. He visited the Holborn Amphitheatre to see the 'wondrous Azella leaping from bar to bar like a man'. He goes on in nearly all his accounts of the acrobats to dramatise their physical androgyny as well as the way in which their performances confuse conventional gender attributes.[16] Thomas Frost's account of the same performance, however, is less starry-eyed and, whilst he acknowledges the 'grace of her evolutions' and the fact that the 'beauty of her person and the novelty of seeing such feats performed by a woman' was certainly a part of her draw, in her case these were also a mask for what he found to be an unconvincing performance since, 'instead of throwing off from one bar, turning the somersault, and catching the next bar, Azella threw off, and somersaulted in her descent from the bar' to the 'board placed for her to alight upon'.[17]

Clearly Munby is not so reliable an arbiter of circus skills and perhaps had not been to see either Léotard or Victor Julien, with whom Frost is able to compare Azella, but his response is revealing of the contemporary excitement, not only at a dress code of flesh-coloured tights and bodice, but at the strange way in which this, which was the most physically revealing of performance outfits, seemed to offer such scope for gender confusion and masquerade.[18]

Some years before, Munby had visited a ten-year-old acrobat, Nathalie Foucart, and her family after a performance at the Alhambra. He declares that she 'proposes to fly from one trapeze to another, like Léotard, and to turn two somersaults in the air between, and not one only like him'. On meeting the girl he describes shaking hands with her, remarking that 'her hand did not feel unusually large or hard at all; but her arms are full of muscle as big as a boy's, I was told.'[19] In another episode he describes going to see a 'sturdy wellknit little fellow' of a trapeze artist with

> broad shoulders and a round plump smiling face ... He showed
> both pluck and skill; he climbed the rope, and hung from the
> trapeze by one hand or one foot ... There was nothing weak or
> feminine about the boy, but remembering how many female
> acrobats there are just now, I asked a girl who stood next to me
> in the crowd ... whether the young performer were a boy or a
> girl. 'It's a girl, Sir!' She answered briskly.[20]

Munby's wrong-footededness here anticipates the revelation that would come two years later in 1871 when the famous trapeze artist Lulu (also the first person to be shot from a stage cannon) who performed at the Holborn Amphitheatre, was discovered to be a young man – Sam Wasgatt, whose childhood stage name had been El Niño.[21] Whereas Adah Isaacs Menken had been, at times, an equestrian male impersonator, this was the first of many cases of female impersonating trapeze artists, a tradition which carried on into the twentieth century with Barbette.[22] Clearly, impersonating a female aerialist in the 1870s was, on one level, an invitation to further controversy since moral reformists were lobbying politicians involved in drafting the Dangerous Performances Act of 1879 and were specifically targeting children and women to be excluded from performing certain kinds of gymnastic and high-wire acts in circuses and theatres. At the same time, such debate no doubt generated publicity so the danger of putting off audiences could be offset against the high levels of sensation and, importantly, sympathy, which a female artist could generate since the vulnerability of a beautiful young woman attempting a treacherous trapeze act would be all the more affecting. This is the central difference between the performers of the 1870s and Barbette. Whereas the former performed as women, Barbette's publicity, in foregrounding his transvestism, meant that his was the performance of a man who was not only performing as an acrobat and aerialist, but who was also overtly performing femininity. Both situations, however, point to further questions about the perception and performance of gender in aerial performances: do such performances in some way erase, blur or transcend visibly recognisable gender codes? Why has so much attention been focused on female over male figures? What kinds of reinforcements or rebellions do such female figures constitute in relation to male desire?

Peta Tait, in an analysis of Australian circus acts of the same period, makes the claim, with reference to Stallybrass and White, that the 'circus was popular because individual circus bodies were perceived as "low-Other", transgressing social categories; entry into the circus tent, therefore, invoked a suspension of social laws so that the circus can be seen as inheriting the Bakhtinian site of the carnivalesque'.[23] For Tait, the popularity of the circus legitimised its capacity to 'contravene social categories of gender' and decency; that is, its resistance to gendered behaviour was consolidated by a symbolic force which the trapeze artist (above all others) acquires precisely because of her apparent ability to defy natural laws, especially those of gravity.

This seems convincing to an extent, yet with reference again to Munby, it also appears idealistic in terms of its conception of class. In his account of another child acrobat, Mlle de Glorion, he finds himself excited by the androgyny of her 'trim and slight and shapely figure' but is soon disturbed by the intervention of a male catcher:

> though it is not well to see a nude man fling a nude girl about as she is flung, or to see her grip his body in mid air between her seemingly bare thighs, I think that an unreflecting audience takes no note of these things and looks on him and her only as two performers.[24]

What is so striking about Munby's account is his perception that he stands *outside* the perceptual space occupied by the rest of the audience by virtue of his superior, because more refined, intellectual sensibility.

He is a voyeur, always importantly to him, in *both* sexual *and* class terms. If the circus were a truly carnivalesque space, such divisional hierarchies would be overturned in favour of, in Bakhtinian terms, a 'free and familiar contact among people', though indeed, as has been argued in the previous chapter, for many critics these terms of Bakhtin's are themselves inherently idealistic. In carnival, he claims, 'what is suspended first of all is hierarchical structure and all forms of terror, reverence, piety, and etiquette connected with it; that is, everything resulting from socio-hierarchical inequality.' [25] In this sense, as we have seen already, the circus is quite clearly not a carnivalesque space. It is very likely that the audience which surrounded Munby that night were just as excited as he was at the sight of two semi-naked torsos in an intimate embrace. The point is, however, that his comments suggest that one of the reasons the circus and circus stage shows were given licence for such excesses was precisely because they maintained class distinctions; that is, the popular music hall audience was allowed its semi-nude performances precisely because its aesthetic appreciation was deemed to be too impoverished to be affected, never mind corrupted, by what, Munby claimed, appears to them to be 'mere athletics'. On the other hand, bourgeois claims that eroticism is acceptable when it is combined with aesthetic sophistication have always served to license certain kinds of erotic display, especially in the realm of high art.

What also emerges from these contemporary nineteenth-century accounts of female trapeze artists is a complex and at times confused and confusing performance of gender which simply becomes more self-conscious and stylised in the twentieth century. The artist's gender is, in Judith Butler's terms, performative, by which she holds that 'acts, gestures, enactments generally construed, are *performative* in the sense that the essence or identity that they otherwise purport to express are *fabrications* manufactured and sustained through corporeal signs and other discursive means'.[26] In the case of the trapeze artist these performative gestures, as Le Roux and Garnier suggest, include a necessary but highly exaggerated mask of feminine actions and costume which surround the performance. At the same time they are the spectacular accoutrements of acts involving uncommon physical strength and danger in which the gestures and tricks in which the aerialists are engaged do not allow for the separate codification of male and female performers. Tait argues that single trapeze acts differ from flying ones in this respect since in the latter the flier 'can only signify gender at the beginning and end of a trick' whereas for the female solo trapeze performer the 'action of gender', in the form of feminised static poses, constitute part of the trick. For Tait, foregrounding of the 'action of gender' as 'a visible segment arranged within the performance' has the effect of 'disrupt[ing] social belief in an innate and fixed identity defined by sexual difference'.[27] So not only were these performances sexually transgressive in terms of the nineteenth-century public stage since they construct a spectacle out of the semi-naked female body, but also because aerial acts provided a stage on which, far from any concessions being made to women's lesser strength, they performed the same moves in the same way as men. Indeed, delicacy and smallness of stature were seen as positive assets since, as we have already seen, at the core of circus entertainment is a championing of the power of human will in competitions between human bodies and objects or natural forces which would conventionally be assumed to be impossibly physically superior, preferably to the extent of being life-threatening.

There is also a congruence between the presentation of the female aerialist's body and the image that the circus as a whole has presented of itself. As I have previously suggested, this circus self-image is at heart a paradoxical one since it promotes an idea of itself in the popular imagination as embodying a lifestyle unfettered by conventionality or by social and legal restraint; a freedom which was echoed in performances which foregrounded the illusion of ease. Behind this image lie levels of physical discipline, bodily regulation and hardship which are unrivalled by any other western performance art. In this sense the fantasy implied in the trapezist's art articulated by Tait is 'the desire of physical bodies to defy the gravity of social categories, before returning to familiar territory when he or she halts the free fall and reinstates gender identity and the material order of bodies'.[28] The aerialist constructs and operates within a fantasy space in which the body is at once made insubstantial and unclassifiable and is thereby liberated from the limitations normally attached to bodies physically marked out in terms of their gender or race.[29] Likewise, this could be argued to be a figure for the circus itself in which, as social anthropologist Yoram Carmeli argues:

The ambiguity of the social and existential condition of the performer is carried out of the text and into other layers of the encounter ... The travellers display life disconnected from place, time, relations, the impossibility of the impossible in the realm of everyday life, their own life experience.[30]

In other words, that apparent physical suspension, those few magic split seconds which audiences first marvelled at in Léotard's performance where he appeared to be held in the air before impossibly flying upwards, are held to be representative of the suspensions of place, time and social relations which is the fantasy offered by the circus and encapsulated by the trapeze artist.

Mary Russo, however, further complicates the image of the aerialist as a socially and sexually transgressive body. In a discussion of Amelia Earhart's flying feats, she identifies a slippage between the two terms 'stunt' and 'stunted':

> The double meaning of the word 'stunt' bifurcates the notion of the extraordinary into 1) a model of female exceptionalism (stunting) described by Arnelia Earhart as comparable to tightrope walking and elaborated in her memoirs as metonymically related to female flying, and 2) the doubled, dwarfed, distorted (stunted) creatures of the sideshow which stand in as the representatives of a well-known cultural presentation of the female body as monstrous and lacking.[31]

The exceptional, in the realm of female physical achievement, may too easily be classified equally as the freakish or the abnormal. The acrobat's body is potentially both awesomely and disturbingly physical. In this sense Carolyn Steedman's account of the child acrobat Mignon in Goethe's *Wilhelm Meister* is a pertinent one since she describes the way that 'it is Mignon's gestures and motions as an acrobat that carry the burden of her oddness'.[32] It is this 'burden of oddness' which is at once the startling register of her supreme skill and, at the same time, an indication of the unnatural efforts and forced training by adult hands which inevitably lies behind the otherwise immaculate performance. This oddness is definitive of the circus body in general which is marked by the will to redefine and challenge what were seen as inherent physical limitations and therefore inevitably not only complicates and questions the performance values of natural poise, grace and ease, but causes us to relate these values also to the gendering of these bodies.

In summary, just as the female aerialist's performance of extreme femininity is shadowed by (or is perhaps, more accurately, the shadow for) a strength of force which might more widely be regarded as being of masculine proportions, likewise the illusion of ease with which they perform is shadowed by a bodily discipline and labour (perhaps enforced labour). Equally, the representational status of the trapeze artist is contradictory in that, although their performance is intensely immediate and visceral, the fact that this labour works to service the illusion of an insubstantial body means that the trapeze artist, above all other circus performers, seems to embody the circus's own more general fantasy of itself as a space of transcendence in which the usual constraints of time and space do not operate. At the same time, the exceptional appearance provides the imprint of their physical oddness; an oddness which, as a trace of the labours imposed on the body, invites sympathy, but at the same time promotes a curiosity about the definition and potential of the 'natural' human body, a curiosity which extends to gender.

Representation

Few artistic renderings of the aerialist in film and literature centre on male figures and those that do, such as *Trapeze* (Carol Reed, 1956) and Franz Kafka's short story 'First Sorrow' (1922), feature damaged men who are injured and hysterical respectively. The portraits of female performers are more multiple and varied, for example Frau Mann in Djuna Barnes's *Nightwood* (1936), Cleopatra in Tod Browning's *Freaks* (1932), Mary in Chaplin's *The Circus* (1928), Fanny in Federico Fellini's *Juliet of the Spirits* (1965), *Lola Montes* (Max Ophuls, 1955) and Fevvers in Angela Carter's *Nights at the Circus*.[33] However, it does seem that in both male and female versions of the aerialist their figure is nearly always a metaphoric one which facilitates exploration of a broader issue; the dynamics of their performance or their relationship to an audience within performance is rarely explored. Lola Montes, for example, is lowered up and down before her circus audience yet she does not (except, we presume, in her final moments) perform for them and the entertainment is provided by the ongoing questioning and story-telling by the ringmaster, Peter Ustinov, who invites the crowd to admire her static, highly fetishised beauty whilst also relishing their superiority over the pathetic spectacle this once glorious woman has now become. Far from transcending social and sexual constraints through performance, the narration weighs her down and humiliates her with her personal history.

What is particularly interesting about Wenders's film, *Wings of Desire*, is that at first it would seem to be deconstructing the myth of the aerialist as an insubstantial figure whose labour of performance is rendered invisible and who exists outside of time, space and society. In the first scene in which she appears we see Marion the trapeze artist being shouted at by an impatient circus manager. The dialogue between the two dramatises the tension outlined above between the labour behind the performance and its concealment during the show. He urges her to 'swing' but 'not with force' and follows this with a reprimand for 'dangling' and a command, 'FLY! You are an angel for heaven's sake.' Marion, who has been forced to wear a pair of tacked-on wings, shouts back that it is impossible to fly 'with these chicken wings', upon which he replies with some familiar rhetoric: 'Imagine you are a dove, Marion, or a lark, or a bunch of sparrows'. When the manager is reminded by a voice in the background that Marion works hard and makes an effort she retorts: 'I am making an effort! What do you think I am doing!' Not only is the labour of Marion's performance being foregrounded here, as well as the theatrical fakery of her ridiculous chicken-winged approximation of a bird in flight, she is also situated cinematically below Damiel, the Angel who is to fall in love with her. He is perched above her in the high wiring of the circus tent and, up to this point, he has been the truly winged and magically transcendental figure of the film.

The fact that Damiel is also an angel (and a real angel in contrast to Marion's performance of one) constructs a complementary relationship between the two which reverberates out towards a series of other connections in the film. They are the mirror image of each other in terms of their relationship to the look; she, the eternal spectacle who says she just wants to 'see the faces', and he, who must spend all his time looking at others whilst never himself being seen. The actual circus in which Marion works may come and go as a narrative presence in the film, yet, as we have seen in Dickens and Fellini, because the circus, and here specifically the trapeze artist, are the central symbolic figures of the film, they are constituitive of the visual language through which other issues are represented.

This is clear from the first few figuratively (rather than narratively) connecting shots of the film. These introduce a series of visual motifs which, in their common circularity of form, in each case contribute to the construction of a trail that leads us ultimately to the circus. Strangely for a film, and for a film about angels and circuses, the film is bookended by the written word. In the pre-title shots we see the refrain 'When the child was a child . . .' being handwritten in ink on a page as a voice reads and sings the subsequent words to us: words fabular in tone. This first line will be repeated throughout the film before the same hand appears again at the end to record a shift in knowledge and status as, we would assume, Damiel inscribes the words, 'I know now what no angel knows.' It is important that we see the words being written on a page in this very individual way, rather than being presented with print. Not only does this give language a personal style and therefore an opacity, but we also see the labour of its composition as a product of thought which might be revised and retold. In this way the film brings writing as close as it can be to a live performance. As an angel Damiel had been stuck in a permanently ideal condition, like a child whose price for being innocent is to be removed completely from influence or involvement in the world, particularly of a sensuous kind. Thus the repeated image of handwritten straight lines on a page almost paradoxically constructs a return within the plot which is circular but which, in terms of their meaning, in fact signals Damiel's escape within the narrative from circularity, repetition and fable/the fabulous. This is reinforced by the fact that, whereas the lines on the page are the first image of the film, they are not quite the last; the recording of Damiel's change in his state of existence is followed by three more: a contrasting shot of the still stranded Cassiel, succeeded by a shot of the storyteller, Homer, walking out into the world with his tales, then a voice-over proclaiming (in French), 'We have embarked!', over a final title ('To be continued'), all of which confirms the idea of a final movement to a new beginning. So the straight lines on the page produce a circularity in the plot, but one which eventually generates its own opening space for a departure and a future.

Next, the opening title sequence is again composed through an approximation of handwritten lettering, but this time they are chalk figures on a blackboard and are written in an almost childlike hand with the final title, 'Wings of Desire', composed in a semi-circular form. This blackness is succeeded and poetically matched as it fades into a shot of a dark, cloudy sky in which the clouds are just covering a bright sun, the circular shape of which is again matched by the next shot as a close-up of an eye is faded on to the previous one so that the iris of the eye exactly covers the space of the sun. This is a visual rhyme which is at the same time a reference to the opening of Luis Buñuel's *Un Chien Andalou* (1928) in which a shot of clouds crossing the moon is followed by a hand drawing an open razor across an eye; where Buñuel's surrealism assaults the eye, Wenders's poetic style pictures the eye open, alert, unblinking and innocent. Finally, an aerial shot of the Berlin cityscape is faded in over the eye, presenting the city to us as though seen through the eyes of an angel overlooking the earth. Again, however, we have a tension between straight lines and circularity as the city's grids of buildings and long, wide roads are filmed by a camera which circles vertiginously as it descends towards earth. These are all circles which will recur throughout the film and which constitute metonymic displacements of the circus: the sun and the moon which represent changing time and therefore mortality, the eye which is the eye of the spectator, of desire and of the witness to history, and the contradictory geographical space of what was West Berlin in which the wide, straight roads which are indicators of the city's modernity and progress are eternally circumscribed by the physical barrier which encircles it (as Marion says, 'I can't get lost. You always end up at the wall') and which is the simultaneous and constant signal of its historical legacy rather than its potential future. Wenders has chosen to focus on the these particular figures which emphasise that Berlin, like the circus space, is as much a symbolic 'site' as a real space and is therefore 'more than a city'.[34]

Two further circles will be important to the film. The first of these is referred to by Homer, who, as several critics have pointed out, is named after the poet Homer, Walter Benjamin's model for the teller of 'epic narrative'.[35] Whilst in the library he internally addresses the 'muse of the storyteller' and laments the passing of his listener/readers who now 'no longer sit in a circle' but 'sit apart now. One knows nothing about the other.' Though his stories still rise from within him in a 'liturgy of words and sentences', they are ineffectual in themselves without the mediating body of an audience to take their meaning into the world. The next circular space, the circus, stands as both a parallel and contrasting formation to Homer's lost circle of listeners in that they constitute exactly a replacement encircling audience, and yet they are absorbed not by narratives of either myth or history, but rather by the pure spectacle of performance and specifically here the aerialist's performance which, as I will argue, stands in tension with the flow of history. At the same time, the film clearly relates the circus to the cinema and to the process of film-making itself. Our first glimpse of the big top comes when Damiel's point of view guides the camera to look round a street corner through what appears to be a long rectangular tunnel at the end of which is the circus. The tunnel functions to present the circus as an image within the film image since its oblong outline is in exactly the same proportions as the larger image, though it is slightly off-centre. From the outset then, the circus is de-naturalised and distanced from us through this highly mediated view which fore-grounds it as a two-dimensional image which is physically cut off from the rest of world. At the same time, a child's voice-over accompanies the image with the line 'And they lived happily ever after'; this, together with the elephant walking past the front of the big top, lends the circus a fabular, childlike quality. This stands in contrast to the real lives of the children in the preceding scene who play without toys on the desolate streets of a Berlin housing estate. Again though, the film presents us with a problem of containment in terms of the incompatible dimensions of straight lines and circular boundaries; it is as though the film image must double itself to contain the circus within an internal black frame.

To a certain extent this tension corresponds to the one identified by David Harvey between the 'power of spatial images (photographs, the film itself, the striving of Damiel and Marion at the end to make an image the world can live by) and the power of the story'.[36] Classical film theory on the 'look' in cinema has argued for the ongoing tension within film narratives between two kinds of looking, both of which are characterised as male: the voyeuristic look which drives the narrative forward through its persistent curiosity over and interrogation of the figures with which it is presented; and the fetishistic look which has the effect of suspending narrative progression in favour of moments of pure spectacle with which it is entranced.[37] Harvey has read this dwelling on still images or moments of spectacle as a facet of the film's postmodernity, suggesting that it is occasionally 'caught in the circularity ... of its own images'. Within the context of this discussion, however, it is possible to see these moments instead as a visual dramatisation of a series of tensions embodied by the circus when it is faced with the problem of representational embodiment – tensions already familiar from the preceding discussions of Dickens and Fellini.[38]

Firstly, the lingering focus on framed and bordered images or photographs reminds us of the melancholy in Fellini's *The Clowns* over the photographic and film records of the now retired or dead clown figures: stilled pictures which simultaneously register the figure and its death or passing. Both Dickens's and Fellini's desire to represent the circus, as we have seen, is flavoured with an inevitable sense of loss or even death when the live charge of the circus is rerouted through immortalising but dead literary or film languages. In the shot I have just described above, Wenders introduces us to his circus, Circus Alekan, but in framing it within the frame he reminds us that it is simply an image of one and in accompanying this with the language of fairy tale he appears to push the circus towards a mythical and symbolic register rather than a realist one. Secondly, in this and through the other instances of still images referred to by Harvey, the circus becomes associated with a profound resistance to classical narrative movement; like Wenders's images of straight roads which are constantly being halted by bending highways or encircling walls, the possibility of straightforward narrative progression and continuum towards a final end is perpetually interrupted and diverted. This is a characteristic that, as I will argue, Marion the aerialist's performance comes to represent as her moments of pure performance put the final brakes on an albeit already digressive narrative. Inevitably, in a film which is overwhelmingly concerned with history and specifically with the connections between past, present and future Berlin, these figures of interruption, diversion, and the arresting of the present moment into moments of pure bodily spectacle have important implications and repercussions.

When Marion says, at the end of her time with the circus, 'I have no roots, no history, no country', she appears to be talking existentially rather than factually since there are photographs of her family in her tent and the final-night party shows her clearly close to the other members of the circus. In this sense she includes herself in what Yoram Carmeli has referred to as the illusory image of the circus which is consolidated by the circus's own publicity and by fictional representations of it, as a place of 'social isolation' which has 'a kind of immunity from social time and history'. For Carmeli the circus's 'performed apartness' allows 'spectators in a modern, fragmented society experientially [to] conjure up a totality they have lost'. [39] This would seem to confirm critics of the film such as Tania Modleski: she reads Marion as an essentially conventional, regressive figure in terms of her femaleness in that, as a potentially maternal figure, she represents 'not only mankind's "future", but the place of return, the locus of nostalgia'.[40] Certainly the film overtly discourses on the contemporary fragmentation of Berlin society, the mutual alienation of its inhabitants and the impossibility of producing a meaningful history or coherent story about it, and only seems to find optimism at the point when Damiel and Marion reach a point of romantic union. However, for a number of reasons, it feels wrong to read their union at the end in personal and sexual terms and as an abandonment of symbol and history. This is partly because their final union is presented in terms of continual speech and reflection but very little physical and no sexual contact and partly because, in her final scene, Marion's representation in her corde lisse performance is significantly altered from her earlier tricks on the trapeze: here she is at her most immortal, symbolic and asexual. Finally, for Damiel to be with Marion, rather representing a return for him to a place of coherence or wholeness, he forfeits his omniscience so that he may be propelled into a future rather than a continual present.

The terms on which Marion and Damiel are finally brought together are crucial to the understanding of the film's concept of history and, more specifically, of the temporal distinctions between past, present and future within the film. Their connection as winged figures sharing the common feature of transcendence (one works hard physically to transcend the circus space, the second who has no real body, is metaphysically transcendent) also makes obvious a the link to Walter Benjamin's 'Angel of History', a figure explicitly cited in the film when Damiel's voice-over mentions Benjamin's purchase of Paul Klee's painting, *Angelus Novus* and his subsequent thesis in which he ponders the picture's allegorical significance.[41]

Benjamin describes his Angel of History in thesis IX as a figure perpetually caught between, hesitating in a flux of contrary directions; he is 'about to move' yet his eyes are 'fixedly concentrating', his 'eyes are staring, his mouth is open, his wings are spread' in the suggestion of expectation, though his 'face is turned towards the past'. Allegorically of course this is also a figure for Benjamin himself and for those forced into exile during the period of his writing who, though they 'would like to stay, awaken the dead and make whole what has been smashed', they are violently expelled by the forces of 'progress'. For this reason, although both Benjamin and the film finish on a note of optimism ('This storm is what we call progress' [Benjamin], 'We have embarked!' [Wenders]), it is hard, as Robert Alter suggests, not to read Benjamin's tone as ironic given the terrible 'wreckage' which would be the immediate future of Europe. However, it is also ultimately double-edged since 'the Marxist and the Messianic in Benjamin would desperately want to give it a more positive meaning'.[42]

Wenders and Benjamin can also be seen to be caught, unknowingly, within a strange historical loop of events involving the Berlin Wall which, in each case, retrospectively effects the way we interpret their texts. Wenders almost occupies the place of the angel himself in making this film which turns back within the history of German philosophical thought to Walter Benjamin for its central image of the angel. Whilst Benjamin wrote this late essay in Paris just before the outbreak of the Second World War, Wenders contemplates the meaning of the Wall three years before it was pulled down in November 1989. Benjamin's impending war of course would, as we now know, finally produce the wall which divided Berlin in two and in this sense the wall (its making and unmaking) represents the unpredictable future(s) which both figures, as they contemplate the wreckage around them, will be propelled towards.

Wenders's filmic angels also explicitly resemble Benjamin's in two important ways. As Alter points out, they are modern, secular figures cut off from their role in Hebrew and Greek tradition as messengers and thereby removed from 'the realms of revelation and divine messages'.[43] Secondly, as Roger Cook has argued, Damiel and Cassiel are both forced 'to observe and verify it as they accompany it into the future with a painful countenance' but are unable to alter or influence it any way.[44] They are in an eternal present but, since they are not a part of it, they cannot produce a vision of its future. At the same time Wenders also constructs his angels in the image of Benjamin's 'chronicler' of history 'who recites events without distinguishing between major and minor ones', following the principle that 'nothing that has ever happened should be regarded as lost for history' because only when 'mankind' has a past which is 'fully citable in all its moments' can it be 'redeemed'.[45] This is exactly Damiel and Cassiel's occupation as they compile their lists of seemingly minor, banal and unconnected but unexpected moments in Berlin life which, they claim, testify 'on the spiritual in people's minds' and it is also what leads them to the circus and, in particular, to Damiel's involvement with Marion the aerialist.

Most importantly for this argument, in thesis V Benjamin describes the 'true picture of the past' in both temporal and spectacular terms; it is something brief and ephemeral which 'flits by' and which always manifests itself in the form of an 'image which flashes up at the instant when it can be recognised and is never seen again' and, if not recognised by the historian, 'threatens to disappear irretrievably'.[46] In the following thesis he makes imperative the need to 'seize hold of a memory as it flashes up at a moment of danger', which is essential if the dialectic process between present and past is to produce a vision of future progress.[47] Later, in thesis XVII, Benjamin describes the importance of moments of 'arrest' within the flow of thought where 'thinking suddenly stops in a configuration pregnant with tensions, it gives that configuration a shock, by which it crystallises into a monad'. This moment of arrest, if fully understood, may have the effect of 'blast[ing] a specific era out of the homogeneous course of history'. In all these respects, it is Marion, the aerialist, who comes to constitute Damiel's 'moment of danger': she is the image, the central source of spectacle in the film who also functions, in her performance or aerial stunts, to arrest the present moment.

I suggested above that the labour and danger of Marion's performance (in contrast with Damiel's ease perched in the ring as a 'natural' angel) is foregrounded and it appears that that at this point Wenders deconstructs the Romantic fantasies which, as I argued in the first half of the chapter, surrounded the figure of the nineteenth-century aerialist. Yet it was also clear that from the accounts of these women that, as Tait argued, they always also harboured a series of profound and troubling ambiguities, even contradictions, which involved their relationship not only to gender and sexuality but also to temporality and history. Part of the double-edged nature of the aerialists' appeal lay in their the idea of their performing 'stunts'; feats which carry both the appeal and the stigma of being exceptional. Russo's account of the 'stunt' also includes a description of the stunt's relationship to time which is relevant here. She quotes Michel de Certeau who contrasts the strategy with the stunt or tactic since the latter 'must be seized on the wing'. She goes on herself, again with reference to Amelia Earhart, to conclude that 'As a temporal category, the tactic, or in Earhart's terms, the practice of stunting, belongs to the improvisational, to the realm of what is possible in the moment.'[48] The stunt, though it may be well practised, maintains its danger and excitement to an audience precisely because it is an opportunistic seizing of the present moment, the live energy of which removes the figure involved from any temporal continuum in which it leaps or at least detaches itself from a past. However, like the moment of danger, since it does not have within it any immanent connection to a specific future, the stunt points only 'to inherent possibility rather than future progress', a possibility which may be either lost or realised.[49]

Almost paradoxically, as *Wings of Desire* progresses, Marion is drawn away from the circus in which, as we have seen, her labour has a kind of grounding function in that, whilst there, she is a character with a family and friends, a job and a society. Gradually, just as Damiel becomes more and more drawn towards an earthly existence and mortality, she becomes less a character and more of a symbol. Her speech to Damiel in the bar makes this very clear as she tells him, 'We are the present day now. The whole town, the whole world is taking part in our decision. We two are now more than us two!' Though she dresses all in red as a classic femme fatale on the night she goes out to meet Damiel, in the crucial scene after this when their union is complete, she cuts a very different figure. This time it is Damiel who looks up at Marion, not the other way round and she who spins this time effortlessly on her corde lisse. In contrast to her previous gaudy, glittery and highly fetishistic circus costumes (even when she performs for the children's show she wears a cat's tail), here she wears a black leotard and tights in which, with her hair tied up, she appears relatively androgynous. Not only does the performance emphasise her lack of gravity, but at one point her body is reduced cinematically to a mere shadow reflected against the wall. As in the first scene, the dialogue is very telling here, partly because this time she has no speech. Only Damiel speaks in an authoritative voice-over which outlines an idealistic vision of spiritual unity and new beginnings. Whilst he has acquired a material body, she has been transformed, in his eyes, into a spirit – 'she was around me' and he is 'in her', he claims. Again, their union produces not a 'mortal child' but rather what he describes as an 'immortal shared image': a reminder both of Benjamin's use of a metaphor which also makes reference to female conception in his account of the moment of danger which is 'pregnant' with meaning and of Le Roux and Garnier's fastidiousness about the need for the female trapeze artist to remain virginal and physically untouched by 'love'. The invasion of Marion's body, and the child produced as a result, are entirely spiritual in this account. Indeed here, as well as in Benjamin and, to an extent, Le Roux and Garnier, conception is displaced from being a biological dimension of the female to being a mental facility for constructing a metaphor for future history (Damiel and Benjamin) or an ideal of the feminine (Le Roux and Garnier) which in each case belongs to the masculine.

It is significant in this respect that Wenders shows Damiel's walking to and fro around the circus tent without leaving the normal footprint trace behind him and later that the first sign of his mortality is Cassiel's sighting of the imprints of Damiel's foot in the dirt behind him. As Peter Stallybrass has pointed out, circus goes further even than ballet in presenting artists who perform the modern fantasy of a 'human whose feet have disappeared' and therefore, because they 'no longer bruise the earth are the logical feet of the bourgeois citizen, the transcendental individual'. In this respect they are the opposite of the clown's lumbering, tripping feet which 'tread[s] on dung' while the aerialist 'walks on air'.[50] Indeed Damiel, almost seems to become a clown in the moment he reawakens as a mortal being. The instant he wakes up he is clobbered on the head with a piece of armoury which falls out of a helicopter (an industrial angel) and which he trades in for some garish badly fitting clothes. He is first seen by a group of children who believe him drunk, has an absurd conversation about colours with a passer-by who, clearly thinking him a tramp or a fool, gives him money and, finally, he gets his timing wrong and misses Marion whose circus has left its site by the time he gets there. This forces him to sit down in the circular space left by the circus in a scene which is a direct visual quotation from the final shot in Charles Chaplin's *The Circus* (1927) when Chaplin, who is a more effective clown outside the ring than in it, choses to abandon the circus and, with it, the object of his impossible love, Merna, also a aerial artist. The removal of physical transcendence with its concomitant return to history and to the mortal body introduces the possibility of collision, breakage and misunderstanding and, with this, humour. Before this, humour in the film comes from mortals and involves Damiel only when he is momentarily shocked by an ironic comment from the roustabouts in Marion's circus about her being an 'angel'. The comment seems to miss Marion and, though it is picked up by Damiel, the joke is that he could momentarily believe that, in being visibly identified by humans as an angel, he has been mistaken for a mortal human when of course human eyes may only ever perceive joke or fake angels such as Marion. In other words, as we have already learnt from Bergson, mortality is the condition of humour and its agency is always both social and 'strictly human'.[51] A transcendent figure (physical or historical), therefore, may never be the source of humour, only ever its subject or its foil, because human subject's are the source of a joke precisely because, weighed down by their human-ness, they fall short of an ideal which is essential to the humour but is, by definition, always impossibly somewhere else.

To conclude, then, Wenders's circus figures function to allegorise Benjamin; that is, the central circus figure of the aerialist to dramatise cinematically moments of danger which are captured by the dutiful chronicler of human behaviour and which spark off in this figure, trapped eternally in the present, a mutual vision of the future. So the film is an allegory about the role of danger in the creation of possibility rather than an image of what might emerge from it. Both the clown and the aerialist are figures within a meditation on the possibility of retrieving a vision of the future from the wreckage of the past (Berlin). Yet the film does not or cannot give us such a vision – only the promise of a journey towards it which, interestingly, is under-taken not by Damiel or Marion but by the old Jewish storyteller, Homer, who is presented in the film as its most authentic connection to all the previously hidden and untold elements from the past.

In this sense the aerialist in her final moments is at her least dangerous and her most abstract; again we have the circus being used as a site of physical danger, sexual excitement and comedy, but these are not ele-ments which the film itself embodies; rather it is interested in these elements as ideas and concepts – precisely as metaphorical figures. Again circus figures are mobilised in a way which confirms the circus as a site of myth, fantasy, symbol and therefore removed from or outside the world, history and reality; of danger which is spectacular and inspiring rather than vital in itself. As we have seen, Dickens and Fellini are careful to present the circus as within realist discourses of economic hardship and commercial opportunism at the same time as they explore the ways in which this image may be in conflict with its symbolic and metaphori-cal potential. Likewise, Wenders initially foregrounds the grim and banal dimensions of the Circus Alekan's existence before his increasingly in-tense focus on the symbolic but ambiguous image of the aerialist means that, following her separation from the circus ring, her abstract and symbolic significance supersedes her physical and sexual presence.

Notes

1 Marius Kwint, 'Astley's amphitheatre and the early circus in England', D.Phil thesis, Oxford University, 1994, pp. 268–9.
2 April 1817, BL *Astley's Cuttings from Newspapers*, vol. 3, item 670. Arthur L. Hayward, *The Days of Dickens* (London, George Routledge & Sons, 1926), p. 169.
3 See Kwint, 'Astley's amphitheatre', pp. 269–70.
4 12 June 1784, BL *Astley's Cuttings from Newspapers*, vol. 1, item 561.
5 5 'W', 'The carnival at Venice', *The Theatrical Journal*, 1849, reprinted in Raymond Toole-Stott, *Circus and Allied Arts: A World Bibliography*, vol. 4 (Derby, Harpur & Sons, 1971), appendix C, pp. 299–300.
6 'W', *Circus. and Allied Arts*, p. 300.
7 'W', *Circus and Allied Arts*, p. 300.
8 'W', *Circus and Allied Arts*, p. 300.
9 Steve Gossard points to evidence suggesting that William Hanlon, one of a troupe of trapeze artist brothers originating from Manchester, claims to have started performing a similar act during a tour of Russia in 1855. *A Reckless Era of Aerial Performance: The Evolution of Trapeze* (Normal, Illinois, the author, 1994), p. 49.
10 George Speaight, *A History of the Circus* (London, Tantivy Press, 1980), p. 73.
11 7 November 1868, *New York Clipper*.
12 See Gossard, *A Reckless Era*, pp. 10–12.
13 Hugues Le Roux and Jules Garnier, *Acrobats and Mountebanks*, trans. A. P. Morton (London, Chapman & Hall, 1890), pp. 209–10.
14 Le Roux and Garnier, *Acrobats and Mountebanks*, p. 210.
15 Again, Gossard suggests that Azella may have been preceded by Mme Senyah (Mrs Haynes). In her memoirs she makes the claim that she performed the leap in 1867. See Gossard, *A Reckless Era*, p. 48.
16 Arthur J. Munby quoted in Derek Hudson, *Munby: Man of Two Worlds: The Life and Diaries of Arthur . J. Munby 1828–1910* (London, John Murray, 1972), p. 252. Another contemporary account of Azella justifies her scant clothing by suggesting that 'flowing female dresses' would simply be a hazard in getting 'caught in the ropes' and at the same time claims that the 'amount of nerve, daring, and muscular strength required for such feats is given but to few men, and, we should have thought until we saw Azella, to no woman,' *The Liverpool Daily Post*, 17 February 1868.
17 Thomas Frost, *Circus Life and Circus Celebrities* (London, Chatto & Windus, 1881), pp. 179–80.
18 Some female performers at the beginning of the century played up the fetishistic appeal of their acts by performing what became known as the trapeze disrobing act in which they would claim to 'disrobe whilst hanging from a trapeze or iron-jaw apparatus though this actually involved taking

off a trick costume underneath which they would be wearing the customary tights and leotard. see Robert C. Allen, *Horrible Prettiness: Burlesque and American Culture* (Chapel Hill, North Carolina University Press, 1991), p. 26.

19 Munby, *Munby*, p. 122.

20 Munby, *Munby*, p. 255.

21 John Turner reports that 'Lulu', the female impersonator, was presented by Farini in Glasgow in March 1875, having first appeared on stage in 1871, but that an accident in Dublin in 1876, of which no details are given, 'led to public knowledge that she was a young man', *Historical Hengler's Circus* (Formby, Lingdales Press, 1989–90), vol. 3, epilogue.

22 George Speaight lists several female impersonators: Alfred Clarke/Mlle Isabella, Alfred Johnson/Miss Beatrice and 'Little Ella, an equestrian whom Speaight supposes was male but who may have been a 'true hermaphrodyte', *History of the Circus*, p. 74 and 106. Shane Peacock cites some interesting references to Lulu's celebrity status in an article on her manager and adoptive father. see 'The amazing life of G. A. Farini', *King Pole*, 79 (1988), pp. 8–9. Barbette (Vander Clyde) was a high-wire and trapeze artist from Round Rock, Texas, who, after circus work in New York, became a cabaret star in Paris in the 1920s where he met Jean Cocteau. He appeared in several films including Cocteau's *Blood of a Poet* (1930), and Hitchcock is said to have based his character of the homosexual/female impersonator/trapeze artist/murderer in *Murder* (1930) on him. see Francis Steegmuller, 'Onward and upward with the arts: an angel, a flower, a bird', *New Yorker*, 45:32 (1969), pp. 130–43, David Lewis Hammarstrom, *Behind the Big Top* (South Brunswick, NJ, A. S. Barnes, 1980), Roy R. Barkley (ed.), *The Handbook of Texas* (Austin, The Texas State Historical Society, 1991) and Lydia Crowson, 'Cocteau and "Le Numéro Barbette"', *Modern Drama*, 19:1 (1976), pp. 79–87.

23 Peta Tait, 'Feminine free fall: a fantasy of freedom, *Theatre Journal*, 48 (1996), p. 30. see Peter Stallybrass and Allon White, *The Politics and Poetics of Transgression* (Methuen, London, 1986), pp. 4–6.

24 Munby, *Munby*, p. 287.

25 Mikhail Bakhtin, *Dostoevsky's Poetics* (Manchester, Manchester University Press [1973], 1984), p. 123.

26 Judith Butler, *Gender Trouble* (London, Routledge, 1990), p. 136.

27 Peta Tait, 'Danger delights: texts of gender and race in aerial performance', *New Theatre Quarterly*, 12:45 (1996), p. 43.

28 Tait, 'Feminine free fall', p. 33.

29 John Whale, in his essay on Hazlitt's 'The Indian Juggler', makes a very similar point when he claims that, to some extent, juggling effaces the recognition of difference. At the same time as triumphing the limits of the body, it triumphs over an overdetermined awareness of racial difference. But when the body makes itself known, as difference becomes apparent,

and the body's colour becomes once again the determining sign of cultural classification and racial identity.' 'Indian jugglers: Hazlitt, Romantic orientalism and the difference of view', in Tim Fulford and Peter Kitson (eds), *Romanticism and Colonialism: Writing and Empire, 1780–1830* (Cambridge, Cambridge University Press, 1998), pp. 207–8.

30 Yoram Carmeli, 'The travelling circus: an interpretation', *European Journal of Sociology*, 29 (1988), p. 275.

31 Mary Russo, *The Female Grotesque: Risk, Excess and Modernity* (London, Routledge, 1994), pp. 22–3.

32 Carolyn Steedman, *Strange Dislocations: Childhood and the Idea of Human Interiority, 1780–1930* (London, Virago, 1995), p. 98.

33 Djuna Barnes, *Nightwood* (London, Faber & Faber [1936], 1985) and Franz Kafka, *The Transformation and Other Stories* (Harmondsworth, Penguin Books, 1992), pp. 199–201.

34 Wenders quoted in Ira Paneth, 'Wim and his Wings', *Film Quarterly*, 42:1 (1988), p. 2.

35 Walter Benjamin, 'The Storyteller' (1936), *Illuminations*, ed. Hannah Arendt, trans. Harry Zohn (London, Fontana Press [1973], 1992), 83–107.

36 David Harvey, *The Condition of Postmodernity: An Enquiry into the Origins of Cultural Change* (Oxford, Blackwell, 1990), p. 321. Several other writers read the film in terms of its postmodernity. see, for example, David Caldwell and Paul Rea, 'Handke and Wenders' *Wings of Desire*: transcending postmodernism', *The German Quarterly*, 64:1 (1991), pp. 46–54 and Robert Philip Kolker and Peter Beicken, *The Films of Wim Wenders: Cinema as Vision and Desire* (Cambridge, Cambridge University Press, 1993), pp. 138–60.

37 For reference see John Ellis, *Visible Fictions* (London, Routledge, 1982), pp. 62–91 and Laura Mulvey, 'Visual pleasure and narrative cinema', *Screen*, 16:3 (1975), pp. 6–18.

38 Harvey, *The Condition of Postmodernity*, p. 321.

39 Yoram Carmeli, 'Text, traces and the reification of totality: the case of popular circus literature', *New Literary History*, 25 (1994), p. 181 and p. 176.

40 Tania Modleski, *Feminism Without Women: Culture and Criticism in a Postfeminist Age* (London, Routledge, 1991), p. 108.

41 Walter Benjamin, 'Theses on the philosophy of history' (1940), *Illuminations*, ed. Hannah Arendt, trans. Harry Zohn (London, Fontana Press [1973], 1992), p. 249.

42 Robert Alter, *Necessary Angels: Tradition and Modernity in Kafka, Benjamin and Scholem* (Cambridge MA, Harvard University Press, 1991), p. 115.

43 Alter, *Necessary Angels*, p. 114.

44 Roger Cook, 'Angels, fiction and history in Berlin: Wim Wenders' *Wings of Desire*', *The Germanic Review*, 66:1 (1991), p. 45.

45 Benjamin, 'Theses on the philosophy of history', p. 246.

46 Benjamin, 'Theses on the philosophy of history', p. 247.
47 Benjamin, 'Theses on the philosophy of history', p. 247.
48 Russo, *The Female Grotesque*, p. 22.
49 Russo, *The Female Grotesque*, p. 30.
50 Peter Stallybrass, 'Footnotes', in David Hillman and Carla Mazzio (eds), *The Body in Parts: Fantasies of Corporealities in Early Modern Europe* (London, Routledge, 1997), p. 313.
51 Henri Bergson, *Laughter: An Essay on the Meaning of the Comic*, trans. Cloudesley Brereton and Fred Rothwell (London, Macmillan [1911], 1935), p. 3.

Bibliography

Fiction

Braddon, Mary Elizabeth, *Lady Audley's Secret*, ed. David Skilton, Oxford, Oxford University Press [1862], 1987.

Carter, Angela, *Nights at the Circus*, London, Vintage [1984], 1994.

Collins, Wilkie, *Hide and Seek*, ed. Catherine Peters, Oxford, Oxford University Press [1854], 1993.

—— *The Woman in White*, ed. Julian Symons, Harmondsworth, Penguin [1860], 1985.

—— *The Moonstone*, ed. Anthea Trodd, Oxford, Oxford University Press [1868], 1982.

Dickens, Charles, 'Astley's' (1835), *Dickens' Journalism: Sketches by Boz and Other Early Papers, 1833–39*, ed. Michael Slater, London, Phoenix, 1996, pp. 106–11.

—— *The Pickwick Papers*, ed. James Kinsley, Oxford, Oxford University Press [1837–7], 1988.

—— ed. *Grimaldi; the Clown*, London, George Routledge and Sons [1838], 1884.

—— *Nicholas Nickleby*, ed. Paul Schlicke, Oxford, Oxford University Press [1838–9], 1990.

—— *The Old Curiosity Shop*, ed. Angus Easson, Harmondsworth, Penguin Books [1840–41], 1985.

—— *Pictures from Italy*, ed. Kate Flint, Harmondsworth, Penguin Books [1846], 1998.

—— A Strange Dance Round a Strange Tree, *Household Words*, 17 January 1852, pp. 385–89.

—— *Bleak House*, ed. Norman Page, Harmondsworth, Penguin Books [1853], 1985.

—— *Hard Times*, ed. Paul Schlicke, Oxford, Oxford University Press [1854], 1989.

Hazlitt, William, 'The Indian Jugglers' (1825), *William Hazlitt: Selected Writings*, Oxford, Oxford University Press, 1991.

Irving, John, *A Son of the Circus*, London, Bloomsbury, 1994.

Bibliography

Mayakovsky, Vladimir, *Moscow Is Burning* (1930), trans. Helen Wilga and Ewa Bartos, repr. in *The Drama Review*, 17:1 (1973), pp. 64–89.

Reade, Amye, *Slaves of the Sawdust*, London, F. V. White, 1892.

—— *Ruby; a Novel, Founded on the Life of a Circus Girl*, London, Author's Co-operative Publishing Company, 1889.

Twain, Mark, *The Adventures of Huckleberry Finn*, ed. Victor Doyno, London, Bloomsbury [1885], 1996.

Wood, Mrs Henry, *East Lynne*, London, Dent [1861], 1984.

Filmography

Birth of a Nation (dir. D. W. Griffith, 1915, US).

Un Chien Andalou (dir. Luis Buñuel, 1928, Fr.).

The Circus (dir. Charles Chaplin, 1928, US).

The Clowns (dir. Federico Fellini, 1970, It.).

The Crowd (King Vidor, 1927, US).

8½ (dir. Federico Fellini, 1963, It.).

Freaks (dir. Tod Browning, 1932, US).

Intervista (dir. Federico Fellini, 1987, It.).

Juliet of the Spirits (dir. Federico Fellini, 1965, It.).

Napoléon (dir. Abel Gance, 1925, Fr.).

Lola Montes (dir. Max Ophuls, 1955, Fr.).

La Strada (dir. Federico Fellini, 1954, It.).

Trapeze (dir. Carol Reed, 1956, US).

Wings of Desire (dir. Wim Wenders, 1986, Ger.).

Bills, press cuttings, programmes and magazine articles

Astley's Cuttings From Newspapers (1768–1856), Scrapbook, 3 vols, Th. Cts. 35–7.

A Collection of Programmes, Cuttings From Newspapers Relating to Performances in Various Circuses from 1772–1858, Scrapbook, 2 vols, Th. Cts. 50.

Ballantine, Bill, Spring's Shameless Ballyhoo, *True, the Man's Magazine*, March 1967, pp. 41–3.

'Burt is back in the big top' (anon), *Friends*, March 1956, pp. 26–7.

Sreedharan Champad, 'The circus in India', *King Pole*, 104 (1994), pp. 35–6.

The Champion, 29 December 1816, p. 132.

Chaudhary, Vivek, 'Campaign aims to outlaw "world of suffering" for circus animals', *Guardian*, 3 August 1993, p. 5.

Circus Fans Association of the United States, 'Position statement on animal welfare', *White Tops*, 63:6 (1990), p. 7.

de Jongh, Nicholas, 'French circus banned', *Guardian*, 21 July 1990, p. 2.

Bibliography

'Gentleman, Amelia Circus lifts girl beggar from low life to high wire', *Guardian*, 30 August 1999, p. 20.

Ghazi, Polly, 'Circus trade thrives on wildlife misery', *Observer*, 11 December 1994, p. 10.

Hubbard, Freeman H., '100 years of circus trains', *Railroad*, April 1956, pp. 12–27.

Illustrated London News, 59, 28 October 1871, p. 407.

Kennedy, Maev, 'Circus runs away to join the Dutch', *Guardian*, 22 March 1990, p. 3.

The Liverpool Daily Post, 17 February 1868.

New York Clipper, 7 November 1868.

New York Times, 6 April 1998.

Ringling Brothers Barnum and Bailey Program 1954, Special Collections, Milner Library, State University of Illinois.

Jeanne Rousch, 'Animals under the big top', *The Humane Society News*, spring 1981, pp. 18–21.

Ruling, Karl G., 'Three ring lighting', *Lighting Dimensions*, November 1995, pp. 95–7.

Steegmuller, Francis, 'Onward and upward with the arts: an angel, a flower, a bird', *New Yorker*, 45:32 (1969), pp. 130–43.

Townsend Walsh Scrapbook, Hertzberg Collection, San Antonio Public Library, San Antonio, Texas.

Vertical Files, Circus World Museum, Baraboo, Wisconsin: Lighting, Advertising, Lillian Leitzel.

Zotti, Ed, 'Circus advertising: the greatest hype on earth', *Advertising Age*, 12 December 1983, p. 11.

Books

Ackroyd, Peter, *Dickens*, London, Sinclair-Stevenson, 1990.

Adams, Anthony, and Leach, Robert (eds), *Talent, Wonder and Delight: A Scrapbook of Victorian Entertainment*, Glasgow, Blackie & Son, 1976.

Allen, Robert C., *Horrible Prettiness: Burlesque and American Culture*, Chapel Hill, North Carolina University Press, 1991.

Alter, Robert, *Necessary Angels: Tradition and Modernity in Kafka, Benjamin and Scholem*, Cambridge, MA, Harvard University Press, 1991.

Altick, Richard, *The Shows of London*, Cambridge, MA, Belknap, 1978.

Angelo, Henry, *Reminiscences of Henry Angelo, With Memoirs of His Late Father and Friends*, 2 vols, London, Henry Colburn, 1828.

Astley, Philip, *The Modern Riding Master: Or, A Key to the Knowledge of the Horse and Horsemanship, with Several Necessary Rules for Young Horseman*, London, 1775.

Axton, William F., *Circle of Fire: Dickens' Vision and Style and the Popular Theater*, Lexington, Kentucky University Press, 1966.

Bibliography

Bakhtin, Mikhail, *Problems in Dostoevsky's Poetics*, trans. and ed., Caryl Emerson, Manchester, Manchester University Press, 1984.

Barkley, Roy R. (ed.), *The Handbook of Texas*, Austin, The Texas State Historical Society, 1991.

Barnum, Phineas, Taylor, *Struggles and Triumphs: or Forty Years' Recollections of P. T. Barnum*, Buffalo, New York, Warren, Johnson & Co., 1873.

Barthes, Roland, *Camera Lucida*, London, Flamingo, 1984.

Bemrose, Paul, *Circus Genius: A Tribute to Philip Astley 1742–1814*, Newcastle-under-Lyme, Priory Publications, 1992.

Bergeron, David, M., *English Civic Pageantries*, London, Edward Arnold, 1971.

Bergson, Henri, *Laughter: An Essay on the Meaning of the Comic*, trans. Cloudesley Brereton and Fred Rothwell, London, Macmillan [1911], 1935.

Booth, Michael, R., *Victorian Spectacular Theatre 1850–1910*, London, Routledge & Kegan Paul, 1981.

Bordwell, David, and Thompson, Kristin, *Film Art: An Introduction*, fifth edition (New York McGraw-Hill, 1996).

Bouissac, Paul, *Circus and Culture: A Semiotic Approach* (Bloomington, Indiana University Press [1974], 1976.

Bowlby, Rachel, *Just Looking: Consumer Culture in Dreiser, Gissing and Zola*, London, Methuen, 1985.

Bradby, David, James, Louis, and Sherratt, Bernard (eds), *Performance and Politics in Popular Drama: Aspects of Popular Entertainment in Theatre, Film and Television 1800–1976*, Cambridge, Cambridge University Press, 1980.

Braun, Edward (ed.), *Meyerhold on Theatre*, London, Eyre Methuen, 1969.

Brooks, Peter, *The Melodramatic Imagination: Balzac, Henry James, Melodrama, and the Mode of Excess*, New Haven and London, Yale University Press, 1995.

Budgen, Suzanne, *Fellini*, London: BFI Education, 1966.

Burch, Noël, *Life to those Shadows*, trans. Ben Brewster, London, BFI Publishing, 1990.

Burke, Frank, *Federico Fellini: Variety Lights to La Dolce Vita*, Boston, Twayne Publishing, 1984.

Butler, Judith, *Gender Trouble*, London, Routledge, 1990.

Carlson, Marvin, *Performance: A Critical Introduction*, London, Routledge, 1996.

Chindahl, George, *A History of the Circus in America*, Caldwell, Idaho, The Caxton Printers, 1959.

Connor, Steven, *Charles Dickens*, Oxford, Oxford University Press, 1985.

Costanzo Costantini (ed.), *Fellini on Fellini*, London, Faber & Faber, 1994.

Cook, David A., *A History of Narrative Film*, New York, W. W. Norton, 1981.

Cook, Pam (ed.), *The Cinema Book*, London, BFI Publishing, 1986.

Corti, Victor (ed.), *Collected Works of Antonin Artaud*, vol. 4, London, Calder & Boyars, 1974.

Costello, Donald P., *Fellini's Road*, Notre Dame and London, University of Notre Dame Press, 1983.

Bibliography

Coxe, Antony Hippisley, *A Seat at the Circus*, London and Basingstoke, Macmillan, 1980.

Croft-Cooke, Rupert, and Cotes, Peter, *Circus: A World History*, London, Macmillan, 1976.

Cross, J. C., *Circusiana; or a Collection of the Most Favorite Ballets, Spectacles; Melodrames, etc. Performed at the Royal Circus, St George's Fields*, 2 vols, London, Lackington, Allen & Co., 1809.

Culhane, John, *The American Circus: An Illustrated History*. New York, Henry Holt, 1990.

Cunningham, Hugh, *Leisure in the Industrial Revolution c. 1780–c. 1880*. London, Croom Helm, 1980.

Cvetkovich, Ann, *Mixed Feelings: Feminism, Mass Culture and Victorian Sensationalism*, Brunswick, NJ, Rutgers University Press, 1992.

Decastro, Joseph, *The Memoirs of J. Decastro, Comedian*, London, Sherwood, Jones & Co., 1824.

Dentith, Simon, *Bakhtinian Thought: An Introductory Reader*, London, Routledge, 1995.

Derrida, Jacques, *Dissemination*, trans. Barbara Johnson, London, Athlone Press, [1972], 1997.

Dibdin, Charles, *History and Illustrations of the London Theatres*, London, J. Moyes, 1826.

Disher, M. Willson, *Clowns and Pantomimes*, London, Constable, 1925.

—— *Fairs, Circuses and Music Halls*, London, Collins, 1942.

John Dungeness Manuscript (unpublished manuscript), Hertzberg Collection, San Antonio Public Library, San Antonio, Texas.

Dyer, Richard, *Stars*, London, BFI Publishing, 1979.

Easton, Susan, Howkins, Alun, Laing, Stuart, Merricks, Linda and Walker, Helen, *Disorder and Discipline: Popular Culture From 1550 to the Present*, Aldershot, Temple Smith, 1988.

Eigner, Edwin M., *The Dickens Pantomime*, Berkeley, California University Press, 1989.

Ellis, John, *Visible Fictions*, London, Routledge, 1982.

Esslin, Martin, *The Theatre of the Absurd*, Harmondsworth, Penguin Books [1961], 1991.

Leslie Fiedler, *Freaks: Myths and Images of the Secret Self*, New York, Simon & Schuster, 1978.

Findlater, Richard, *Memoirs of Joseph Grimaldi* (1838) London, Macgibbon & Kee, 1968.

—— Grimaldi: King of Clowns, London, Macgibbon & Kee, 1955.

Frost, Thomas, *The Old Showmen and the Old London Fairs*, London, Tinsley, 1875.

—— *Circus Life and Circus Celebrities*, London, Chatto & Windus, 1881.

Gallagher, Catherine, *The Industrial Reformation of English Fiction: Social Discourse and Narrative Form 1832–1867*, Chicago, Chicago University Press, 1985.

Bibliography

Gossard, Steve, *A Reckless Era of Aerial Performance: The Evolution of the Flying Trapeze*, Normal, Illinois, the Author, 1994.

Greenwood, Issac, *The Circus: Its Origins and Growth*, New York, Dunlop Society, 1898.

Hammarstrom, David Lewis, *Big Top Boss: John Ringling North and the Circus*, Urbana and Chicago, Illinois University Press, 1992.

Harris, Neil, *Humbug: The Art of P. T. Barnum*, Chicago and London, University of Chicago Press, 1973.

Harvey, David, *The Condition of Postmodernity: An Enquiry into the Origins of Cultural Change*, Oxford, Blackwell, 1990.

Hayward, Arthur, L., *The Days of Dickens*, London, George Routledge & Sons, 1926.

Hinchcliffe, Arnold, P., *The Absurd*, London, Methuen, 1969.

House, Madeline, and Storey, Graham (eds), *The Letters of Charles Dickens vol. II, 1840–41*, Oxford, Clarendon Press, 1969.

Hudson, Derek, *Munby: Man of Two Worlds, The Life and Diaries of Arthur J. Munby 1828–1910*, London, John Murray, 1972.

Ricky Jay, *Learned Pigs and Fireproof Women*, New York, Villard Books, 1986.

Keel, Anna and Strich, Christian (eds), *Fellini on Fellini*, trans. Isabel Quigley, London, Eyre Methuen, 1976.

Kiley-Worthington, Marthe, *Animals in Circuses and Zoos*, Basildon, Little Eco Farms Publishing, 1990.

Kolker, Robert Philip, and Beicken, Peter, *The Films of Wim Wenders: Cinema as Vision and Desire*, Cambridge, Cambridge University Press, 1993, pp. 138–60.

Larrabee, Eric, and Meyersohn, Rolf (ed.), *Mass Leisure*, Glencoe, Illinois, The Free Press, 1958.

Leprohon, Pierre, *The Italian Cinema*, London, Secker & Warburg, 1972.

Liehm, Mira, *Passion and Defiance: Film in Italy from 1942 to the Present*, Berkeley and Los Angeles, University of California Press, 1984.

The Lives and Portraits of Remarkable Characters, Drawn From the Most Authentic Sources, 2 vols, London, W. Lewis, 1819.

Loxton, Howard, *The Golden Age of the Circus*, London, Grange Books, 1977.

Lukens, John, *The Sanger Story: Being George Sanger Coleman's Story of his Life with his Grandfather 'Lord' George Sanger*, London, Hodder-Stoughton, 1956.

Le Roux, Hugues, and Garnier, Jules *Acrobats and Mountebanks*, A. P. Morton, trans. London, Chapman & Hall, 1890.

McCabe, Colin (ed.) *High Theory/Low Culture: Analysing Popular Television and Film*, Manchester, Manchester University Press, 1986.

Malcolmson, Robert W., *Popular Recreations in English Society 1700–1850*, Cambridge, Cambridge University Press, 1973.

Mannix, Dan, *Memoirs of a Sword-Swallower*, London, Hamish Hamilton, 1951.

May, Earl Chapin, *The Circus from Rome to Ringling*, New York, Dover Publications [1932], 1963.

Bibliography

Meisel, Martin. *Rèalisations: Narrative, Pictorial and Theatrical Arts in Nineteenth-Century England*, Princeton, Princeton University Press, 1983.

Mills, Cyril Bertram, *Bertram Mills Circus: Its Story*, Bath, Ashgrove Press, 1983.

Modleski, Tania, *Feminism Without Women: Culture and Criticism in a Postfeminist Age*, London, Routledge, 1991.

Murray, Marian, *Circus! From Rome to Ringling*, Westport, CT, Greenwood Press [1956], 1973.

Newton, Douglas, *Clowns*, London, George G. Harrap and Co., 1958.

Nietzsche, Friedrich, *Thus Spoke Zarathustra: A Book For Every One and No One*, trans. R.J. Hollingdale, Harmondsworth, Penguin Books [1885], 1969.

Ogden, Tom, *Two Hundred Years of the American Circus*, New York, Facts on File Inc., 1993.

Oxberry's Dramatic Biography; Or, The Green-Room Spy, vol. 1, London, G. Virtue, 1827.

Pykett, Lyn, *The Sensation Novel from 'The Woman in White' to 'The Moonstone'*, Plymouth, Northcote House Publishers, 1994.

Ritter, Naomi, *Art as Spectacle: Images of the Entertainer since Romanticism* Columbia and London, University of Missouri Press, 1989.

Royle, Edward, *Modern Britain: A Social History 1750–1985*, London, Edward Arnold, 1987.

Rudlin, John, *Commedia dell'Arte: An Actor's Handbook*, London, Routledge, 1994.

Rudnitsky, Konstantin, *Russian and Soviet Theatre, 1905–1932*, trans. Roxane Permar, New York, Harry N. Abrams, 1988.

Russo, Mary, *The Female Grotesque: Risk, Excess and Modernity*, London, Routledge, 1994.

Said, Edward, *Orientalism*, Harmondsworth, Penguin Books [1978], 1995.

Sanger, 'Lord' George, *Seventy Years a Showman*, London, J. M. Dent & Sons, 1927.

Saxon, A. H., *Enter Foot and Horse: A History of the Hippodrama in England and France*, New Haven and London, Yale Univeristy Press, 1968.

—— *The Life and Art of Andrew Ducrow and the Romantic Age of the English Circus*, Hamden, CT, Archon Books, 1978.

Schlicke, Paul, *Dickens and Popular Entertainment*, London, George Allen & Unwin, 1985.

—— (ed.), *Oxford Reader's Companion to Dickens* Oxford, Oxford University Press, 1999.

Sedgwick, Eve, *The Coherence of Gothic Conventions*, London, Methuen, 1986.

Sontag, Susan, *On Photography*, Harmondsworth, Penguin Books, 1979.

Speaight, George, *A History of the Circus*, London, Tantivy Press, 1980.

Stallybrass, Peter, and White, Allon, *The Politics and Poetics of Transgression*, London, Methuen, 1986.

Steedman, Carolyn, *Strange Dislocations: Childhood and the Idea of Human Interiority 1780–1930*, London, Virago, 1995.

Bibliography

Stewart, Susan, *On Longing: Narratives of the Miniature, the Gigantic, the Souvenir, the Collection*, Durham, NC, and London, Duke University Press, 1993.

Thayer, Stuart, *Annals of the American Circus*, vol. 1, Manchester, Michigan, Rymack Print Co., 1976.

—— *Annals of the American Circus*, vol. 2, Seattle, Peanut Butter Publishing, 1986.

—— *Annals of the American Circus*, vol. 3, Seattle, Dauven & Thayer, 1992.

Thompson, E. P., *The Making of the English Working Class*, London, Penguin Books [1963], 1988.

Toole-Stott, Ray, *Circus and Allied Arts: A World Biography*, 4 vols, Derby, Harpur, 1958–71.

Lietta Tornbuoni (ed.), *Federico Fellini*, New York, Rizzoli International Publications, 1995.

Turner, John, *Historical Hengler's Circus*, 4 vols, Formby, Lingdales Press, 1989–90.

Tyler, Parker, *Chaplin: Last of the Clowns*, New York, Vanguard Press, 1948.

Truzzi, Marcello (ed.), *Sociology and Everyday Life*, Englewood Cliffs, NJ, Prentice Hall, 1968.

Vail, R. W. G., *Random Notes on the History of the American Circus*, Worcester, MA, American Antiquarian Society, 1934.

Walvin, James, *Leisure and Society 1830–1950*, London, Longman, 1978.

Westervelt, Leonidas, *The Circus in Literature*, New York, the Author, 1931.

Williams, Raymond, *Keywords: A Vocabulary of Culture and Society*, London, Fontana [1976], 1984.

—— *Culture and Society 1780–1950*, Harmondsworth, Penguin Books [1958], 1984.

Willson Disher, Maurice, *Fairs, Circuses and Music Halls*, London, William Collins, 1942.

Withington, Robert, *English Pageantry*, vol. 2, Cambridge, MA, Harvard, University Press [1926], 1963.

Zizek, Slavoj, *Enjoy Your Symptom!: Jacques Lacan in Hollywood and Out*, London, Routledge, 1992.

Theses

Kwint, Marius, 'Astley's amphitheatre and the early circus in England, 1798–1830', Oxford University D. Phil, 1994.

Articles

Amidon, C. H., 'Behind the scenes with John B. Ricketts', *Bandwagon*, November/December 1974, pp. 16–19.

Artaud, Antonin, 'Oriental and Western theatre' (1935) and 'On the Balinese

Bibliography

theatre' (1932) trans. Victor Corti in Victor Corti (ed.), *Collected Works of Antonin Artaud*, vol. 4, London, Calder & Boyars, 1974.

Bazin, André, 'La Strada' (1956), trans. Joseph E. Cunneen, repr. in Peter Bondanella (ed.), *Federico Fellini: Essays in Criticism*, Oxford, Oxford University Press, 1978, pp. 54–9.

Benjamin, Walter, 'The work of art in the age of mechanical reproduction' (1935), repr. in Gerald Mast and Marshall Cohen (eds), *Film Theory and Criticism*, Oxford, Oxford University Press, 1982, pp. 848–70.

—— 'The Storyteller' (1936), in *Illuminations*, ed. Hannah Arendt, trans. Harry Zohn (London, Fontana Press [1973], 1992, pp. 83–107.

—— 'Theses on the philosophy of history' (1940), in *Illuminations*, ed. Hannah Arendt, trans. Harry Zohn, London, Fontana Press [1973], 1992, pp. 245–55.

Bogdan, Robert, 'Circassian beauties: authentic sideshow fabrications', *Bandwagon*, 30:3 (1986), pp. 22–3

Braathen, Sverre O., and Faye O., 'The advance could make or break a circus', *Bandwagon*, January/February 1971, pp. 11–25.

Burch, Noël, 'Charles Baudelaire v. Dr. Frankenstein', *Afterimage*, 8/9 (1981), pp. 4–23.

Burke, Frank, 'The three phase process and the white clown–Auguste relationship in Fellini's *The Clowns*', *Film Studies Annual* (1977), pp. 124–42.

Caldwell, David, and Rea, Paul, 'Handke and Wenders' *Wings of Desire*: transcending postmodernism', *The German Quarterly*, 64:1 (1991), pp. 46–54.

Carmeli, Yoram, 'Why does the 'Jimmy Brown Circus' travel? A semiotic approach to the analysis of circus ecology', *Poetics Today*, 8:2 (1987), pp. 219–44.

—— 'The travelling circus: an interpretation', *European Journal of Sociology*, 29 (1988), pp. 258–82.

—— 'Performance and family in the world of British circus', *Semiotica*, 85: 3–4 (1991), pp. 257–89.

—— 'Text, traces, and the reification of totality: the case of popular circus literature', *New Literary History*, 25 (1994), pp. 175–205.

Champad, Sreedharan, 'The circus in India', *King Pole*, 104 (1994), pp. 35–6.

Cook, Roger, 'Angels, fiction and history in Berlin: Wim Wenders' *Wings of Desire*', *The Germanic Review*, 66:1 (1991), pp. 34–46.

Coxe, Antony Hippisley, 'Equestrian drama and the circus', in Bradby, David, James, Louis and Sherratt, Bernard (eds), *Performance and Politics in Popular Culture*, Cambridge, Cambridge University Press, 1980, 109–18.

Crowson, Lydia, 'Cocteau and "Le Numéro Barbette"', *Modern Drama*, 19:1 (1976), pp. 79–87.

Dahmane, Razak '"A mere question of figures": measures, mystery, and metaphor in *Hard Times*', *Dickens Studies Annual*, 23 (1994), pp. 137–61.

Davies, David, 'Circus in the USSR', *King Pole*, 79 (1988), pp. 12–14.

Bibliography

Dulles, Foster Rhea, 'Farm and countryside', in Larrabee, Eric, and Meyersohn, Rolf (eds), *Mass Leisure*, Glencoe, Illinois, The Free Press, 1958, pp. 54–68.

Eisenstein, Sergei, 'Montage of attractions; for Enough Stupidity in Every Wiseman', trans. Daniel Gerould, *Drama Review*, 18:1 (1974), pp. 77–84.

Hardy Ivamy, E. R., 'Circuses and the law', *The Law Journal*, 102 (1952), pp. 115–16.

Ionesco, Eugene, 'The avant-garde theatre', *World Theatre*, 8:3 (1959), pp. 171–202.

Jamieson, David, and Davis, David, 'Animals in the circus', *King Pole*, 120 (1998), pp. 12–15.

Jamieson, David, et. al., 'Animals in the circus: a *King Pole* special', *King Pole*, 67 (1985), pp. 3–19.

Jones, Charles Henry, 'Transporting the Greatest Show on Earth; the 1898 tour of England', *The Ludgate*, September 1898, repr. in *Bandwagon*, March/April (1968), pp. 13–16.

Kindem, Gorham, 'Hollywood's movie star system: a historical overview', in Gorham, Kindem (ed.), *The American Movie Industry: The Business of Motion Pictures*, Carbondale, Southern Illinois University Press, 1982, pp. 79–93.

Hunt, Leigh, 'On Pantomime', 5 January 1817, repr in *Leigh Hunt's Dramatic Criticism; 1801–1831*, ed. Lawrence Huston Houtchens and Carolyn Washburn Houtchens New York, Columbia University Press, 1949, pp. 140–3.

—— 'On Pantomime, continued from a late paper', 26 January 1817, repr as a footnote to 'On pantomime' in *Leigh Hunt's Dramatic Criticism*, pp. 312–3.

Kracauer, Siegfried, 'Photography' (1927), trans. Thomas Y. Levin, repr. in *Critical Inquiry*, 3 (1993), pp. 421–36.

Linfors, Bernth, 'Circus Africans', *Journal of American Culture*, 6:2 (1983), pp. 3–19.

Loeffler, Robert, 'Candles, flares, gas, electric all used to light the circus', *White Tops*, May/June (1984), pp. 27–38.

Lougy, Robert E., 'Dickens's *Hard Times*: the romance as radical literature', in Harold Bloom (ed.), *Charles Dickens's Hard Times*, New York, Chelsea House, 1987, pp. 12–15.

Mansel, Henry, 'Sensation novels', *Quarterly Review*, 113 (1863), pp. 482–514.

Meyerhold, Vsevolod, 'The fairground booth' (1912), in Edward Braun (ed.) *Meyerhold on Theatre*, London, Eyre Methuen, 1969, pp. 119–42.

Mills, Cyril Bertram, 'Bertram Mills Circus: rail travel in Great Britain', *Bandwagon*, November/December (1983), pp. 36–8.

Moy, James S., 'Subverting/alienating performance structures', in James Redmond (ed.), *Themes in Drama*, vol. 9, Cambridge, Cambridge University Press, 1987, pp. 161–76.

Mulvey, Laura, 'Visual pleasure and narrative cinema', *Screen*, 16:3 (1975), pp. 6–18.

Oliphant, Margaret, 'Sensation novels', *Blackwood's*, 91 (1862), pp. 564–84.

—— 'Novels', *Blackwood's*, 102 (1867), pp. 257–80.

Bibliography

Paneth, Ira, 'Wim and his wings', *Film Quarterly*, 42:1 (1988), pp. 2–8.

Peacock, Shane, 'The amazing life of G. A. Farini', *King Pole*, 79 (1988), pp. 8–9.

Parkinson, Bob, The circus and the press, *Bandwagon*, March/April (1963), pp. 3–9.

—— 'Concerning mechanisation of the circus', *Bandwagon*, June 1967, pp. 30–1.

Parsons, Neil ' "Clicko" or Franz Taaibosch: South African bushman entertainer in Britain, France, Jamaica and the USA: his life from 1908–1940', African Studies Association Conference Paper, 21 November 1992.

Pfening, Fred D. Jr, 'Tractors and trucks on circuses', *Bandwagon*, January/February 1965, pp. 16–17.

—— 'Circus bill posting and advance car advertising', *Bandwagon*, November/December 1973, pp. 4–16.

John Schad, 'Dickens's cryptic Church: drawing on *Pictures from Italy*', in John Schad (ed.), *Dickens Re-Figured: Bodies, Desires and Other Histories*, Manchester, Manchester University Press, 1996, pp. 5–21.

Schlicke, Paul, 'Dickens in the circus', *Theatre Notebook* 47:1 (1993), pp. 3–19.

Sharpe, Stephen, '100 years ago: Barnum & Bailey on tour', *King Pole*, 121 (1998), p. 18.

Speaight, George, 'Some comic circus entrées', *Theatre Notebook*, 32 (1978), pp. 24–7.

—— Astley's amphitheatre, *Theatre Notebook*, 42 (1988), pp. 75–8.

Stacey, Don, '100 years of cinema and the circus: part 1', *King Pole*, 113 (1996), pp. 6–9.

Staiger, Janet, 'Seeing stars', in Christine Gledhill (ed.), *Stardom: Industry of Desire*, London, Routledge, 1991, pp. 3–16.

Stallybrass, Peter, 'Footnotes', in David Hillman and Carla Mazzio (eds), *The Body in Parts: Fantasies of Corporealities in Early Modern Europe*, London, Routledge, 1997, pp. 313–25.

Stubbs, John C., 'The Fellini manner: open form and visual excess', *Cinema Journal*, 32: 4 (1993), pp. 49–64.

Tait, Peta, 'Feminine free fall: a fantasy of freedom', *Theatre Journal* 48 (1996), pp. 27–34.

—— 'Danger delights: texts of gender and race in aerial performance', *New Theatre Quarterly*, 12:45 (1996), pp. 43–9.

Turner, John, 'Pablo Fanque: "an artiste of colour" ', *King Pole*, 89 (1990), pp. 5–9 and 90 (1991), pp. 3–5.

Truzzi, Marcello, 'The decline of the American circus: the shrinkage of an institution', in Marcello Truzzi (ed.), *Sociology and Everyday Life*, Englewood Cliffs, NJ, Prentice Hall, 1968, pp. 314–22.

Whale, John, 'Indian jugglers: Hazlitt, Romantic orientalism and the difference of view', in Tim Fulford and Peter Kitson (eds), *Romanticism and Colonialism: Writing and Empire, 1780–1830*, Cambridge, Cambridge University Press, 1998.

Index

Note: all texts are indexed under author's or director's names.

Index

Index

Index

Index